Dear Daryl,
I hope this book is a blessing to you.
Perhaps I will see you sometime
again. With love and prayers
Gisela Yohannan

LET ME WALK WITH YOU

GISELA YOHANNAN

LET ME WALK with YOU

LETTERS OF FAITH AND STRENGTH

BOOKS

a division of Gospel for Asia

www.gfa.org

Library of Congress Control Number: 2014932514

ISBN: 978-1-59589-132-7

Published by gfa books, a division of Gospel for Asia
1800 Golden Trail Court, Carrollton, TX 75010
1-800-WIN-ASIA

First printing, 2014

Printed in the United States of America

For more information about other materials, visit our website: www.gfa.org.

DEDICATION

I dedicate this book to my dear sister
Jeena, who has led the Women's Fellowship
ministry since it first started in 2005.

It is through her commitment to the Lord, love
for the sisters and hard work that this program
has succeeded and become a great blessing to tens
of thousands of women across South Asia.

We have traveled together to many places, and I
have very much enjoyed her friendship and our
times of sharing, dreaming and planning for the
future of our Women's Fellowship.

TABLE OF CONTENTS

Acknowledgments

Let Me Walk with You is a continuation of the letters of hope and encouragement that were first published in my *Dear Sister* book. This new book represents the next eight years of my journey with the Lord and the faith and strength I found in His Word. I wrote these letters to thousands of women who serve the Lord. We have now published them so they can be a blessing to many more of God's people.

I sincerely thank Heidi Chupp, Kim Smith, Tricia Bennett . . . and all the others who helped produce this book. And I am grateful to my dear husband, K.P. Yohannan, for his support and advice.

INTRODUCTION

The title of this new book, *Let Me Walk with You,* expresses the desire of my heart to come alongside my sisters who serve the Lord and to speak words that will fill their hearts with faith and strength. With each letter, I want to remind them that they are not walking alone and that the Lord is well able to strengthen them and fulfill all He has purposed to do through their lives.

The letters I wrote over the past eight years include specific lessons from God's Word. I have collected them into this book to make it possible for anyone to study them, whether on their own or with others in a Bible study group.

I have kept the letters in their original form, including dates, family references, travel reports and prayer requests, to preserve the time frame and personal touch. Because our ministry is changing and growing fast, the events and statistics mentioned in this book correspond only to the dates of the letters in which they appear.

My prayer is that this book will be a source of faith and strength to my sisters and many other believers who seek to serve the Lord and honor Him with their lives.

Gisela Yohannan

1

WE HAVE A GOD OF NEW BEGINNINGS

FEBRUARY 2006

Dear Sister,

God has given us a new year and with it, this promise: *"I will never desert you, nor will I ever forsake you"* (Hebrews 13:5). That means we don't have to be afraid. No matter what we may encounter, Jesus will be right there with us and His hand will hold ours.

I would like to ask you a personal question: How did this past year end for you? Could you rejoice over the progress you made in your spiritual life, the victories you won, the blessings you received and the prayers God answered? Or do you look back over the bygone year with disappointment, a heavy heart, deep hurt, tears or regrets?

My dear sister, if you were one who could not rejoice, I want to encourage you to say each morning when you get up: **"This day and this year will be different, because my God is a God of grace, hope and new beginnings!"** That's what the Bible teaches us from the first to the last book, and that's what we must believe in our hearts, confess with our mouths and act upon daily.

If you want 2006 to become different from last year, you need to leave three things behind:

1. Your failures

The devil wants to keep you a prisoner of your past, and that's why he fills your mind with lies like these: "Even if God forgave you, you can never recover from your failures. You missed your chance; God can no longer use you or fulfill the plan He once had for your life." Nothing could be further from the truth of God's Word! The Bible clearly says:

> *If we confess our sins, He is faithful and righteous to forgive us our sins and to cleanse us from all unrighteousness* (1 John 1:9).
>
> *For I will forgive their iniquity, and their sin I will remember no more* (Jeremiah 31:34).
>
> *There is therefore now no condemnation for those who are in Christ Jesus* (Romans 8:1).

If you truly humbled yourself before God and repented of your sin, then God immediately and freely forgave you because of Jesus. In His sight you are completely cleansed and free of condemnation, just as if you had never failed at all.

Your responsibility is to receive His full pardon, rejoice in it, live from now on in obedience to God's Word and never look back. If the devil, people or your own heart still condemns you, you must reject the condemnation and choose to believe what God's Word says about your cleansing. Even if you face consequences as the result of your failures, don't get discouraged, but commit yourself to the Lord and trust

Him to see you through. I guarantee you He will. Above all, honor Jesus' sacrifice on the cross by leaving your failures and all condemnation behind and walking in the freedom He purchased for you.

2. Your hurts

Perhaps this last year or several years ago, someone whom you loved and trusted hurt you deeply. You hoped the wounds the person inflicted on your heart would heal with time, but they haven't.

Now you have stepped into the new year, still chained to the hurts of your past. My dear sister, unless you forgive that person completely and release him of the wrong done to you, your wounds will never heal.

Maybe you forgave in the past, but you are still hurting. I urge you to search your heart. If you find any bitterness or resentment toward that person or you blame him for what became of you, or you wish he would feel the same hurt as you experienced or you desire to see him punished, then your forgiveness is incomplete and you are still in chains.

The only way for you to find freedom and healing is to choose to let go of *all* those things and forgive *"just as God in Christ also has forgiven you"*(Ephesians 4:32). Christ did not hold back anything, not even a grudge. He even prayed for God's mercy on those who drove the nails in His hands. My dear sister, it's not worth going through another day or year with wounds that God is able to heal if you forgive completely. Did you know that bitterness and unforgiveness will affect your physical health and also hinder God from blessing you?

Let this year of 2006 become for you the year of freedom from hurt!

3. Your low expectations

God wants to establish His kingdom in your village, city, state and nation. He wants to do it through His people—and that includes you. The perception and expectation you have of yourself as a child of God determine the extent to which you will permit God to use your life. If you are convinced that you can't do anything and that others are more talented, spiritual minded and courageous to share the Gospel and disciple others, you leave no room for God to use you.

Let me tell you what God's Word says about you as a believer:

> *It is no longer I who live, but Christ lives in me* (Galatians 2:20).
>
> *You shall receive power when the Holy Spirit has come upon you; and you shall be My witnesses* (Acts 1:8).
>
> *For God has not given us a spirit of timidity [fear], but of power and love and discipline* (2 Timothy 1:7).
>
> *But in all these things we overwhelmingly conquer through Him who loved us* (Romans 8:37).
>
> *I can do all things through Him who strengthens me* (Philippians 4:13).
>
> *For whatever is born of God overcomes the world; and this is the victory that has overcome the world—our faith* (1 John 5:4).

My dear sister, you need to leave your low expectations behind and agree with and believe what God says you can do through Christ. It will cause you to volunteer like Isaiah: *"Here am I. Send me!*" (Isaiah 6:8). And it will enable God to use your life in ways you never imagined.

———————— ❋ ————————

Let us pray for one another, that during this new year we will walk with Jesus in such a way that we will bring honor to His name.

Your sister in Christ,

Gisela

2

WALKING WORTHY OF HIS NAME

APRIL 2006

Dear Sister,

I think about you often, and I pray that you will become steadfast in your commitment to the Lord and represent Christ well in this world. Let me share with you a few thoughts on this subject.

When the Lord Jesus went back to heaven, He left His disciples behind to give leadership to the Church that was born on Pentecost. The Church was to represent Jesus here on earth and to proclaim the Gospel to the rest of the world.

Something wonderful happened, and we read about it in the book of Acts: *". . . and the disciples were first called Christians in Antioch"* (Acts 11:26).

The remarkable thing is that the believers did not choose the name "Christians" for themselves; it was given to them by the people of their society. What caused the people to select this name? The reason was this: They remembered how Christ acted and talked while He was on earth, and these believers behaved exactly like Him.

That means these believers loved like Jesus, showed compassion like Jesus, walked in humility like Jesus, spoke the truth like Jesus, prayed in faith like Jesus, cared for others like Jesus, healed the sick and cast out demons like Jesus, obeyed God's Word like Jesus, preached with authority like Jesus and were faithful until death like Jesus.

What name does the world give us? If the people around us closely observed our private lives—the way we talked and dealt with our parents, husband, children, neighbors, co-workers, pastor, leaders, fellow believers and others we come in contact with—what name would they give us to identify us?

Would they call us pretender, gossip, self-seeker, lover of money, unsubmitted, prideful or covetous, or would we truly qualify to be called Christians?

We often excuse our un-Christlike attitude and behavior by pointing out that no one is perfect and that we are no different than anyone else in church. It may be true that other believers are as sorry Christians as we are, but that should never be our justification or satisfy us to stay as we are. We must desire with all our heart to become someone worthy to be called a Christian.

There are specific things we must do or change in our lives to become more like Jesus:

1. Jesus must become our measuring rod. Romans 8:29 tells us that *"He [God] also predestined [us] to become conformed to the image of His Son."*

Therefore, the cry of our heart must be, "Lord Jesus, I want to become like You, so I can bring honor to Your name." This means we will no longer use our culture, our family background, our past failures and other people's poor examples as excuses to stay as we are. But we will look at Jesus alone to tell us what God destined for us to become, through His grace and the power of the Holy Spirit.

2. We must decide to obey the Word of God regardless of what others practice. If other believers gossip, we will not join them. If they do not submit to authority or exhibit a critical spirit, we will not have any part in it. Why? Because we choose to do the will of God as His Word instructs us.

3. We need to surround ourselves with people who live what we desire to become. There is an old proverb that says, "Tell me who your friends are and I will tell you who you are."

We may think it doesn't really matter who our close friends are or who we spend time with, as long as we follow our own convictions. My dear sister, this may well be one of the most successful deceptions the Enemy uses to keep us from becoming like Jesus. We may not believe or admit it, but the negative behavior, critical spirit and rebellious attitude of those we associate with will surely rub off on us. It will not happen overnight, but over time and without us realizing it, our heart is being poisoned little by little.

Perhaps we think we are strong enough and this will never happen to us. We are wrong. The Apostle Paul wrote, *"Do not be deceived: 'Bad company corrupts good morals' "* (1 Corinthians 15:33).

My dear sister, if we want to become like Jesus, then we must surround ourselves with people who live what we desire to become. We may have to make a deliberate choice to let go of some of our old friends and choose to spend time with sisters who will influence us toward godliness, walking in the light and in obedience to God's Word. We need to choose those people as our friends who have the same desire as we do to become like Jesus, and encourage and correct each other as we pursue this goal.

Yes, we will hurt some feelings, including our own, when we dissolve some friendships that pull us the wrong direction. We need to let them know that their influence is causing us to become as negative and critical as they are and, therefore, we can no longer maintain close friendship with them.

4. We must draw near to God. God put a wonderful promise and invitation in His Word for us: *"Draw near to God and He will draw near to you"* (James 4:8).

If we desire to become like Jesus, we must be faithful to spend time with Him in prayer and in reading His Word. We will find that His presence and character will transform our thoughts, hearts and actions in such a way that we become authentic Christians.

Let us pray together for the new television channel we will launch in a few months:

- Pray for the team that is working to get everything ready for the launch date.
- Pray for the ongoing production of the various programs.
- Pray that the Lord will be honored and millions of people will be blessed through this channel.

My dear sister, may God's love and grace strengthen you to follow Jesus.

Your sister in Christ,

Gisela

3

WATCH OVER YOUR HEART

Dear Sister,

This morning I had some workers from a nursery come to our house to plant two trees in our backyard. One is an oak tree, and the other one, a purple ash. Before the gardeners left, they told me how much and how often I needed to water the trees. In addition, the nursery gave me a whole page of tree maintenance instructions I am supposed to implement over the next few years.

I am determined to carefully follow all those directions, and I'll tell you the reason why. You see, last year we bought and planted three trees, but only one survived. The two trees planted today are replacements for the ones that died. I really don't want the same thing to happen again, because it's too expensive and time-consuming and my backyard keeps lacking shade.

You know, when we dug up the dead trees to make space for the new ones, I thought about how the Lord has to do the very same thing in our lives.

God sows the seeds of His Word into our hearts, yet so often the plants that come up don't survive. Consequently, He has to go back and replant again and again, until finally the plants take root, grow tall and bear fruit.

Just look at your life: For how many years now has God been trying to grow the plants of faith, honesty, compassion, holiness and obedience in your heart? You read daily about them in your Bible, and you have heard a hundred sermons on the subjects. Yet these plants never seem to develop in your life, though you have been a Christian for more than 5, 10 or 20 years. Why is that?

In the parable of the sower, Jesus explains that the problem lies in the condition of our hearts. We so often blame God, our pastor, fellow believers, our husband, parents, team leader, upbringing or difficult circumstances for our lack of spiritual development. We even feel sorry for ourselves and wish we could go to one of those big crusades where an anointed preacher lays hands on us and prays, so we can become instantly spiritual.

My dear sister, even if you had such an opportunity, no permanent change would happen in you, because your real problem is the condition of your heart. Please read carefully what Jesus says in Matthew 13:3–8 and 18–23, and identify which one of these soils is your problem.

Roadside: The seed never makes it into the ground at all. It's lying on top of, or right beside, the hard pavement and has no chance to even sprout. It's easily and immediately snatched away by the birds.

This is the picture of a heart that is totally unprepared to receive anything. The person either doesn't understand the

Word he heard or, in the case of a believer, something is blocking the Holy Spirit from penetrating his heart. Two things that will cause this are unconfessed sin and an unteachable spirit (which is the result of pride, unbrokenness and an unsurrendered self-will).

Rocky ground: The seed falls into the soil and sprouts. However, the layer of soil is very shallow and underneath is hard rock. The root of the little plant is unable to penetrate the rock and get to the water source. As soon as the sun comes up, it withers away and dies.

This is the picture of a heart that wants spiritual blessings and benefits, but has no intentions of carrying the cross. There are plenty of believers with such a shallow commitment. They gladly receive forgiveness of sin, deliverance from bondage, healing, peace, joy, material benefits and the promise of a heavenly home. They also want the church to pray and care for them when they are in need. However, when they must choose to accept inconvenience, suffering and sacrifice for the sake of Christ, they are unwilling to make the step from being a believer to becoming a disciple of Christ. A disciple is one who follows Christ wherever He goes, even if it means Calvary.

Thorny ground: This ground has no hardness or rocks. It's made up of good soil, soft and deep enough for a plant to put down roots and grow. However, the ground is not weeded. It has thorn bushes that overgrow and choke the life out of the little plants that came up from the seeds that were sown.

This is the picture of a heart whose ground has all the right conditions to receive the seed of God's Word and develop healthy plants that yield fruit. However, the person has permitted other seeds to take root in his heart as well. Jesus identified them as the worry of the world and the deceitfulness of riches. Is it possible for these plants to peacefully coexist beside the Word of God? No—because their nature is that of a thorn bush: to spread and take over the entire ground and choke all other plants to death. Worry kills our faith, and without faith we cannot please God, so nothing in our Christian life works. The lure of riches takes our affection away from the things of God and causes us to desire the things of this world. Our love will grow cold, and our usefulness to God will die away.

But is there a way to turn bad soil into good soil and bring much fruit? Yes, there is!

If your heart is hard like the pavement of the road and you are unteachable, the only thing that will help you is to repent of sin, stop justifying yourself and humble yourself before God. Confess your pride and give the Holy Spirit permission to break you in all those areas where you are unyielding. Lay down your self life, and deliberately choose His will over your own. If you do this, He will make the soil of your heart fruitful and 2 Chronicles 7:14 will become your personal testimony:

> *[If] My people who are called by My name humble themselves and pray, and seek My face and turn from their wicked ways, then I will hear from heaven, will forgive their sin, and will heal their land.*

If your heart has only a thin layer of good soil and your commitment has no depth because of the rock underneath, then go to the Word of God and learn what it says. Ask the Holy Spirit to reveal to you what it cost Jesus to redeem you and what the lordship of Christ is. If you submit to God's Word, you will find that it is *"like a hammer which shatters a rock,"* the hard rock of your heart (Jeremiah 23:29).

If your heart is invaded by thorns, start weeding and pulling them *all* up by the roots. Don't entertain thoughts or listen to people whose words turn into thorn bushes. *"Watch over your heart with all diligence"* (Proverbs 4:23) and immediately pull up even the smallest thorns.

My dear sister, may God's grace be with you always.

With love and prayers,

Gisela

4

WHEN WE HAVE
NO ANSWERS

Dear Sister,

How are you doing? I am writing this letter to you on my way to Hyderabad in India. Sister Jeena and I are traveling together to conduct four training seminars for the state Women's Fellowship teams from every state of India and from Nepal. So far we have finished two seminars. The state Women's Fellowship teams are responsible to develop the Women's Fellowship program and give leadership to all the local and district Women's Fellowships in their states.

We are very encouraged to hear all the good reports of what God is doing through our sisters in the local Women's Fellowships in different parts of India. For example, in the state of Madhya Pradesh, the Women's Fellowship sisters from a local Believers Church went for mission outreach to a remote village where everyone is illiterate. God gave them grace to win eight families to the Lord.

This morning I read a scripture from the book of Zechariah that encouraged me. So I thought I would share with you what I learned.

There are things and circumstances in our lives for which we have no answers. They may be very personal, such as health issues and uncertainties about our future, or they may have to do with our family, children, relatives, co-workers and the ministry.

This morning I was thinking about some of those things in my life for which I have no answers. You know, each time I dwell on these issues, my mind tries to find solutions but can't. What happens next is this: My mind starts imagining the worst possible outcome.

I wonder if your mind does the same to you.

As a result, we get discouraged, anxious, fearful and our heart becomes heavy. This often happens to us not at first, but after we prayed and trusted God to intervene. However, when weeks and months go by and we haven't seen any positive changes, our mind tells us that there is no solution.

In addition, if we pray for someone specific, we are confronted with the fact that God can only work in people's lives and circumstances if they permit Him to. And if they refuse, then all our faith on their behalf will do no good. At least that is what our mind concludes.

Did you know that God asks us a specific question if we think there is no solution possible? The Old Testament tells us the story how God's people were taken into captivity as the result of their sin. They were far away from their homeland. For 70 years their land was desolate, their cities destroyed and Jerusalem (along with the temple) in ruins. Then God told them that He would bring the people back and restore everything as it was before. Even after many of them returned, it was impossible for them to imagine that such a restoration could happen. In response, God asked them this question:

If it is too difficult in the sight of the remnant of this people in those days, will it also be too difficult in My sight? (Zechariah 8:6).

What God wanted to tell them—and us—is this: "Just because you can't think of any answers and solutions, don't conclude that I can't either. Remember I am God, and for Me, all things are possible."

We are supposed to focus and meditate on the greatness of our God instead of the conclusions of our limited minds. Let's start with these stories:

- God brought Noah and his family safely through the flood.
- He made a way for His people through the Red Sea by dividing it.
- He fed them with manna through 40 years of wilderness travel.
- The Lord kept Daniel safe in the lions' den.
- He protected Shadrach, Meshach and Abednego in the midst of the fiery furnace.
- He provided food for the prophet Elijah through ravens.

- He cleansed Naaman from leprosy.
- Jesus gave sight to blind Bartimaeus.
- He healed the paralyzed slave of a centurion.
- He silenced the wind and the waves with a word.
- He freed the daughter of a Canaanite woman from demons.
- He raised Lazarus from the dead.

Do you know what all these events have in common? They are problems for which we as human beings have no answers. Yet none of these things was too difficult for our God! He is almighty, and there is absolutely nothing He cannot do, including changing the laws of nature, if it fits His purpose.

What will happen when we meditate on the greatness of our God? Our faith and trust in Him will grow far beyond the limited solutions our mind can produce.

As a result, we will not give up believing that God knows a way to change the circumstances and the hearts of the people for whom we are praying. He has done it before, and He purposely recorded it in His Word so we may know that He is willing and able to do it again.

How privileged we are to serve a God whose power has no limits!

—————— ❈ ——————

Please join us in prayer for our Women's Fellowship program:

- Pray for all the state Women's Fellowship teams as they start their ministry this month.
- Pray that Sister Jeena will find two capable sisters who can serve together with her on the national Women's Fellowship team.
- Pray that we will know the mind of the Lord for all the programs that need to be developed.

My dear sister, may the Lord strengthen you by His grace.

Your sister in Christ,

Gisela

5

POSSESSING WHAT IS OURS

Dear Sister,

By the time you get this letter, I will be back in India for some teaching and for a special meeting with Sister Jeena and several other sisters from our Women's Fellowship. We will discuss and plan next year's Women's Fellowship curriculum. Please pray for God's guidance for this meeting.

This morning I read a few verses in the book of Joshua that have an important message for us.

Israel stopped short of possessing the land. God had delivered the people of Israel out of Egypt and brought them into the promised land. Under the leadership of Joshua, they had defeated all the kings and nations that lived there. However, only a few of the tribes of Israel went ahead and possessed the land God had given to them. The rest of them just lived within a small part of their new land and put off taking full possession of what God had already given them.

Why? Perhaps they were tired of waging war and wanted to take a break, relax and enjoy their lives. Maybe the piece of land and the homes they now occupied were big enough for their present needs and it seemed troublesome and unnecessary to go after more. They might have thought, "Why should we be in such a hurry to occupy it all? Let the next generation finish the job in 10, 20 or 30 years."

They didn't consider the consequences of not possessing their whole land; otherwise, they would have seen the wisdom of doing it immediately. Right after the conquest of Canaan, Israel was in the best position to occupy the entire land because the majority of their enemies were dead or had fled. The few common people who still lived in some settlements would surely have run away or could have been easily wiped out as soon as the Israelites took over their areas. And strongholds still controlled by enemy resistance fighters would have stood no chance because they were cut off from any outside help.

However, if Israel failed to possess and occupy their entire land, the situation would look very different in 10 to 30 years: Their borders would not be secure, and any outside nation could invade their land. The enemies that fled before Israel would have time to regroup, elect new leaders, make alliances with other nations, raise up new armies and come against Israel to take back their land. The resistance fighters in the strongholds would establish outside connections and support and be a constant threat by waging guerilla warfare. The common people who were not driven out would multiply and become a snare to Israel with their idol worship and pagan lifestyles. Without being inhabited, the conquered cities would deteriorate and the fruitful land without being cultivated would turn into a wilderness.

God urged them to finish possessing their land because He could see the trouble they were going to have in the future. He spoke to Joshua, and Joshua in turn called the tribes of Israel and said to them, *"How long will you put off entering to take possession of the land which the Lord, the God of your fathers, has given you?"* (Joshua 18:3).

They listened to Joshua and went ahead and started to possess their land.

Israel's story is given to us for our instruction because what they encountered in the physical realm, we encounter in the spiritual one. Jesus brought us out of the kingdom of darkness into God's kingdom of light. He has given us, His children, an incredible inheritance. Along with being conformed into the image of Christ, we have become heirs of everything God promises in His Word. Here are just a few examples of what is ours:

- Salvation
- Freedom from any bondage
- Victory over sin
- Authority over the devil
- Power to be a witness
- The ability to live a holy life through the indwelling of the Holy Spirit
- Faith that overcomes the world
- His strength to be able to do all things
- Divine love and forgiveness for one another and for our enemies
- Christ's humility to be a servant of all
- The mind of Christ to become obedient until death

- The authority to pray in Jesus' name and receive answers
- Spiritual gifts to serve
- The authority to heal the sick, cast out demons and speak on behalf of Christ

We often stop short of possessing what is ours. We are happy and satisfied with our salvation and the knowledge that we can go to heaven when we die. So we sit back and simply enjoy God's blessings instead of growing up in Christ and becoming fully equipped to serve Him as it is the will of God for our lives (see Ephesians 4:11–15).

We don't consider the consequences for our personal life and the kingdom of God. This is what happens if we neglect to possess what God purposed for us to have:

- We will be weak Christians who have little or no power to overcome anything.
- We will be immature in our behavior and unable to take responsibility.
- Our marriage and family life will not have the testimony it should have.
- Our children will not learn from us what it means to serve God fully and walk in faith, holiness and obedience to God.
- We will selfishly pursue blessings and have little concern or burden for the lost world.
- We will be a hindrance to others and a burden to the Body of Christ.
- We will delay God's plan and blessings for our lives.

- We will deprive the church of our service.
- We will rob God of the glory He is supposed to receive from our lives.

God urges us to finish possessing what He has freely given us through Jesus. My dear sister, what is it that you fail to possess from your inheritance as a believer? Look at the first list of things God promises are ours. How much longer will you put off overcoming a sin, forgiving someone who hurt you or walking in faith?

How, then, should we go about possessing our inheritance? This is how the Apostle Paul did it, and he finished well: *"Not that I have already obtained it, or have already become perfect, but I press on in order that I may lay hold of that for which also I was laid hold of by Christ Jesus"* (Philippians 3:12). This scripture tells us that we must never be satisfied with less than what God intended for us to have. And we must desire and go after it until we lay hold of it.

May the Lord bless you and keep you in His grace.

Your sister in Christ,

Gisela

6

JOY TO YOU!

Dear Sister,

As I write this letter to you, it's almost Christmas.

I don't know how you celebrate Christmas with your family, your Gospel team and your church—but I wish with all my heart that you experience the joy and peace the angels proclaimed 2,000 years ago when they announced the birth of the Savior to the shepherds.

This year our family will celebrate Christmas together in India. It will be very special, because our family has grown to six members!

Our daughter, Sarah, got married on the 11th of December. Her husband's name is Daniel Johnson. He is a godly young man who desires to use his training as a medical doctor to serve the Lord here in India. As a family, we were blessed that so many of our leaders and friends from across India and other countries came for the wedding. Daniel and Sarah very much valued their love and prayers. Now we two Daniels in our family, our son and our son-in-law.

It is our desire and prayer as a family that the Lord will use all six of us together to reach the unreached of Asia with the Gospel and to be a blessing to the Believers Church and the whole Body of Christ.

This Christmas season, I would like to share with you a little bit about the joy the angels announced to the shepherds with these words:

> *Do not be afraid; for behold, I bring you good news of a great joy which shall be for all the people; for today in the city of David there has been born for you a Savior, who is Christ the Lord* (Luke 2:10–11).

Did you know that God designed us to experience joy? When God created the first people into His own image, He gave them the capacity to experience joy just like He does. He wanted them and their descendants to continuously live in the joy of His presence.

Before sin came into this world, Adam and Eve experienced a level of joy we cannot even imagine. Their joy was always present, perfect, pure and undisturbed.

In comparison, our joy is mostly short-lived and clouded by burdens, pain, disappointments and grief. How much it must have hurt our Heavenly Father to see His creation lose that wonderful joy He intended for them to have.

God gave every person on earth a reason for great joy. God in His great love didn't leave us without hope. He not only made a way for our salvation, but He also decided to restore our joy. When the angel first spoke to the shepherds, he said:

I bring you good news of a great joy which shall be for all the people (Luke 2:10).

In the midst of darkness, sin and despair, God gave the people of the earth a great joy: He sent His Son to be our Savior. From that moment on, Jesus became the reason for our joy. Now, even in the midst of difficult circumstances, nothing and no one can rob us of our joy, because Jesus our Savior never leaves us nor forsakes us.

The saddest thing is that half of this world has not yet heard about God's love for them and that Jesus, their Savior, was born 2,000 years ago.

Our relationship to Jesus creates joy. The Apostle Peter talks about the joy that is ours because we love Jesus and we believe in Him:

Though you have not seen Him, you love Him, and though you do not see Him now, but believe in Him, you greatly rejoice with joy inexpressible and full of glory (1 Peter 1:8).

As we abide in Jesus and His Word abides in us, the fruit of the Spirit will develop in our lives. This will cause our joy to grow much more:

But the fruit of the Spirit is love, joy, peace . . . (Galatians 5:22).

My dear sister, what I wish for you to learn from this little Christmas study is this: The more you love Jesus, believe in Him and abide in Him, the more your heart will be filled with joy! If it is joy you long for, this is the way you will get it.

A personal prayer request: Two days ago I got the news that my sister, Edith, is seriously ill. She is only 57 years old, and the doctors' prognosis is not good. If their diagnosis is correct, there is no cure and she has only two to five years to live. Edith is my only sister. I have no brothers, and my parents are already with the Lord. I will be cutting my time in India short and going to Germany to be with her while she spends time in the hospital for further tests. Would you please join our family and ask the Lord to touch her and heal her? He is well able to do a miracle.

Please share this prayer request in your Women's Fellowship meeting as well. Thank you so much.

My dear sister, may the Lord bless you this Christmas and may you experience the joy of His presence every day of the new year.

With love and prayers,

Gisela

7

DEALING WITH OTHERS' WEAKNESSES

FEBRUARY 2007

Dear Sister,

I count it a privilege to write to you, and I hope my letter will encourage you.

Last month I was in Germany with my sister, who has been ill. After extensive testing, the doctors confirmed that she indeed has an illness for which there is no cure and the life expectancy is but a few years. However, we as a family are praying that the Lord will heal her. We would be grateful if you would continue to intercede for her as well. From now on I will need to visit my sister more often.

These past few days, I have thought about how impatient and unloving we often are toward people when dealing with their weaknesses. The Bible teaches us a lot about this subject.

Since the fall of Adam, none of us is perfect. As human beings, we all have areas of strength in our lives—and areas of weaknesses. This is true of our physical body, our mind and our character. For example, one person can easily run 10 miles, while another one is exhausted after only 300 yards. One is very gifted in music, while another one is unable to keep a simple tune. One has great patience, and another one has none at all.

When we become followers of Christ, we are brand-new creations—in our spirit. However, we are still living in the same imperfect body and have the same intelligence, natural gifting and character traits. For the rest of our lives, the Holy Spirit works in us to conform us into the image of Christ. That means, praise God, we are changing and gradually taking on Christ's character, but we have a long way to go. In fact, the Bible declares that we won't be perfect until we reach heaven.

So how do we treat others when their weaknesses show up? This is what usually happens: If others have the same weaknesses as we have, we treat them with some understanding and compassion. However, if they are weak in the areas where we ourselves are strong, we condemn them quickly. We show little mercy and understanding for their struggles because we don't have the same problem. In fact, we lecture them and challenge them to exercise faith, follow our example and change at once. Should they fail, we are likely to write them off and not give them a second chance.

The Apostle Paul was the most bold, fearless, determined and hard-working missionary leader of the first century. Nothing, not even death threats, beatings, stonings, imprisonment, shipwrecks, wild animals, robbers, sleepless nights, hunger, thirst, cold and much labor could stop him from proclaiming the Gospel and planting churches (see 2 Corinthians 11:23–28).

Naturally, Paul expected and demanded the same level of boldness, commitment and hard work from anyone who joined his missionary team. John Mark, a young man, traveled with Paul and Barnabas on their first missionary journey, but he only lasted through a few adventures before he left them to go back home. You see, his weaknesses were fear and lack of commitment to hard work, and he couldn't handle the intense situations and workload the team encountered.

Later on, when Paul was about to set out for his second missionary journey, he refused to give Mark a second chance to accompany him. He even called him a deserter and one who had not gone with them to the work (see Acts 15:38). You see, at this time in his life, Paul had no compassion for Mark's weaknesses in the areas where he himself was so strong.

How does Jesus treat us when our weaknesses show up? Jesus doesn't write us off. Instead, He has understanding and compassion on us and offers us His grace and help to overcome our weaknesses:

> *For we do not have a high priest who cannot sympathize with our weaknesses, but one who has been tempted in all things as we are, yet without sin. Let us therefore draw near with confidence to the throne of grace, that we may receive mercy and may find grace to help in time of need* (Hebrews 4:15–16).

He even put it in writing that He will complete the work He started in us:

> *For I am confident of this very thing, that He who began a good work in you will perfect it until the day of Christ Jesus* (Philippians 1:6).

This promise gives us the assurance that the Lord will indeed succeed in changing us into His likeness, even in the areas of our present weaknesses. He did it for John Mark. Consider this: Near the end of Paul's life, he wrote in a letter to Timothy:

Pick up Mark and bring him with you, for he is useful to me for service (2 Timothy 4:11).

What tremendous work the Holy Spirit must have accomplished in Mark's life that the Apostle Paul wanted him for service while he was in prison awaiting his execution! No doubt it was a dangerous mission for Mark, but he was no longer fearful and unwilling to work. In fact, Mark had become so useful in service that God chose him to write one of the four Gospels.

What does the New Testament teach us concerning how we should deal with others' weaknesses? Exactly as Jesus deals with ours!

Now we who are strong ought to bear the weaknesses of those without strength and not just please ourselves (Romans 15:1).

We urge you, brethren, admonish the unruly, encourage the fainthearted, help the weak, be patient with all men (1 Thessalonians 5:14).

Incidentally, these instructions were written by the Apostle Paul after the Holy Spirit helped him to recognize that he too had a weakness he needed to overcome: He lacked Christ's love, compassion and patience with people who were weak in the areas where he was strong.

My dear sister, let us learn to be compassionate with each other until the Lord has completed His work in us.

Please join me in prayer for the many thousands of Bible college students in our Bible colleges:

- For wisdom as they write their final exams.
- For clear guidance where each one should serve the Lord after graduation.
- For the Lord to empower them as they go for summer outreach or their permanent assignment.

May the Lord bless you and keep you close to Himself.

I love you in Jesus,

Gisela

8

WHO IS ON TOP
OF OUR LIST?

APRIL 2007

Dear Sister,

During the past six weeks I was in three different countries. For much of the time our family was together, for which I am grateful. We had a great time traveling together. Now I am at home for a while and I hope to catch up with my writing assignments.

This month we celebrated the resurrection of the Lord Jesus, the foundation of our faith. How much Jesus must love us to have come to earth and laid down His life for our redemption! He did it out of His free will, considering us more important than all the glory of heaven He could have enjoyed instead.

God desires that Christ's love, humility and selflessness become part of every believer's character. If it does, it will be the most powerful Christian testimony we can have in this world. So let's take a good look at our hearts and find out where we are in reflecting Jesus.

To ourselves, we are the most important person in this world. As human beings, we evaluate everything and everyone we encounter in relationship to ourselves. Whether we are rich or poor, educated or uneducated, famous or unknown, we appraise everything in relation to how it will benefit, bless and promote us, or how negatively it will affect our circumstances, plans or wishes. We try to get the best seat on the bus, the biggest cucumber in the market and the highest-paying job for ourselves! And we regard others who are after the very same things as our competition.

Even as Christians, we expect God, the pastor and the church believers to put our name on top of the priority list when it comes to blessings and care.

But Jesus' mindset was different. He thought of others before He thought of Himself. The Apostle Paul wrote how we should follow Christ's example:

> *Do nothing from selfishness or empty conceit, but with humility of mind let each of you regard one another as more important than himself; do not merely look out for your own personal interests, but also for the interests of others* (Philippians 2:3–4).

Who is our neighbor? As believers, we are commanded to love our neighbor as ourselves (see Luke 10:27). When Jesus first made this statement, one of His listeners inquired whom He meant by neighbor. Perhaps he expected Jesus to say that his neighbor was a close family member, a dear friend, the person living next door or perhaps a member of his synagogue.

To the man's surprise, Jesus told him the story of the Good Samaritan. Through this story, we learn that God expects us to regard all fellow human beings we come in contact with as our neighbors, even if they are total strangers or belong to a different ethnic, social and religious background.

This means that the poor woman in the marketplace, the rich banker, the important politician, the servant girl, the homeless beggar, the school principal, the man afflicted with leprosy, the slum dweller, the scientist and the illiterate bonded laborer—all are our neighbors, whom we are to love.

God's interpretation of whom our neighbor is presents us with the tremendous challenge of reaching with His love across all social and cultural barriers, including a 3,000-year-old caste system.

What does it mean to love others as ourselves? It means that we begin to see every person as God sees them: created in His own image, their souls more valuable than the whole world, loved by God so much that He sent His only Son to die on the cross for their redemption, called to become children of God and destined to be the Bride of Christ.

It means that we recognize that others are just as valuable as we are, regardless of their earthly social standing. It means we must treat them with the same dignity, respect and understanding we want for ourselves. And it also means that we reach out with Christ's love and compassion to help them in their need.

Where do we start? Across Asia, we are surrounded by millions of people who have countless spiritual and physical needs. Even if we wanted to, it would be impossible for us to reach out to all of them. So how do we begin to love others as ourselves?

In the story of the Good Samaritan, who did God hold responsible to help the man who fell among the robbers? Those who *traveled the same road* and saw his desperate condition. In the same way, God arranges for people in need to cross our path and puts it within our grasp to love and help them in the name of Jesus.

It may be the lady who sits next to us on the bus holding a sick child, the college student attending our class who failed her exam, the old woman living down the road whose husband recently died or the new believer in our church whose parents rejected her for her faith in Christ.

So how could we love those people as ourselves? We could offer to pray for the mother and her sick child on the bus. We could encourage the student and help tutor her in the subject she failed. We could visit the old woman and comfort her with God's Word. We could invite the new believer to our home for dinner and fellowship.

How far have we come? If we know Christ's teaching about loving our neighbor as ourselves, why do we struggle to live it practically, like Mother Teresa did, with such dedication and joy? The reason is that deep down in our hearts, we still regard ourselves better than others.

You see, for those of us who come from a lower social background, Christ's command is good news and a wonderful step up in acceptance, value, equality and dignity. But for those who come from a higher social class, it means taking a step down in humility in order to be like Jesus and to be one with the Body of Christ.

If you feel sorry for yourself, that you have to lay down some of your earthly privileges, just look at how much the Lord Jesus gave up to become your Savior:

> . . . *who, although He existed in the form of God, did not regard equality with God a thing to be grasped, but emptied Himself, taking the form of a bond-servant, and being made in the likeness of men. And being found in appearance as a man, He humbled Himself by becoming obedient to the point of death, even death on a cross* (Philippians 2:6–8).

What an honor and a privilege have been given to you by God to lay down something for Jesus' sake so you can reflect and represent Him to a lost world!

My dear sister, let us determine to follow Christ in humility and love for others.

With love and prayers,

Gisela

9

TRUSTING THAT HE WILL

JUNE 2007

Dear Sister,

This morning while I was drinking my coffee, I was reading in the book of Psalms about the greatness of our God and about His lovingkindness toward those who trust in Him. Look what David wrote:

> *For to Thee, O Lord, I lift up my soul.*
> *For Thou, Lord, art good, and ready to forgive,*
> *And abundant in lovingkindness to all who call upon Thee.*
> *In the day of my trouble I shall call upon Thee,*
> *For Thou wilt answer me.*
> *There is no one like Thee among the gods, O Lord;*
> *Nor are there any works like Thine.*
> *For Thou art great and doest wondrous deeds; Thou alone art God.*
> *I will give thanks to Thee, O Lord my God, with all my heart,*
> *And will glorify Thy name forever.*
> *For Thy lovingkindness toward me is great,*
> *And Thou hast delivered my soul from the depths of Sheol.*
> —Psalm 86:4–5, 7–8, 10, 12–13

This song of praise reminds me of a scripture in the New Testament: *"He who did not spare His own Son, but delivered Him up for us all, how will He not also with Him freely give us all things?"* (Romans 8:32).

God is not stingy. When we face troubles, we often pray to God as if He were unwilling to grant us our request. We agonize, shed tears and plead with Him, as if we have to wrestle the answer from His tightly closed hand.

Nothing could be further from the truth! The two scriptures we just read tell us that our Heavenly Father loves us dearly and is eager to answer when we call upon Him. He is more than willing to use His great power to deliver us out of our present trouble. After all, He delivered us before—out of hell, the greatest trouble of all! To save us, He made the most costly sacrifice in the universe: He gave up His only Son, Jesus, to die for our sin on the cross.

The Apostle Paul says that if God paid such a high price for our redemption, we can be sure He will *freely* give us everything else we need also. God doesn't get upset over the many times we ask for His help. He hasn't put up a sign by His throne that reads: "Four prayer requests allowed per day, per person." There is no limit as to how often we can come to Him with our needs. We are always welcome and accepted. In fact, He invites us to come to Him with *all* our needs and burdens:

> *Come to Me,* **all** *who are weary and heavy-laden, and I will give you rest* (Matthew 11:28).
>
> *. . . casting* **all** *your anxiety upon Him, because He cares for you* (1 Peter 5:7).
>
> *. . .* **in everything** *by prayer and supplication with thanksgiving let your requests be made known to God* (Philippians 4:6).

None of our problems is beyond His power. Think about how God created the heavens and the earth out of nothing. He simply spoke them into existence. He gave the breath of life to all the animals and the people He created. Ever since, the whole universe and all life have been sustained by His power.

When Jesus walked on this earth, we could see the power of God up close: He stilled the raging storm, multiplied bread to feed the hungry multitudes, walked on water, cast out demons, opened the eyes of the blind and the ears of the deaf, cleansed the lepers, healed every kind of sickness and raised the dead.

There was not one sick or demon-possessed person He could not heal or deliver. Even a legion of demons had to immediately leave a man when Jesus commanded them to go. Lazarus was already dead for four days when Jesus called him out of the grave, and he immediately came back to life.

Because of sin, Satan held all mankind captive, and we were destined for hell. Yet the power of the blood of Jesus cleansed us from all sin and set us free to become sons and daughters of God. And God wants us to know that He is willing to freely use the same divine power on our behalf if we cast our cares, needs and problems upon Him.

What's there left for us to do? Our part is to trust Him completely that He not only *can* deliver us from our troubles, but that He *will*. That's called faith!

Now, because our Heavenly Father is taking care of our problems, we can stop worrying. He has all power and authority at His disposal; He doesn't need our help or advice to come up with a solution. The very best thing that will honor Him is for us to start thanking Him for answering our prayers, even before we see the evidence of His intervention.

If we do this, His peace will fill our hearts and protect us from fear and despair, even in the midst of the storm. That's His promise:

> *Be anxious for nothing, but in everything by prayer and supplication* **with thanksgiving** *let your requests be made known to God. And the peace of God, which surpasses all comprehension, shall guard your hearts and your minds in Christ Jesus* (Philippians 4:6–7).

Our natural human response to problems is the opposite of the instructions we read in this scripture. We get anxious, worry and imagine the worst outcome. That's why we have to purposely retrain ourselves according to God's Word.

My dear sister, I encourage you to deliberately practice this new response the next time you encounter a problem in your home, with your children or in your ministry. It will change your life.

———— ❊ ————

Let us pray together for the new school year in our Bridge of Hope centers:

- For the children, that they will do well in their studies.
- For the teachers to be able to love each child as Jesus would.
- For the parents and children to get to know Jesus.

May the Lord bless you with His presence and grace.

Your sister in Christ,

Gisela

10

WHAT'S YOUR TESTIMONY ABOUT GOD?

AUGUST 2007

Dear Sister,

I am so glad to be back home after being gone to Germany for more than three weeks during the month of July.

My parents passed away a few years ago, and it was the responsibility of my sister and me to clear out the home they lived in for 50 years and give away their possessions. Because my sister is seriously ill, she could no longer help me with this task, and so I needed to go and take care of it by myself. I am so thankful that the Lord was with me and answered my prayers to finish the job.

Since I got back, I have started again to work on my writing assignments and preparation for upcoming meetings and seminars. I would like to ask you to please keep my sister in your prayers, that God would touch and heal her by His grace.

In this letter I would like to share with you a few thoughts from Psalm 144:

Blessed be the Lord, my rock,
Who trains my hands for war,
And my fingers for battle;
My lovingkindness and my fortress,
My stronghold and my deliverer;
My shield and He in whom I take refuge.
—Psalm 144:1–2

This psalm contains David's testimony of what God is in his life. We often read powerful declarations of praise like this one in our Bibles, and we borrow them for our own prayers and worship songs. David, however, didn't copy these statements about God from a prayer book. Each expression was a personal testimony of how he experienced God when he was in trouble and cried out to Him for help.

My rock: After David killed Goliath and Saul became envious of him, David's peaceful life was over. His whole world turned upside down, and there was not a place in Israel where he could stay in safety. Because of constant danger to his life and that of his family, he even had to relocate his parents outside the borders of Israel.

In all this turmoil, David found someone he could rely on, count on for help and completely trust in—and that was his God. He experienced Him as his unmovable rock in an ocean of trouble, confusion and uncertainty.

My trainer: When David went out to fight Goliath, he wasn't an experienced soldier who could handle sword and spear. He was a shepherd boy with a sling, some stones and faith that God would give his enemy into his hand.

Even later on, when David became a mighty warrior, he attributed all his success to God and not to any captain of

Saul's army who taught him the basics of warfare. He said: *"For by Thee I can run upon a troop; and by my God I can leap over a wall"* (Psalm 18:29).

My lovingkindness: David loved God and had a humble and teachable heart. Even when he sinned, he always humbled himself before God. That's why God could shower him with His grace and lovingkindness and call him a man after His own heart.

This is how much David valued God's love and compassion toward him: *"Thy lovingkindness is better than life"* (Psalm 63:3).

My fortress, my stronghold: Think about how many years King Saul hunted for David to kill him. David was constantly on the run and had to hide in caves and in the wilderness. He didn't have a fortress with towers and a high wall to protect him inside and keep Saul out. But he experienced how God became his fortress and stronghold and kept him safe. Saul with all his army could not penetrate God's protection around David.

My deliverer: More than once David was betrayed, surrounded by enemies or outnumbered in battle. Yet each time, God delivered him and those who belonged to him.

My shield: David had many close encounters where he could have easily been killed, such as when Saul threw a spear at him while he was playing the harp. At those times, he experienced God as his shield, which no enemy weapon could penetrate.

My refuge: Being a fugitive, where could David have gone for protection and help? People were afraid to give him a place to stay, because Saul had even killed a priest and 85 of his relatives for giving David supplies. God became David's place of refuge and defense when he was in danger, discouraged or weary.

What is *our* personal testimony about God? It's wonderful to know Jesus as our Savior, but the Bible says He wants to be so much more in our lives. Do we know Him yet as our strength, comfort, wisdom, peace or any of the names we just looked at?

Like David, each time we walk through a time of difficulty or blessing in our lives, we should be able to add one more name of God that testifies, in praise, what He has become to us.

My dear sister, I hope these thoughts from Psalm 144 will encourage you to get to know Jesus in a much more personal way.

Please pray with us for the upcoming state Women's Fellowship training seminar in the month of September in India. Pray for:

- Safe travel for the teams.
- The Lord's presence to be with us.
- The training to strengthen our Women's Fellowship program.

May the Lord bless you and fill you with His joy.

Your sister in Christ,

Gisela

11

GOD PUT US IN A FISHBOWL

OCTOBER 2007

Dear Sister,

Recently, a friend sent me an interesting letter. She wrote about the time she met our family when our children were still small. And then she wrote, "I know you, Brother K.P., Daniel and Sarah have made a sacrifice living in a 'fishbowl,' as it were." What she meant was that because of my husband's ministry, people watch our lives very closely—much of the time. I thought: That's true, and now Erika and Danny, our daughter- and son-in-law, have also joined us in the fishbowl!

Being on display came with the call of God on our lives—and it is the same with your life as well. God wants to make each of His servants an example of a Christian whom others can follow, even though He knows we are not perfect. In this letter, we will consider how mindful we must be of our conduct and calling so we will bring honor to Jesus and not discredit His Church.

When the Lord Jesus called His 12 disciples, He simply invited them to follow Him. He didn't reason, threaten or plead with them to become His disciples; nor did He promise them position, power and money. He didn't give a demonstration of His divine powers or tell them that He was the Son of God and the promised Messiah of Israel.

Jesus simply walked by Peter and Andrew's fishing boat and said: *"Follow Me, and I will make you become fishers of men"* (Mark 1:17). In a similar way, He called the others to become His followers.

Jesus allowed them to be with Him and observe Him closely. The disciples were with Him 24 hours a day for more than three years. They watched every aspect of His private life and His public ministry.

They saw the attitude He woke up with in the morning, they listened to what He said about others in private, and they watched His reaction when the food didn't taste good, when the sleeping arrangements were terrible and when He was tired and exhausted.

The disciples learned what made Him happy, serious or sad. They watched how He handled disappointments, misunderstandings, opposition, persecution—as well as praise, fame and the contributions people gave to His ministry.

Each time they heard Jesus teach God's Word, they could check to see if He followed His own teaching. And when He cast out demons, healed the sick, cleansed the lepers, gave sight to the blind and raised the dead, they noticed if He gave God the glory or took it for Himself.

Living and traveling with Jesus, the disciples observed how much of a prayer life He had and whether or not His personal holiness and devotion to God's Word were real.

What was their conclusion? As eyewitnesses of Jesus' private and public life, they came to the conclusion that Peter expressed: *"Lord, to whom shall we go? You have words of eternal life. And we have believed and have come to know that You are the Holy One of God"* (John 6:68–69). The apostles never changed their confession, not even when they faced opposition, persecution or martyrdom.

What did people say about the disciples and the believers of the first-century Church? After watching their private and public lives closely, they called them Christians (see Acts 11:26). They did so because these believers lived and behaved just like Christ.

What do people say about us? Most of us would get a pretty good report card if someone would ask the people in our community and local church about our Christian testimony. After all, we follow the rules of our society, pay our taxes and don't make any trouble. And at church we teach Sunday school, sing in the choir, give our tithe and help the poor.

However, I imagine our report card would get a few deductions if someone asked our friends and neighbors about our Christian character. They know us a whole lot closer and see us daily.

But we would receive our most accurate report card if someone asked our parents, brothers and sisters, husband, children, daughter-in-law or son-in-law regarding our Christian walk. They know who we really are behind closed doors. They could testify to our uncontrolled anger, the sharp words we use to criticize others, how defensive we get when we are corrected, our lack of submission, the unforgiveness we harbor when our feelings get hurt, how often we neglect to pray and read God's Word and the many times we fail to practice what we tell others to do.

What would happen if 12 new believers moved in with us and copied everything we practiced? If they didn't know the Word of God and we were the only believers they could observe and learn from, what kind of Christians would they turn out to be? They would become exactly what we are!

Do you think the Lord Jesus would be honored by the conduct of these disciples if they lived in public what we practiced at home? And would they be a blessing or a headache for the church? If, like Jesus' disciples, they were to become the future leaders of the church, the church would be a reflection of them and those who had trained them.

It is our responsibility to produce authentic followers of Christ. We may feel very insignificant in the work of God. However, we must remind ourselves daily that the future of the Church depends on us providing the correct example. Paul wrote to Timothy, and to us, how we should go about it: *"In speech, conduct, love, faith and purity, show yourself an example of those who believe"* (1 Timothy 4:12).

What if we mess up and make mistakes? We will not be perfect, and those who watch us will surely point out our failures. This is what we must do when we fail: We must humble ourselves, ask forgiveness from God and those we hurt, accept correction and continue to walk in God's grace. God put us in a "fishbowl" so those who watch us can learn this crucial lesson by our example as well.

My dear sister, let us be careful how we represent the Lord Jesus to our generation.

———— ❀ ————

Let us unite in prayer for all our pastors and missionaries. Pray for them:

- That they will maintain a close personal walk with God.
- That their lives will reflect Christ's character.
- That their families will have a testimony in the community that honors Jesus.

May the Lord bless you and keep you close to Himself.

Your sister in Christ,

Gisela

12

WHY DID HE LOVE US?

Dear Sister,

I t's the middle of December, and soon all our family will arrive home. I am excited that we all can spend Christmas together. It will be fun to cook, bake and make our home look nice for the holidays.

It will be so great to do these things together with Sarah and Erika. Of course, my husband, Daniel and Danny will also have their parts in making our Christmas celebration special.

In the first week of January, I will travel to Germany to be with my sister for about two-and-a-half weeks. She is very ill and needs for the Lord to heal her. Please keep her in your prayers. From Germany, I will travel on to India for our state Women's Fellowship seminars and other programs. It looks like I will be gone for almost two months.

In just a few days, Christians all over the world will celebrate Christmas and rejoice over the birth of our Savior, the Lord Jesus Christ. Though this event took place 2,000 years ago, it still fills us with amazement: God loved us so much that He sent His own Son to live among us and then die for our sins.

What was it that God saw in us that was so lovable and deserving that He would make this ultimate sacrifice?

Nothing mankind did was worthy of God's amazing love! Just like today, people broke every one of God's commandments. They turned away from the Living God and worshiped nature and self-made idols. They were selfish, unthankful, corrupt and rebellious, hating, lying, cheating and shedding innocent blood. God's assessment of everyone on earth was: "*There is none righteous, not even one*" (Romans 3:10).

Were we worthy to be redeemed because God created us in His image (see Genesis 1:26) or because He created us for Himself (see Colossians 1:16)?

He also created the angels for Himself, one-third of which joined Lucifer in his rebellion against God and, together with him, were cast out of heaven. Likewise, Adam and Eve joined Satan by listening to him and sinning against God; they consequently were thrown out of Eden. Why did God send Jesus to redeem us, while none of the fallen angels got a second chance?

So why is it that *"God so loved the world,* that He gave His only begotten Son, that whoever believes in Him should not perish, but have eternal life"* (John 3:16)?

We really don't know the answer to why God's love for us is so great. But we know that it is real when we look at His Son lying in a manger. That's why we celebrate Christmas with such joy, hope and thankfulness.

What is our response to God's greatest demonstration of His love for us? If we consider the extent of God's love and the sacrifice God made on our behalf to send His Son to become our Savior, our response should be the very same as that of the wise men who followed the star to Bethlehem: "*They fell down and worshiped Him*" (Matthew 2:11).

This Christmas and every day of the new year, our hearts will overflow with praise and worship if we daily allow the Holy Spirit to reveal God's amazing love to us.

———— ❄ ————

Please pray with us for our leader in Myanmar. His dear wife, Susanna, recently went home to be with the Lord. Pray that the Lord would comfort him and his family and be near to them during this difficult time.

My dear sister, I wish you God's blessing for Christmas and for the coming year. May the Lord watch over you and fill your heart with His joy and peace.

With love, your sister,

Gisela

13

Hope beyond Death

Dear Sister,

A few days ago we celebrated Easter, the day the Lord Jesus rose from the dead. For us as believers, Jesus' resurrection is the proof of His victory over sin, the devil and death. It is also the source of all our hope, comfort and assurance that we too will rise again should we die before the Lord comes back.

This Easter I spent more time thinking about the resurrection of Jesus and all those who belong to Him—because of what happened in February.

Perhaps you remember that in my last letter I told you I was planning to visit my sister in Germany in January and then go on to India for our state Women's Fellowship seminars.

I arrived in Germany on the 4th of January, and I found that my sister had become much more ill and weak than when I saw her last summer. Two years ago she had been diagnosed with an illness that has no cure, and I had asked all the sisters who receive my letter to pray for her.

It was very sad to see her suffer and struggle. While I was there, I helped take care of her. She could no longer walk or speak, and she had great difficulties swallowing food and increasing problems with breathing. However, she was very brave, and she used a speech computer to communicate. She would type in what she wanted to say and then press a button for the computer to speak out what she had written.

One day, while we were sitting together in her living room, she typed in that she believed she would not live much longer. I cried, and then I asked her about her faith in Jesus. I told her that I needed to know if I would see her again. She replied that I didn't have to worry, and that she was sure she will see me again.

To make certain she understood why I was concerned, I said to her: "When you were a child, you made a beginning with the Lord, but later you lived your own life. What happened to that faith you had as a child?" She replied: "I came back to it." When I asked her when that was, she told me: "This sickness brought me back."

When I heard her answer, it became so clear to me how God had answered the prayers of all the thousands of believers who were praying for my sister's healing: He had brought her back to Himself, so she could be forever with Him.

On January 23, in the early morning before I left for India, I prayed with my sister. She wrote "come back soon" on a piece of paper, and then she waved good-bye to me.

When I landed in Delhi, I got the news that the same day I had left Germany, my sister had to be hospitalized because of severe breathing problems. For the next two weeks, her condition changed daily, sometimes bad, sometimes critical and sometimes stable.

In the meantime, Sister Jeena, our national Women's Fellowship leader, along with our regional leaders and I held our first state leaders' seminar in Delhi. It was such a blessing to hear the reports of what the Lord was doing through our Women's Fellowship sisters and the plans God had put on their hearts for this year.

After our time in Delhi, Sister Jeena and I traveled to Nagpur, where we had our second leaders' seminar, and then on to Kerala to take part in the Women's Fellowship program at the Kerala Believers Church state convention.

However, early the next morning I got a call from Germany with the sad news that my sister had passed away. My daughter, Sarah, and I traveled to Germany for my sister's funeral. Sarah was such an encouragement and joy to have with me.

I had to leave Sister Jeena alone to do the speaking and teaching at the Women's Fellowship program during the convention and the rest of the state seminars. I praise God for how well it went.

My sister's funeral was a sad event. She was only 58 years old, and our family and her friends will miss her a lot. For me it is strange to think that now all my immediate family members are gone. But I am so glad that my grandmother, father, mother and sister confessed their faith in Christ—and that I can know they are with the Lord and one day I will see them again.

Christ's victory over death and His promise that those who believe in Him shall live even if they die (John 11:25) turn our tears and mourning into joy. My dear sister, as believers in Jesus, we are so privileged to have a hope that goes beyond death and the grave.

Thank you so very much for all your prayers on behalf of my sister over these past two years. The Lord answered according to His greater wisdom and purpose.

Please pray with us for our brothers and sisters who are facing severe persecution in the Indian state of Orissa. Recently, many churches and believers' homes were burned down, and hundreds of believers had to flee for their lives into the jungle. Please pray:

- That the Lord will keep them safe.
- That their needs for food and shelter will be met.
- That their faith will remain steadfast.
- That those who persecute them will come to know Christ.

May the joy of the Lord be your strength.

Your sister in Christ,

Gisela

14

JUDGING OTHERS

Dear Sister,

I t's early in the morning. I just made myself a cup of coffee, and now I am sitting at my kitchen table to write to you. The other day I read a scripture about not judging others, one that so many believers do not take seriously. I would like to share with you a few thoughts on this subject. Jesus said: *"Do not judge lest you be judged. For in the way you judge, you will be judged; and by your standard of measure, it shall be measured to you"* (Matthew 7:1–2).

The Bible is given to us for our instruction and correction (see 2 Timothy 3:16). God clearly told us in His Word how we should live on this earth as His children. He gave us moral laws to keep and instructions for our personal walk with God, marriage, family, raising children, work, church, missions and our conduct in society.

God's Word is the foundation for our Christian lives and is the measuring rod by which we must evaluate ourselves and everything we encounter in this world as well. Following

God's instructions guides us safely through all the dangers of this fallen world and protects us from wrong decisions. Even if we have taken a wrong turn, God's Word will correct us and put us back on the right path.

We like to measure and judge the spirituality and performance of other believers. We use what we have learned from the Bible as a measuring rod to highlight the faults of other believers and pass judgment on them. We find their speech and behavior not dignified enough, their prayers too lengthy, their spiritual understanding too shallow, their home too fancy or too unkempt, their dress and hairstyle too worldly and their children not as well behaved as ours.

How does it look when we judge others? We are irritated by their behavior, and we condemn them in our hearts. We try to correct them by criticizing or scolding them without truly caring for them. We don't consider their circumstances and have no real compassion or love for them. We get together with other believers and discuss their wrong behavior, inappropriate clothing or lack of spirituality, while we lift up our own righteousness and excellent performance.

Why does Christ not want us to judge others? Because:

- We will be judged by God with the same measure we judge others (see Matthew 7:1–2). The truth is, we often condemn others for the very same things we do ourselves, but we justify *our* behavior with explanations and excuses.

- When we judge, we elevate ourselves above others, and pride and self-righteousness take hold of our heart.

- We forget that it is only God's grace, and nothing in ourselves, that keeps us from making the very same mistakes.

- When we judge others, we destroy the opportunity to speak into their lives and help them change.

- Our judgment may not be accurate! We may have added our own cultural interpretations and religious traditions to what God's Word actually says. This was the mistake the Pharisees made. They burdened people with their many extra laws and regulations (see Mark 7:13).

- The person we judge may be a new believer who loves the Lord dearly but has not yet had time to grow in his faith. It is totally unfair of us to judge him by what took us 5, 10 or 20 years to learn. Our judgment will discourage this new believer and harm his spiritual development.

So what should we do when others don't measure up?

- Don't condemn, criticize or scold them in order to change their performance. True change must always come from the heart; otherwise, the "godly" behavior we scolded them into is only a façade.

- Don't discuss their shortcomings and failures with other believers. Love them enough not to make them the subject of gossip. Instead, seek to cover their failures. If you get any satisfaction out of discussing others' weaknesses, it proves that you lack love for them. *"Above all, keep fervent in your love for one another, because love covers a multitude of sins"* (1 Peter 4:8).

- Show them compassion and mercy like Jesus did when He dealt with others' failures. I guarantee you that the time will come when you will make mistakes and will need others' compassion and mercy. *"As those who have been chosen of God, . . . put on a heart of compassion, kindness, humility, gentleness and patience; bearing with one another, and forgiving each other"*(Colossians 3:12–13).

- Pray for them diligently, and allow the Lord to fill you with His love for them.

- Take them aside privately and talk to them without condemnation. Show them from the Word of God where they fall short. Teach, correct and counsel them with love and gentleness. Encourage them and build them up instead of tearing them down. Pray with them.

- If you find they have a problem that is too difficult for you to counsel, put them in contact with an experienced pastor or a mature believer who can help them.

- Teach them godly behavior by your example rather than by your many words (see 1 Timothy 4:12). You only qualify to teach and correct others if you live in public and private what you proclaim.

- Seek to be a friend and mentor whom they can trust and love rather than a judge who passes sentence on them.

If you practice these things in your church or Bible study group, you will see many positive changes in your life and the lives of others.

———————— ❀ ————————

Let us pray for the country of Myanmar, which just experienced a devastating cyclone:

- For the thousands of people who lost loved ones, are injured or are homeless.
- For supplies to reach those who are suffering and are threatened by disease and starvation.
- That God will enable our leaders, believers and churches to help, comfort and share His love.

May God's peace be with you always.

Your sister in Christ,

Gisela

15

Evidence of Repentance

Dear Sister,

On June 16, our first grandbaby arrived! Her name is Esther Hope, and she is so sweet and beautiful. I just like to look at her and watch her sleep. We all are so grateful to the Lord that our daughter-in-law Erika's delivery went well and that she and the baby are healthy. Of course, little Esther keeps her parents busy. Her favorite things are eating, sleeping and being held. Our son, Daniel, took nice pictures of her, and I wish I could send you one. We feel so blessed to have little Esther in our family.

And very soon she will have a cousin!

This morning I read the message John the Baptist preached when he was baptizing people in the Jordan River. It was quite a fiery sermon, and he wasn't shy in pointing out people's sins. No wonder he was arrested by Herod later on. The statements John the Baptist made regarding repentance are very relevant for us as followers of Christ. He said:

Therefore bring forth fruits in keeping with repentance, and do not begin to say to yourselves, "We have Abraham for our father," for I say to you that God is able from these stones to raise up children to Abraham (Luke 3:8).

After our salvation, we still need to repent. Though we were cleansed from all our sin and saved by grace through faith in the Lord Jesus Christ, we still need to repent each time we act contrary to the will of our Heavenly Father.

As Christians, we live in a fallen world, and the devil tries to trick us into sin every chance he gets. However, our greatest challenge is to be transformed into the image of Christ *in every area* of our lives. In order for this to take place, our mind must be renewed by the Word of God.

For such a long time, our thinking was wrong and led us to wrong actions and habits. Once we receive Christ, the Holy Spirit shows us, one area at a time, where we need to change. This is a process that takes our willingness to leave our old ways and adopt Christ's ways. We will still fail at times—and when we do, God expects us to repent and receive cleansing. The Apostle John explains how this works: *"If we confess our sins, He is faithful and righteous to forgive us our sins and to cleanse us from all unrighteousness"* (1 John 1:9).

What is insincere or unbiblical repentance?

- When we ask forgiveness because we made a mess of things and we want God to rescue us from the consequences.

- When someone confronts us with our unbiblical conduct and we admit our wrong but at the same time defend our old habits.

- When we make excuses with our repentance such as, "This is normal behavior in my culture," "I was brought up in this way," "It is due to the temperament I was born with," "Everybody in my family acts like this," or "The hurtful experiences in my life made me this way."
- When we confess our wrong actions to God but have no intentions of changing them.
- When our mouth admits our un-Christlike behavior, but our heart doesn't see the ugliness of our sin.

What do people rely on when they don't change their old ways? In John the Baptist's time, the religious Jews relied on being descendants of Abraham for their salvation and eternal security. They believed that this fact automatically included them in God's covenant with Israel. Therefore, their repentance was often insincere, and nothing changed in their lives as a result. John the Baptist had a message for those Israelites: *"Do not begin to say to yourselves, 'We have Abraham for our father,' for I say to you that God is able from these stones to raise up children to Abraham"* (Luke 3:8).

In our time, many born-again Christians rely on the love, mercy and grace of our Lord and the fact that indeed they are already saved and going to heaven. Thus they take their remaining un-Christlike behavior lightly. Their repentance is often insincere, and nothing changes in their lives as a result.

But such an attitude is not without severe consequences for ourselves and for the kingdom of God: By clinging to our old ways, we will not grow in many areas of our Christian life, and our usefulness to God becomes very limited. This will result in not fulfilling God's plan for our lives and consequently missing out on many of the rewards God wants to give to us in heaven. Most of all, we will not be able to represent the Lord Jesus in this world in the way we should. This will bring dishonor to God's name and the Church. It will cause people to mock Christ and His Church and will also give them an excuse for rejecting Jesus and the Word of God.

What is true repentance?

- We see our un-Christlike attitudes, habits, behavior and actions in the light of God. We recognize and are deeply convicted by how ugly, offensive and sinful they really are.

- We confess them as sin to the Lord and to others, and we make no excuses for ourselves.

- We ask sincerely for God's forgiveness, and we receive His cleansing by faith.

- We turn from our sinful habits and behavior with all our hearts, and we desire never to go back.

- We renew our mind with what God's Word says, and with the help and power of the Holy Spirit, we replace our old behavior with what we see modeled by Christ.

What is the visible evidence of true repentance? John the Baptist gives the answer: *"Therefore bring forth fruits in keeping with repentance"* (Luke 3:8). It's the new fruit we produce that will grab people's attention and point them to Jesus. They will recognize our new Christlike attitude and behavior and understand that our old ways are gone.

What are the "old ways" you need to sincerely repent of and replace with Christ's life? Is it gossip, envy, laziness, complaining, criticizing others, dishonesty, disobedience, immorality, unforgiveness, selfishness, lack of submission, rebellion, greed, backbiting or pretense? Perhaps your "old ways" are not on this list, but you know what they are.

Today, make a decision to truly repent and remove these un-Christlike ways, and put on the life that is in the Lord Jesus Christ, as the Apostle Paul wrote:

> *Let us therefore lay aside the deeds of darkness and . . . put on the Lord Jesus Christ. . . . In reference to your former manner of life, you lay aside the old self . . . and put on the new self, which in the likeness of God has been created in righteousness and holiness of the truth* (Romans 13:12, 14; Ephesians 4:22, 24).

My dear sister, let us desire to become all that God has planned for us to become in Jesus.

With love and prayers,

Gisela

16

WHAT DOES GOD SAY ABOUT GRANDMOTHERS?

OCTOBER 2008

Dear Sister,

I am writing this letter to you on my way back from India. For the past two months I had the joy of being with our daughter, Sarah, and our son-in law, Danny, for the arrival of their first baby. Little David Jeremiah was born on the 5th of September. He is so cute and beautiful, and it was so special to watch and hold him. As a family we thank God for this healthy little boy and for watching over Sarah during the delivery.

The birth of David made my husband and me grandparents for the second time in three months! I am still learning how to be a mother-in–law, and now I need to learn how to be a grandmother.

Perhaps you wonder: What is there to learn about being a grandmother? Does this role not come naturally to us? Can't we just follow the example of our own grand-mothers, who are the most wonderful people on earth? They love us unconditionally, cook our favorite food, buy us those presents our parents won't get, rescue us when we make mistakes, comfort us when we are sad, tell us we are wonderful even if we are not, pray for us when we are in trouble and believe in us when nobody else does.

Are these not the most important qualities we should seek to imitate when our time comes to be a grandmother—or is there more we should do?

What does the Bible say about the role of a grandmother? Actually, so far I haven't found very many scriptures on grandmothers. However, the Bible has a lot to say about the specific qualities God desires for a godly woman to have and how older sisters should teach younger sisters His principles for their personal life, marriage, work, family and raising children (see Titus 2:3–5).

Surely this means that by the time we are grandmothers we should have acquired those godly qualities God talks about in His Word: *"Let it be the hidden person of the heart, with the imperishable quality of a gentle and quiet spirit, which is precious in the sight of God"*(1 Peter 3:4).

It also means that by then we should have succeeded in applying in our own life the principles we are supposed to teach and pass on to the younger women in the church. Certainly among those younger women are the mothers of our own grandchildren: our daughters and daughters-in-law.

God expects grandparents and parents to pass on their faith to their descendants. Our grandchildren will have to grow up in a world that is full of sin and controlled by the Evil One. Yet God desires that they will know Him early and choose to follow Him. God said about Abraham: *"For I have chosen him, in order that he may command his children and his* *household after him to keep the way of the Lord by doing righteousness and justice . . ."* (Genesis 18:19).

God also instructed the children of Israel not to forget the things He did for them, *"but make them known to your sons and your grandsons."* They were also to remember the words He spoke to them, *"that they may teach their children"* (Deuteronomy 4:9–10). According to this scripture, grandparents are given the responsibility by God to pass on their faith to the next two generations!

The Bible tells us about a grandmother whose example we can follow. It is Lois, the grandmother of Timothy who was the most trusted and faithful "son in the faith" of the Apostle Paul. In fact, Timothy carried on Paul's life work after the apostle was martyred.

Timothy was the son of a Jewish mother and a Greek father. Yet this is what Paul wrote about him: *"From childhood you have known the sacred writings. . . . For I am mindful of the sincere faith within you, which first dwelt in your grandmother Lois, and your mother Eunice, and I am sure that it is in you as well"* (2 Timothy 3:15; 1:5).

Because Timothy grew up in a Gentile nation with a non-Jewish father, who would have taught him the Word of God and helped him to believe in the God of Israel? It was his grandmother Lois who passed on her sincere faith to his mother and, together with her, to Timothy. This grandmother went against all odds with her efforts. Amazingly, she succeeded to see her daughter follow the Lord in spite of her marriage and her grandson serve the Living God in the midst of an idol-worshiping society. What a joy that all three of them received Jesus as their Messiah.

How did Lois pass on her sincere faith? She lived it every day before Eunice and Timothy. Lois not only had faith, but she had *sincere* faith. This means that her faith was genuine, pure, honest, reliable and trustworthy. There was no hypocrisy in her walk with God or her conduct with others. Eunice her daughter followed her example. What Timothy saw in his grandmother and in his mother was genuine godliness and faith, and he too became like them.

When we become grandmothers, we too must model the same kind of godliness and sincere faith to our grandchildren. When they look at us, they should be able to learn from our example what it means to follow Christ, be faithful in all things, have a gentle and quiet spirit, walk by faith and obey God's Word.

Why am I writing to you about how to be a grandmother, even if you may be still unmarried or you are a young wife and mother? My first reason is because I am a new grandmother and I myself need to get a clear understanding of what God expects from me. The second reason is that someday you, too, will be in my place! Let me assure you of this: What you live and practice right now will determine what you become 10 or 20 years from now.

You see, in spiritual things you can only teach others what you genuinely live yourself. Your life, not your words, is the most powerful testimony you have to your children and grandchildren. What you model will transfer, not what you lecture at them!

I want to encourage you to choose now to develop those godly qualities that honor the Lord and that are worthy to pass on.

May the Lord give you much grace to walk with Him with all your heart.

With love and prayers,

Gisela

17

DON'T TAKE GOD'S CALLING LIGHTLY

FEBRUARY 2009

Dear Sister,

H ow are you doing since the new year started? Our family had a wonderful Christmas, and we especially enjoyed that our children and grandchildren were here to celebrate with us. Now it's already February, and I am busy with writing projects and preparations for meetings, a trip to India and a Women's Fellowship seminar next month.

This morning I read in the New Testament how the Lord Jesus called the tax collector Levi to become His disciple: *"As He passed by, He saw Levi the son of Alphaeus sitting in the tax office, and He said to him, 'Follow Me!' And he rose and followed Him"* (Mark 2:14).

Levi's instant obedience changed his life forever. He became the Apostle Matthew who wrote the Gospel of Matthew.

What would have happened if Matthew hadn't obeyed immediately? He could have said to himself, "I need to finish my obligations in the tax office before I can leave. When Jesus passes by next time and calls me again, I will go with Him then."

But what if Jesus never again came along this same road? Even if He passed by a second time a year later, what guarantee was there that the spot among Jesus' 12 disciples was still open? After all, Jesus had only three-and-a-half years to complete His ministry on earth, train His disciples and then die for our sins. He needed disciples who were ready to follow Him right now.

As long as we live on this earth, we are governed by time. We have only a few years for each stage of life. We pass from birth through childhood, youth, adulthood, middle age and old age in a few decades.

Many of the opportunities in life come our way only once. That's why it is crucial that we think deeply and make our decisions with eternity in mind. Especially as Christians, we must take very seriously what we choose to live for during this brief time we have on earth. Levi the tax collector recognized the privilege God offered him and he never looked back, even when things got difficult.

Don't take lightly God's call to serve Him. Did God call you to serve Him in any capacity, whether on a team, in the ministry office, at the church, in the Women's Fellowship or with your husband? Take it very seriously, even if it is just one single task, such as welcoming visitors, discipling a new believer, giving out Gospel tracts, or encouraging and praying for your husband when he goes for ministry.

Consider this: The God and Creator of the universe has chosen *you* among more than 6 billion people on earth to do something for Him. He easily could have given the job to thousands of other people more qualified and able than you. But He wanted to bless you with the awesome opportunity to serve Him and help win souls for God's kingdom. There is absolutely nothing in this world, nor in the universe, that is of greater value than the smallest task Jesus entrusted to you.

Don't quit—or trade your calling for something else. Over the years, I have seen many brothers and sisters who started so well walk away from fulfilling their calling. Here are just a few of the reasons:

- Being offended by someone
- Not being given the recognition or position they thought they deserved
- Not wanting to humble themselves and accept correction from their pastor or leader
- Harboring bitterness and developing a critical spirit
- Someone betraying their trust
- Feeling lonely and discouraged
- Financial struggles and fear of the future
- Unwillingness to serve in a place that is not near their home
- Misunderstanding between co-workers
- Having a materialistic mindset and looking for opportunities for personal gain
- Making a mistake and covering it up instead of confessing and repenting from it
- Difficulties adjusting to a new mission field
- Losing heart because someone spread lies or gossips about them

- Pressure from parents and relatives who want their son or daughter making a lot of money instead of doing ministry
- Constant complaints and tears from a wife who does not submit to her husband's leadership
- Being lured away from the ministry by someone who offers them an important position, money, travel and other material benefits

My dear sister, Jesus and the apostles faced many of these struggles in their ministry, and we will too. The Enemy always wants to use problems to cause us to quit our calling, or at least to make us bitter and unfruitful. Jesus, on the other hand, desires that we overcome each of these trials and temptations and become stronger and more Christlike in our character and usefulness to God.

God's Word declares that we as Christians are not helpless or too weak to overcome all these trials: *"For whatever is born of God overcomes the world"* (1 John 5:4). Jesus promised to be with us always (see Matthew 28:20), and we have received the Holy Spirit, who lives in us and empowers us to be His witnesses (see Acts 1:8).

> But in all these things we overwhelmingly conquer through Him who loved us (Romans 8:37).

> I can do all things through Him who strengthens me (Philippians 4:13).

Therefore, let us never entertain the thought of quitting or trading our calling for anything else! Instead, let us make a lifetime decision to be faithful to Jesus and fulfill our calling no matter what we may encounter.

It's worth it to finish the race and win the prize. Shortly before he was martyred, the Apostle Paul wrote, *"I have fought the good fight, I have finished the course, I have kept the faith; in the future there is laid up for me the crown of righteousness, which the Lord, the righteous Judge, will award to me on that day; and not only to me, but also to all who have loved His appearing"* (2 Timothy 4:7–8).

My dear sister, let us pray for one another that we will all be found faithful in finishing what God has entrusted to each of us.

With love and prayers,

Gisela

18

HE DEALS GENTLY WITH US

APRIL 2009

Dear Sister,

This letter comes to you from Kerala, India, where I arrived at the beginning of March. I had the privilege of attending the graduation of our seminary students and also meeting many of our Believers Church leaders during the leadership meeting that took place afterward. From March 15–18 we held a seminar for our Believers Church Women's Fellowship state leaders from India, Nepal and Sri Lanka. Sister Jeena and I were very encouraged to hear the good reports of what the Lord is doing through our Women's Fellowship sisters in the local churches and through our district, state and regional Women's Fellowship teams.

This month, a new literacy training book will be printed in the Hindi language and will be available for our local Women's Fellowship teams to order and use for their literacy classes. It will be such a blessing to thousands of sisters who haven't yet had a chance to learn how to read and write. Please encourage all the illiterate sisters in your church to participate in the literacy classes, so they will soon be able to read the Bible.

Plans are already under way to translate this literacy training book into five other languages. Please pray with us for this important project.

While I am here, I have the joy of spending time with our children and grandchildren. Little Esther is now nine months old, and little David is six months old. They are so sweet and fun to watch, especially when they smile at me or play with their toys.

Yesterday morning I read something in the book of Hebrews that I would like to share with you.

> *For every high priest taken from among men is appointed on behalf of men in things pertaining to God, in order to offer both gifts and sacrifices for sins; he can deal gently with the ignorant and misguided, since he himself also is beset with weakness* (Hebrews 5:1–2).

In the Old Testament, God chose a high priest to stand before Him on behalf of His people. This high priest was not perfect. Like everyone else, he made mistakes, and in one way or another, he too transgressed God's laws. That's why he had to offer sacrifices for his own sins as well as for those committed by the people of Israel.

God desired that this high priest would deal gently with His people! God loves and cares for His people like a shepherd for his sheep. Psalm 23 is a true picture of how God leads and looks after them with great compassion and understanding of their needs.

God doesn't want His sheep to be beaten, judged or destroyed if they do wrong or get sick or hurt. Instead, He wants them rescued and restored to health. That's why God wanted the high priest to care for His people with the same loving heart as His.

In fact, God expected the high priest to deal extra gently with those who sinned out of ignorance or because they were misguided by their own hearts or the influence of others. The high priest's gentleness and compassion toward others were to come from recognizing that he, too, was plagued by weaknesses and needed forgiveness and mercy.

In the New Testament, Jesus, the Son of God, became our High Priest. When Jesus died on the cross for the sin of the whole world, He was the final, perfect and sinless sacrifice God accepted for our redemption. Since that point, our sins have been completely forgiven, and we can become sons and daughters of God through faith in Jesus. There is no further sacrifice needed, ever. And if there are no more sacrifices, then there is also no need for a human high priest to offer them. The Bible says that when Jesus went to heaven, He became our High Priest, constantly interceding for us (see Hebrews 7:25).

Jesus, our High Priest, deals gently with us! As long as we live on this earth, we will be surrounded by the results of the fall of man: sin, sickness and death. Our world is full of corruption, unspeakable suffering, poverty, diseases, abuse of innocent children, injustice, slavery, child labor, cruelty, wickedness, violence, murder, wars, dishonesty, lies, gossip and any other evil thing we can imagine. As a result, we face fear, discouragement, economic struggles, sadness, burdens and constant pressure from the world around us. In addition, each one of us has weaknesses and we face temptations. Though we are saved and we have the power of the Holy Spirit to overcome the world and temptations, we still fail at times.

When that happens, our greatest comfort is that Jesus understands us completely and has compassion and mercy on us. He deals gently with us because He lived in a human body in this corrupt world for 33 years, experiencing everything we go through.

> For we do not have a high priest who cannot sympathize with our weaknesses, but one who has been tempted in all things as we are, yet without sin. Let us therefore draw near with confidence to the throne of grace, that we may receive mercy and may find grace to help in time of need (Hebrews 4:15–16).

As servants of God, we are likewise expected to deal gently with others! How do we deal with others when they make small mistakes or fail miserably? So often we are disgusted, angry and ready to cut them off from our love, care and fellowship. Yes, we must hate sin, the consequences it brings and the dishonor it causes for the name of the Lord. However, we must also remember that God has no pleasure in the destruction of a child of God who has sinned, but rather in his restoration. To find compassion for the one who failed, we must look at our own weaknesses and in humility admit that we are capable of failing just like him. The only thing that keeps us safe is the grace of God. This perspective helps us to be humble and deal gently with the already bruised reed (see Isaiah 42:3).

The Bible teaches that gentleness must be part of the character of a servant of God. If we cannot deal gently with others, we are not qualified to look after God's people. Helping others does include rebuke, correction and instruction, but it must come from a heart of compassion and love:

Pursue righteousness, godliness, faith, love, perseverance and gentleness (1 Timothy 6:11).

The Lord's bond-servant must not be quarrelsome, but be kind to all, able to teach, patient when wronged, with gentleness correcting those who are in opposition (2 Timothy 2:24–25).

Remind them to be . . . gentle, showing every consideration for all men (Titus 3:1–2).

Dear sister, let us watch over our heart, cultivating the fruit of the Spirit of gentleness, so that our ministry will be according to the will of God.

With love and prayers,

Gisela

19

FOR THE SAKE OF PEACE

JUNE 2009

Dear Sister,

How are you getting along with your brothers and sisters in your church or ministry? Sometimes it is not easy to maintain the unity and love God wants us to have for each other.

This morning I read the story of how Abraham and Lot separated because their herds and flocks had grown too large for the grazing land available. There are some important things we can learn from this story that will help us when another believer takes advantage of our love and kindness. Please read Genesis 13:5–17.

Abraham addressed the issue. Abraham did not pretend that everything was fine while there was ongoing strife between his and Lot's herdsmen. He recognized that something had to be done to end the conflict. That's why he took the initiative to talk to Lot, his nephew, about the problem.

Abraham's main goal for finding a solution was to maintain peace between them. *"Please let there be no strife between you* *and me, nor between my herdsmen and your herdsmen, **for we are brothers**"* (Genesis 13:8).

Abraham offered a solution: *"Is not the whole land before you? Please separate from me: if to the left, then I will go to the right; or if to the right, then I will go to the left"* (Genesis 13:9).

Abraham was God's chosen servant, a respected leader, a powerful chief of his people and Lot's uncle. As such, he had the full authority to tell Lot what to do and expect him to follow his orders without question.

However, Abraham's love and desire to live in peace with his "brother" caused him to humble himself before Lot. Rather than giving him an order, Abraham twice, gently but urgently, appealed to Lot with a request. And when Abraham offered a solution to their problem, he took the risk of ending up with a bad deal.

Abraham left the choice of land to Lot, who shamelessly took advantage of his uncle's generosity and chose *all* the best land for himself (see vv. 10 and 11).

Didn't Abraham see it coming? No doubt Abraham must have known Lot's character. After all, the young man had lived with Abraham since his father, Haran (Abraham's brother), died. Perhaps he hoped that Lot had learned and changed since he too believed in Abraham's God, and Abraham wanted to give him a chance to succeed in life.

How did Abraham respond when he was exploited by his "brother"? He was silent when Lot took advantage of his love and generosity. Surely Abraham must have been disappointed, hurt and sad, yet he didn't complain to God, to his wife, Sarah, or to anyone else about Lot.

And he didn't scold or slap his nephew for his utter selfishness, lack of respect and ungratefulness. Abraham easily could have gone back on his word and fairly divided the good and bad land between his nephew and himself, but he didn't. He chose rather to suffer loss and be considered foolish in order to maintain peace with his brother.

In addition, Abraham didn't keep any bitterness in his heart toward Lot. Instead, he loved and cared for him enough to risk his own life and that of his men to rescue Lot when Lot was taken captive during a war. And he pleaded and bargained with God to spare Sodom on behalf of his nephew and his family.

Why did Abraham not fight for his rights? Abraham trusted God with all his heart. He believed that the God who called him and promised to give him all the land (which included the portion Lot took) would surely fulfill His word. He was not worried about his present disadvantage, Lot's greediness or what he should do to get the fertile land back in his possession. He placed himself and his future into God's mighty hand and left it up to Him to defend his rights and fulfill His promise at the right time. That's faith!

God reconfirmed His promise to Abraham. Read Genesis 13:14–17. God was pleased with Abraham's choice to humble himself and suffer loss in order to maintain peace— and to trust God to be his defender.

God encouraged Abraham by repeating and reconfirming his former promise: *"For all the land which you see, I will give it to you and to your descendants . . ."* And then God rewarded Abraham by adding a new promise: *"forever"* (Genesis 13:15). Even today, God still stands by this promise to Israel.

Choose to follow Abraham's example! We too will encounter situations when other Christians take advantage of our love and kindness, even if we never make them a generous offer like Abraham. Perhaps you lend money to a needy sister in the church, but later on when she is doing well, she has no intention of paying it back. Or maybe your co-worker or team member takes credit for your good work and gets the recognition and reward you deserve.

If the fellow Christian who took advantage of your good heart is unwilling to change, you have only two choices:

1. You can fight for your rights by proving them wrong and force them to do the right thing, but you will end up with a broken relationship.

2. Or you can choose to suffer injustice, forgive them and entrust yourself to the Lord and thus maintain peace in the Body of Christ.

If you choose the second option, you are following Abraham's example, and God's blessing will surely rest on you. Don't fear that your fellow believer got away with defrauding you. God will deal with him in His own time, for he too is His child and needs transformation of his character.

Let us thank God together for the release of Brother Manja from prison in Nepal. Pray for him and his family, that God will bless them abundantly and use their testimony to strengthen His people.

With love and prayers,

Gisela

20

TRAVEL, SEMINARS
AND FAMILY

Dear Sister,

When I landed in Delhi, India, last month, I had the joy of receiving a copy of the printed Women's Fellowship (WF) literacy training book in the Hindi language. A team of our WF sisters and a pastor who is trained in literacy work wrote and designed this book. It will be used to teach our illiterate sisters and others in the local churches how to read and write. The book has already been shipped to all the states where the Hindi language is spoken. Our WF leaders are now working on the task of getting it translated and adapted into six other major Indian languages.

On September 8, World Literacy Day, we will start our WF literacy teachers training. Sisters from six Indian states will come together to learn how to use the literacy book in order to start literacy classes in our local churches. A recent survey of our churches in 14 states in India shows that 54 percent of our dear believers are illiterate. There is much work to be done to help these first-generation Christians to be able to read the Bible for themselves. It's vital not only for their own spiritual growth, but also for the stability and future of the Church.

The literacy course will be an ongoing Women's Fellowship program. Even if all the current believers become literate, we will continually gain new illiterate ones as each church grows in numbers.

A week ago, Sister Jeena (our national Women's Fellowship leader for India) and I returned to Kerala, India, from our trip to Myanmar and Tamil Nadu.

In Myanmar we had a five-day Women's Fellowship training seminar. The sisters were so eager to learn and participate, and we are very confident that they will do well in implementing the program. The Believers Church leadership was very supportive, and we had wonderful fellowship with our sisters and brothers. We felt like family. During our stay, we had the opportunity to eat all kinds of food we had never seen or tasted before. It was a lot of fun.

One afternoon we visited the first church that Adoniram Judson established, named after the first Burmese Christian he won to Christ. Judson's life and sacrifice were not in vain. The believers throughout Myanmar are the fruit of this man's willingness to become the grain of wheat Jesus talked about: *"Unless a grain of wheat falls into the earth and dies, it remains by itself alone; but if it dies, it bears much fruit"* (John 12:24).

Our second training seminar in Chennai was for pastors' wives. About 225 sisters came from all the different districts of Tamil Nadu. We were encouraged by their eagerness to learn lessons that will help them in their personal walk with the Lord and improve their effectiveness as pastors' wives. We were grateful for the help, advice and support we received from our Believers Church state leader and our state WF team.

Pastors' wives seminars are part of the WF program. They are designed as an ongoing program in every district where we have churches. The goal is to encourage and train each pastor's wife to be able to help her husband in his ministry and to be a blessing to the church.

In a number of places, our state and district WF teams have already held pastors' wives seminars, and we have heard good reports as a result. However, before we can implement the seminars everywhere, we need to complete the curriculum for the first series of seminars. These are biblical lessons and practical ministry training sessions that need to be taught systematically in all of the seminars. That way all the pastors' wives receive the same ongoing training. We hope to be able to complete the curriculum needed within the next two months.

Right now, I am in Kerala for a few weeks. My husband was also here when I came. At the moment he is traveling for two weeks to speak in meetings.

While he is gone, I work in the morning hours on some WF writing projects, and in the afternoon and evening, I spend time with our daughter, Sarah, and her family. I was so looking forward to seeing them and especially little David. When I saw him last in April, he was just starting to figure out how to crawl. This time he is walking and running. He is so busy playing and discovering things and smiling at everybody. He has a lot of friends at the campus.

Each morning he goes with his mother to the seminary office, and while he takes a nap, Sarah works as part of the administration team. At lunchtime they go home, and Sarah does the rest of her work in the evening when David is asleep. He likes his mom the best when he is sad, tired or hungry.

David is especially excited when his daddy comes home from his work at the ministry. He wants to play hide-and-seek with him and other noisy games. With me, he likes to read books, bounce on my knees to nursery rhymes and clap his hands to songs. In two weeks he will have his first birthday. I am happy that my husband and I can be here for this event.

Little Esther, David's cousin, was one year old in June. She walks and "reads" books to herself and goes to sleep hugging her little doll. She is a very happy little girl. When she visits me, she likes to play with my purse, my keys and some teddy bears I have in my kitchen. She is such a sweet little angel, and I miss her while I am here in India. I look forward to when I can enjoy both of my grandchildren together at the same place!

Dear sister, I wish I could also know something about your life, family and ministry. Perhaps I will meet you somewhere at a conference or seminar.

Please join us in prayer for some of the things I mentioned in this letter:

- The upcoming training of literacy teachers for our local churches in September.
- That soon the WF groups in all our local churches will be able to start the literacy course.
- The training of teams to adapt and translate the literacy book into other languages.
- For our sisters in Myanmar as they implement the WF program in their churches.
- For the completion of the curriculum for the pastors' wives seminars.
- For several dedicated sisters to help Sister Jeena in the head Women's Fellowship office.
- **And let's thank God** together for the printing of the literacy book in the Hindi language.

May the Lord bless you and use your life to reach others with His love.

Your sister in Christ,

Gisela

21

DIVERSE BUT ONE

Dear Sister,

I t has been a while since you received my last letter. How are you doing? I trust that you seek the Lord each day and find encouragement and strength in His Word.

Time has gone by so fast, and we have already passed the first month of the new year. Since I wrote to you last time, our family has grown—my husband and I became grandparents for the third time. On the 27th of October, little Jonah was born to our son, Daniel, and his wife, Erika. We thank God for a safe delivery for Erika and for a healthy, beautiful grandson. Little Esther, Jonah's sister, is excited to have a baby brother.

About a week before Jonah was born, our daughter, Sarah, her husband, Danny, and little David came for a visit. We all had a few wonderful weeks together, and we enjoyed watching Esther and David play. They were so busy discovering the world around them, and they made us smile a lot.

Thank you for your prayers for our family and especially for our grandchildren. Our hearts' desire is that they will come to know the Lord early in their lives and serve Him.

My husband and I were in Kerala during most of December and January. We celebrated Christmas together with Sarah and her family. Little David was so happy about all the lights, stars and decorations of the season.

January 3–10 was our Believers Church General Assembly. More than 3,000 delegates from all the people groups and nations where we have churches came together and celebrated God's goodness and our oneness as His family. The sessions were translated into 15 languages.

Personally, what blessed me the most was to see the diversity of our church and watch how much these first-generation Christians love the Lord and one another. The wonderful diversity among our brothers and sisters came alive each evening during the cultural programs and during the rallies at the beginning and the end of our General Assembly, when everyone wore their traditional clothing. The one thing I was most grateful for were the many godly leaders the Lord has given to our church. We are indeed blessed beyond measure.

Because our church is so diverse, I thought to share a few thoughts with you about how we as Christians should treat others who are different from us. This does not just apply to a conference, but also to our life in society and in the local church.

When we meet others from different social backgrounds and cultures, we must always keep two things in mind:

1. All people were created by God and in His image. That makes them all equally precious in the sight of God—so much so, that Jesus died for each one of them (see John 3:16). Social divisions such as classes and castes were invented by people in order to keep others out of their own group or to dominate each other.

2. God created each person different from anyone else in this world because He wanted him or her to be different! That means you are made unique. Everything about you was specifically chosen by your loving Heavenly Father according to the plan and task He has for your life. That includes your people group, language, looks, skin color, gender, gifts and talents (see Psalm 139:13–16). There never was, and never will be, another you! And the same is true of every person you meet!

If we keep these two things in mind, we will be able to treat others with respect and kindness. It also will keep us from pride and from exalting ourselves above others. And it will prevent us from trying to make others into something they were not created or gifted to be. That's something parents need to remember when they raise their children.

Being different is not the same as being wrong! Each culture or ethnic group has its own way of doing things, such as food preparation, dress, social interaction, family relationships, entertainment, art and the things they value. Each group believes they have the best way of life and that their view on things is the right one.

What happens when we meet others who come from a different background? Often, we automatically judge their behavior by the values and customs we were taught. That's the reason why we look down on others, despise and reject them, question their values, criticize their behavior and dress, condemn their views and discriminate against them.

We must learn that being different is not the same as being wrong! According to God's Word, "wrong" is when we transgress God's unchanging moral laws such as "you shall not kill" or "you shall not commit adultery." There is nothing wrong in being different in the way we dress, eat or interact, unless one of these things violates God's moral laws.

Diversity in the Body of Christ makes us richer and stronger. This is true about the gifts of the Holy Spirit (see 1 Corinthians 12:7). It is also true about the various cultures within our church: Believers Church can broadcast the Gospel in 110 languages and work among 300 people groups only because we have brothers and sisters from each of these cultures and languages in our churches.

We can learn from each other. Instead of being proud and criticizing others' differences, thank God for an opportunity to learn something new about them and from them. The more you understand others, the more effective your witness for Christ will be. You will find that each group has good things worthy of learning.

How is it possible for such a diverse church like ours to be one in Christ? It is possible only if each of us follows what Jesus told us to do: *"A new commandment I give to you, that you love one another, even as I have loved you, that you also love one another"* (John 13:34).

Love is not proud, does not judge and knows no discrimination. Love accepts others as they are and seeks to bless and serve them, just like Jesus did when He walked on this earth.

My dear sister, let's pray for one another that above all else, we will love one another as Jesus loved us.

Your sister in Christ,

Gisela

22

FEARLESS AND AFRAID

MAY 2010

Dear Sister,

Last month, little David and his parents came to visit us. It was wonderful to have our family all in one place. David and Esther (his cousin) had such fun playing together. Jonah, who is now 6 months old, enjoyed watching them. All three made us laugh a lot. I thank God for giving us this time together with our children and grandchildren.

These past few days I have been reading the story of the prophet Elijah in the Old Testament. He seems to be one of those spiritual superheroes who stands far above all of us. Yet this is what the Bible says about him: *"Elijah was a man with a nature like ours, and he prayed earnestly that it might not rain; and it did not rain on the earth for three years and six months. And he prayed again, and the sky poured rain, and the earth produced its fruit"* (James 5:17–18).

If indeed Elijah was a man with a nature like ours, what was it that made him such a spiritual giant? We find the answer in the events recorded in 1 Kings 17–19.

Elijah didn't have an easy ministry in the days of King Ahab and Jezebel. In fact, he was on their "most wanted list" and had to spend much of his time in hiding to save his life. The message God gave him for Ahab and Israel was not prosperity and blessing, but rebuke and severe judgment for their idolatry and wickedness. It surely wasn't easy for him to preach to a hostile audience and not get any applause or appreciation for his sermon. Yet Elijah never altered his message to please people.

He saw incredible miracles in his ministry. Just in these three chapters alone, we read how according to Elijah's word, it didn't rain for three years, and how it only rained again when he said it would; how ravens brought him food during the drought; how the flour and oil in the house of the widow of Zarephath didn't run out and how her dead son came back to life when Elijah prayed; how on Mount Carmel God answered Elijah's prayer with fire; and how he even outran, on foot, Ahab's chariot.

He was bold and fearless one day, and afraid the next. On Mount Carmel, Elijah boldly stood alone for God against King Ahab, 400 prophets of Baal and the people of Israel. He challenged them to a contest that proved to everyone that the Lord was God. And he killed all the prophets of Baal. However, the very next day when he received Jezebel's death threats, Elijah was so afraid that he ran for his life into the wilderness.

He even wanted to quit the ministry and die. Elijah's expectations may have been a national repentance after the Mount Carmel victory. Instead, Ahab, Jezebel and the people resumed their idol worship, and Jezebel did her best to hunt him down. Elijah got so depressed and discouraged that he prayed, *"It is enough; now, O Lord, take my life, for I am not better than my fathers"* (1 Kings 19:4).

How did God respond to His fearful and discouraged servant? God in His grace remembered that Elijah was human. The Bible tells us, *"For He Himself knows our frame; He is mindful that we are but dust"* (Psalm 103:14).

God sent an angel to bring the weary prophet food, so he could go on a long journey to the mountain of God. There God met with Elijah in a gentle way. He let him pour out his heart and patiently listened to all his complaints and discouragements. He didn't interrupt him, condemn him for his weakness, preach a 10-point sermon at him or rebuke him for his wish to die.

Then what did God do? He simply allowed Elijah to be in His presence, and ultimately, He sent him out with new ministry assignments. The time Elijah spent in the presence of God renewed his strength, and he was able to resume his ministry.

God's presence always restores us; that's why it is so important that we come to Him daily. Please read 1 Chronicles 16:11, 27 and Isaiah 40:29–31.

What do we learn from Elijah's story?

To have a nature like ours means: Elijah was not born a super human. His fear, weakness and discouragement prove it. He was a fragile vessel of clay, just like we are. That means all the boldness, power, glory and miracles we see in his life and ministry were of God and not of himself (see 2 Corinthians 4:7).

What, then, made him a spiritual giant? Each time this clay vessel trusted God and prayed in faith, God stood by His Word, empowered His servant, answered his prayers and performed miracles. It was Elijah's faith in his God that made all the difference. Elijah believed and acted on what God said, with full assurance that God would do what He said He would do.

God still acts on faith! As Christians, we have Jesus as our example, God's Word for our instruction and the Holy Spirit to empower us. However, God is still looking for that "Hebrews 11:1" kind of faith to act on our behalf and to fulfill His promises. Without faith we cannot please Him, nor can we expect to receive anything He promised in His Word (see Hebrews 11:6 and James 1:6–7).

My dear sister, God recorded Elijah's story of weakness and faith for us, so we will know what incredible things God can do with even the most fragile vessels of clay—when we believe.

God is our example for how to deal with Christians who are discouraged and weary. Deal with them gently, with grace. *Listen* patiently and with compassion. Let there be no condemnation or 10-point sermon. Take them with you into God's presence and help them to wait upon the Lord until their strength is renewed.

Let us pray together for:

- Recruitment of committed students for our Bible colleges.
- Teams working on translating and adapting the literacy book in seven languages.

I am grateful to God that you love the Lord and seek to serve Him with all your heart.

Your sister in Christ,

Gisela

23

THE VALUE OF DIFFICULTIES

Dear Sister,

This letter comes to you right after my return from India. In July I had the privilege to be part of our Women's Fellowship leaders' seminar in Kerala and then to travel with Sister Jeena to Sri Lanka for a training program for Women's Fellowship district teams. Both seminars went very well, and we are excited and encouraged by all the good things the Lord is doing through the Women's Fellowship program.

A few days ago I read Psalm 119, and I would like to share some thoughts with you.

The writer of Psalm 119 earnestly prayed to God to teach him His statutes:

Blessed art Thou, O Lord; teach me Thy statutes (v. 12).

Open my eyes, that I may behold wonderful things from Thy law (v. 18).

Teach me Thy statutes. Make me understand the way of Thy precepts (vv. 26–27).

Remove the false way from me, and graciously grant me Thy law (v. 29).

Give me understanding, that I may observe Thy law, and keep it with all my heart (v. 34).

Teach me good discernment and knowledge (v. 66).

The law, statutes and precepts are the commands, principles and guidelines God has given us in His Word to live by. If we follow them, our lives will be blessed: They protect us from wrong and harmful ways, and they guide us in the path of righteousness.

God answered the psalmist's prayers by letting him encounter afflictions. When the psalmist prayed, he may have thought God would answer him by giving him a special revelation through an angel, a dream or a vision like some of the prophets had. But none of these things happened. Instead, God allowed him to go through afflictions—this means sufferings, problems, pain, difficulties and hardships.

At first, he may have been confused and wondered why God did not prevent these afflictions from coming his way. After all, he loved God and was seeking to learn His ways and serve Him with all his heart. Should that not qualify him to be blessed by God and receive the very best from Him in his daily life?

But then he discovered that these afflictions were the very best God allowed him to have for a season, because they taught him the very things he so much wanted to learn:

- Through the trials he faced, he learned to search out God's promises and to cling to them (vv. 49, 50, 52).

- He learned to walk by faith and trust God to fulfill His Word (vv. 107, 116).

- He discovered how he could keep from sin and walk in purity (vv. 9, 11).

- He experienced that God was his hiding place and his shield when he could not protect himself (v. 114).

- He found out that God's Word gave him light for his path, understanding and wisdom (vv. 98–100, 104, 105, 130).

- He learned that God was good, faithful and righteous (vv. 68, 137–138, 142).

- He learned that his greatest treasure was God's Word, and that all of God's Word was truth (vv. 127, 142, 160).

And this man experienced that God was faithful to bring him safely through every single storm and affliction he described in this psalm.

When he realized what he had learned, he was thankful to God for the afflictions through which He led him. He told God: *"Before I was afflicted I went astray, but now I keep Thy word. . . . It is good for me that I was afflicted, that I may learn Thy statutes"* (Psalm 119:67, 71).

He looked at his life before and after he faced all those difficulties and sufferings, and he came to the conclusion that going through those trials was well worth it. They taught him important lessons that he may not have learned any other way. Most of all, before those afflictions he so easily went off course, but now he was able to obey God's Word and stay on the right path.

We, too, ask God to teach us His ways, but we seldom appreciate when He answers by leading us through trials. Why?

1. Because we expect God to teach us through one earthly blessing after another. This may include getting an A+ in our exams, having the best house, job and car or making a lot of money so all our dreams can come true. There is no doubt that God is kind to us and He blesses us with many good things. *However, we rarely seem to learn deep spiritual lessons and obedience through an ongoing series of earthly blessings.* The children of Israel didn't, though it was definitely God's first choice for them to hear His Word and keep it forever and thus avoid all bitter consequences. We seem to have the same struggle with obedience that they did.

2. Because we often don't understand the value of learning through difficulties. If you look back at your Christian life, you will discover that you learned more through a short time of struggles and trials than in 10 years of an "easy life." For example:

- The persecution and rejection you faced from your family when you received Christ caused you to learn to cling to the Lord for strength, comfort and help. It also caused you to learn to trust the Lord for your future.

- When you were misunderstood and falsely accused, it caused you to learn to commit yourself into the hand of God and allow Him to defend you in His own time.

There is something about suffering that teaches and changes us. God used the same teaching method for His Son when He came to earth, though He was without sin: *"Although He was a Son, He learned obedience from the things which He suffered"* (Hebrews 5:8). And Philippians 2:7–8 tells us that Christ's obedience went from laying down all His glory in heaven until His death on the cross.

3. Because we don't recognize that it is God's love that doesn't give up on us. God could easily let us go astray if we didn't abide by His Word. Yet it is His great love for us that uses afflictions so we will learn to keep His Word and live.

As parents, we love our children in a similar way. If our 3-year-old son runs across the street by himself, a car may hit him. If our words have no effect to restrain him, we discipline him. It hurts momentarily, but it teaches him to abide by our command. We love him enough to "afflict" him to save his life.

The writer of Psalm 119 recognized God's love behind the afflictions he faced. That's why he wrote, *"In faithfulness Thou hast afflicted me"* (v. 75). If you can look back on the afflictions God has led you through and see His faithfulness, then you, too, will become thankful for the work He has accomplished in your life.

Dear sister, there is a lot more we need to consider about afflictions in order to have a good balance on this subject. We will do so in my next letter.

With love and prayers,

Gisela

24

GOD KNOWS WHAT
HE IS DOING

NOVEMBER 2010

Dear Sister,

S ince I wrote to you last time, I spoke at several women's
retreats and visited our ministry offices in England and Germany. It was so nice to meet our brothers and sisters who work
so diligently to help reach Asia with the love of Christ.

Last month, Sister Jeena wrote me the good news that the
Women's Fellowship literacy books have been completed and
published in seven new languages. Let us thank God together
for making this possible. Soon thousands of our illiterate believers will be able to read God's Word. Please pray for the
training of all the literacy teachers in those languages.

In August, I sent you the first part of a lesson on affliction.
Here is the second part:

In our last lesson we learned about a man who had trouble
staying on the right path. When he asked God to teach him His
ways, God led him through afflictions. In the end, this man was

thankful that he was afflicted because it taught him to abide by the Word of God. He also recognized that it was God's faithfulness and love that led him through this experience.

We, too, can trust God when we go through afflictions.

God does not create the afflictions we face in this fallen and corrupt world! He is *not* the author of evil. The devil is. When Adam sinned, he and the whole human race suffered the consequences. That's why people in this world face problems, sickness, tragedies and death. We also suffer because of the ungodliness, unrighteousness and injustice of world systems as well as individuals' corruption, perversion and slavery to every kind of sin.

As believers, we must not fear when God permits afflictions to come our way. The Bible teaches us that we have a loving Heavenly Father who does not enjoy torturing or persecuting us for His entertainment! We are His beloved children, and He deeply cares for us. He hurts when we hurt, and He is near to the brokenhearted and compassionate toward the afflicted and suffering.

The afflictions we face as children of God are carefully measured by God.

They cannot come without His permission. We see this very clearly in Job's life. We read that God had put a hedge of protection around this man, and the Enemy could not touch him, his family or his possessions. Even when God permitted afflictions to come his way, He set definite limits that Satan could not cross (see Job 1 and 2).

They are temporary afflictions. Job's afflictions were for a limited time, and so were Joseph's sufferings as a slave in

Egypt and David's struggles because of King Saul. The writer of Psalm 119 clearly states: *"Before I was afflicted I went astray, but now I keep Thy word"* (v. 67). The words "was" and "now" tell us that his afflictions passed. Even if someone's affliction continues until death, we must remember that death marks the end of all suffering for a child of God. From the perspective of eternity, all our earthly afflictions are temporary.

God uses our temporary earthly afflictions to teach us His ways. The intention of the devil is always that the afflictions we face in this world would cause us to walk away from God (see Job 1:11 and 2:5). God, on the other hand, uses the very same afflictions to draw us closer to His heart, strengthen our faith and cause us to know Him in a deeper way.

The Bible is full of incredible truths that people learned through difficult times:

- **Job** declared by faith: *"As for me, I know that my Redeemer lives"* (Job 19:25). After his encounter with God, he said: *"I have heard of Thee by the hearing of the ear; but now my eye sees Thee"* (Job 42:5).

- **Joseph** told his brothers: *"Now do not be grieved or angry with yourselves, because you sold me here; for God sent me before you to preserve life"* (Genesis 45:5).

- **David** wrote: *"For by Thee I can run upon a troop; and by my God I can leap over a wall"* (Psalm 18:29).

- **The writer of Psalm 119** concluded: *"It is good for me that I was afflicted, that I may learn Thy statutes"* (v. 71).

We can trust God 100 percent that He knows what He is doing and that He does not make a single mistake. How can we be sure? There is so much we don't understand when we encounter suffering and pain. Often we ask, how could a loving and all-powerful God let this terrible thing happen to an innocent child or to a dedicated believer?

When we have no answers, we must always go back to the basic things we know for sure about God:

- God is love (see 1 John 4:8).
- God is good (see Psalm 136:1).
- God never changes (see Hebrews 13:8).

He always will be love and He always will be good. This has to be enough for us until we reach heaven. Then our perspective will be different, and all our questions will be answered. Only God knows and understands everything about afflictions. We are not God!

We must be careful not to judge others when they go through suffering! If someone is afflicted, we cannot simply say, "This sister suffers because she didn't learn to obey God. Now God has to teach her the hard way. She brought this on herself." Remember, there are a million other reasons why someone may go through emotional or physical pain, such as an injury, a child going astray, a tragic death of a loved one or the effects of old age.

The disciples judged a blind man wrongly, thinking his condition was the punishment for his or his parents' sin. Jesus told them that his blindness was *"in order that the works of God might be displayed in him"* (John 9:3).

We must not give wrong advice to someone who suffers. We will cause a lot of confusion and damage if we wrongly evaluate someone's afflictions and then tell the person, "It's your own fault that it takes so long for you to be healed. The faster you learn your lesson, the sooner your afflictions will be over."

We must not deliberately bring afflictions upon ourselves or others for the sake of learning spiritual truth. In many religions, people inflict physical and emotional suffering upon themselves in the hope of gaining spirituality. Nowhere in the Bible does God ask us to torture our bodies, forsake normal life and deprive ourselves of any joy so we can become spiritual. If we do these things, we only damage ourselves and others.

We must never conclude that if God teaches us through afflictions, then it would be wrong to interfere and ease someone's pain. This kind of faulty thinking would prevent us from alleviating any pain and suffering in this world. It would cause us to not use doctors and medicine to get well, set broken bones, feed the hungry, save a child from drowning, comfort people in their distress, stop a crime, end a war or even pray for those who suffer. This is an entirely wrong and unbiblical way of thinking.

Wherever Jesus found suffering, He responded to it with the Good News of God's love, healing, deliverance and restoration. He fulfilled the scripture:

The Spirit of the Lord is upon Me, because He anointed Me to preach the gospel to the poor. He has sent Me to proclaim release to the captives, and recovery of sight to the blind, to set free those who are downtrodden, to proclaim the favorable year of the Lord (Luke 4:18–19).

On the cross, He bore not only our sin, but also our sorrows, grief and sickness (see Isaiah 53:4–6). When Jesus sent His disciples out for ministry, He commanded them to respond to suffering just like He did (see Matthew 10:8).

In conclusion, God is good! Though He uses the afflictions we face as human beings to teach us spiritual truth, at the same time, He is also our Healer, Deliverer and Savior.

Dear sister, this letter became longer than usual in order to conclude our lesson. May the Lord bless you and keep you close to Himself.

With love and prayers,

Gisela

25

GOING FORWARD

Dear Sister,

I trust you experienced God's blessing at Christmas and for the start of the new year. Our family celebrated Christmas together. We had a wonderful time with our children and grandchildren. Esther, David and Jonah entertained us with their play, words and accomplishments. We are so grateful for God's love and care for our family. Thank you for your prayers on our behalf. It is our desire that God may continue to use our lives to serve His people.

For the new year, a scripture from Paul's letter to the Philippian Christians stands out to me: *"But one thing I do: forgetting what lies behind and reaching forward to what lies ahead . . ."* (Philippians 3:13).

Paul was talking about God's goal for his life. Jesus had saved him and taken hold of him for a specific purpose and calling: knowing Jesus. Paul said in his letter that he had not yet reached this goal. But he was going to pursue it with all his might. In fact, he purposed to forget *all* the things that were past and reach forward to what lay ahead. He even said that this would be the only goal he would pursue (see Philippians 3:10–14).

The Apostle Paul's ministry was the result of truly getting to know Jesus. Each of his letters and instructions for the Church came out of this deep relationship. He became so close to the Lord that he understood His heart.

In turn, God was able to fulfill everything He had planned for Paul's life on earth. The apostle himself wrote shortly before he died as a martyr: *"I have finished the course"* (2 Timothy 4:7).

What made it possible for Paul to go forward with God? It was his decision to forget what lay behind! There was so much in Paul's past that could have held him back. There was his prestigious ancestry, his superior education, his perfect report card as a Pharisee and his zeal for the law. These things gave him the highest respect of his nation. However, when he became a Christian, he gave up all those honors. And then there was his ruthless persecution of the Church, for which God had forgiven him. Paul recognized that if he was going to go forward with God, he had to make a choice to leave all of his past behind—the good and the bad.

God has a plan for this new year for each of us. There are specific things God wants to do through our lives. Even if we consider ourselves insignificant, we are an important part of God's plan for our generation. God needs for us to go forward with Him to build His kingdom.

However, we cannot go forward as long as we are chained to the past. All of us wish to grow in our Christian life and to be used of God. But as long as we hold on to something in our past, or something in our past holds on to us, we wear a chain that pulls us back each time we try to take a step forward with Jesus.

Perhaps you find your chain in one of these examples:

- The high caste or importance of your family that holds you back from becoming a servant of all.
- The low caste or poverty of your background that makes you feel unaccepted by others.
- Your college education that causes you to consider yourself more important than others.
- Your lack of education that makes you feel inferior.
- Disappointment because you failed to accomplish the goals you set for yourself last year.
- Someone you loved deeply hurt your feelings and you are unable to get past your pain.
- Your grief over a loss in your life (the death of a loved one, a lost friendship, finances, job, reputation, health) and you blame God and others for your loss.
- A sister in the church whom you trusted betrayed you and you are unable to forgive and love her.
- Something bad happened in your life and you can't understand why God allowed it.
- You prayed for a specific matter and God did not answer your prayer.
- Last year you tried to overcome a temptation or sin in your life and you didn't succeed.

If we don't leave these chains behind, we will go round and round in a circle. And by the end of 2011, we will discover that we could not even take one step forward with God.

How do we get rid of our chains? Just like the Apostle Paul, we must make a decision to forget what is past:

1. We must stop clinging to positions, honors and accomplishments that will hinder us from picking up the cross and following Jesus.

2. We also must leave our failures and losses in the past. We cannot make one thing undone by reliving it, mourning about it or blaming others for it.

As children of God, we have received God's complete forgiveness for *all* our failures. And He already has given us His grace and the power of the Holy Spirit to forgive others who wronged us and leave all the chains of our past behind.

How do we go forward with God? Just like the Apostle Paul, we must focus on what lies ahead and not look back. We must pursue knowing Jesus, and out of this relationship with the Lord will come our ministry, our usefulness to God and the fulfillment of our calling.

What if the past tries to come back? Practice this:

• Right away, cast down any thoughts and imaginations that will bring back past failures and griefs.

• Actively refuse to dwell on anything from the past you have left behind.

• Immediately replace fear, doubts and hurts with words of faith from Scripture.

• Commit to God the things you don't understand about your life. Leave them there and trust Him.

• Continually fill and occupy your mind with the things of God; then you have no place for the past.

Determine to go forward with God in 2011. My dear sister, what are the things that chain you to the past and hinder you from going forward? It's not worth holding on to any of it. Cut the chains to your past and experience the freedom to reach for the things that lie ahead. I want you to know that God's power and grace are sufficient for you to be more than a conqueror in 2011!

May the Lord bless you and surround you with His love.

Your sister in Christ,

Gisela

26

BECAUSE HE HAS RISEN

Dear Sister,

This month we celebrate Easter, the day when our Lord Jesus rose from the dead.

The resurrection is incredibly important for our Christian faith. Without it, we would not even know if Jesus' death on the cross was enough for our redemption. But now that He has risen from the dead, we should be the most joyful people on earth, for our hope and faith are in the living Savior!

Let's look together at Christ's resurrection and what it means to us as believers.

Jesus' resurrection is God the Father's approval. It tells us that the price Jesus paid on the cross was indeed enough for our redemption. God raised Jesus up and, through Him, made salvation freely available for us.

The God of our fathers raised up Jesus. . . . He is the one whom God exalted to His right hand as a Prince and a Savior, to grant repentance to Israel, and forgiveness of sins (Acts 5:30–31).

It's the fulfillment of prophecy. King David spoke these prophetic words about the resurrection of the Messiah: *"For Thou wilt not abandon my soul to Sheol; neither wilt Thou allow Thy Holy One to undergo decay"* (Psalm 16:10).

Jesus told His disciples that He would rise from death: *"The Son of Man must suffer many things and be rejected by the elders and the chief priests and the scribes, and be killed, and after three days rise again"* (Mark 8:31).

The resurrection proves that Jesus is indeed the Son of God. After Martha's brother, Lazarus, had died and was in the tomb for four days, Jesus told her: *"I am the resurrection and the life"* (John 11:25).

And when Jesus talked about laying His life down for us, He said: *"I lay down My life that I may take it again. No one has taken it away from Me, but I lay it down on My own initiative. I have authority to lay it down, and I have authority to take it up again"* (John 10:17–18).

Only God Himself can say this and back up His words by raising Lazarus from the dead—and later, by walking out of the tomb alive Himself, after being crucified and dead for three days.

Jesus' resurrection proclaims His victory over death. After Adam sinned, the entire human race was subjected to death. Throughout all generations, no one could escape death or come back from the grave on his own. Even those few who were brought back through a miracle of God would die again after a short time.

But when Jesus rose from the tomb, He defeated death for all of us for all eternity. Now death cannot hold us in its power any longer. We live because He lives.

Death is swallowed up in victory. O death, where is your victory? O death, where is your sting? (1 Corinthians 15:54–55).

Jesus . . . abolished death, and brought life and immortality to light through the gospel (2 Timothy 1:10).

The resurrection gives us the assurance that we too will rise again. Jesus is our resurrection and our life. He said about us: *"He who believes in Me shall live even if he dies, and everyone who lives and believes in Me shall never die"* (John 11:25–26). That means when we leave this world and we are with the Lord, we will never have to face death again.

It tells us that everything else Jesus said about us being with Him is the truth. Jesus promised us: *"In My Father's house are many dwelling places. . . . I go to prepare a place for you. . . . I will come again, and receive you to Myself; that where I am, there you may be also"* (John 14:2–3).

The resurrection sets Christianity apart from any other religion. Out of all the founders of any religion, only Jesus rose from the dead. His grave is empty. He is alive. If we call upon His name, He saves, delivers and heals us, and He answers our prayers.

It calms our fear of death. For a believer, death is just the moment he walks as through a door right into the presence of the Lord. The Apostle Paul wrote: *"I . . . prefer rather to be absent from the body and to be at home with the Lord"* (2 Corinthians 5:8).

The resurrection lets us look forward to the glory that awaits us. *"Things which eye has not seen and ear has not heard, and which have not entered the heart of man, all that God has prepared for those who love Him"* (1 Corinthians 2:9).

My dear sister, I hope this reflection on the resurrection of our Lord fills your heart with joy and comfort. Soon we will see the Lord face-to-face.

———— ❁ ————

Take some time and thank the Lord for:

- His amazing love for you.
- His willingness to suffer and die for your sin.
- The hope you have because He is your resurrection and life.
- His promise that He will come again, so you can always be with Him.

May the Lord bless you with His peace.

In Christ's love, your sister,

Gisela

27

HE CREATED YOU
FOR YOUR OWN TIME

SEPTEMBER 2011

Dear Sister,

I t's now been a few months since you received my last letter. I didn't forget you, but I was recovering from hip surgery. Thank you so much for all your prayers. God answered, and after more than three months, I am able to put full weight on both legs. I still have to improve in strength and ability to get around before I can travel overseas, but by God's grace and diligent exercise on my part, I believe that I will be able to do so by next year. Please keep on praying for my full recovery.

In this letter, I would like to share with you a few thoughts on God's call to serve Him in our lives. I have talked to some of my sisters who have expressed fear that God may one day require sacrifices or a ministry lifestyle from them that they neither desire nor feel strong enough to live.

Where does this fear come from? Perhaps we read about the persecution of the Christians in the first century. Many were burned alive, crucified or thrown to wild animals.

Or we heard of the immense suffering of pioneer missionaries like Adoniram Judson, who had to bury his wife and children on a hostile and disease-ridden mission field. Or we remembered the story of Corrie ten Boom, who was imprisoned in one of the worst Nazi concentration camps during World War II.

Then we met brothers and sisters serving in our own ministry who had been persecuted, beaten and imprisoned for sharing their faith. Others were called by God away from a good life to serve in a slum, a remote tribal area or a travel ministry that caused their families to be often alone.

In the end, we compared ourselves with those we read about or met and concluded, "I could never do or endure what they did." Then fear set in and told us, "But what if God is asking me to do the exact same thing?"

Before we shed tears of fear, we need to know a few things about God:

God is doing something new with every generation. God has a definite timeline for this earth and for mankind. There was a beginning in the Garden of Eden, and an end is outlined in the book of Revelation. Along this timeline, God has planned many events to occur to fulfill His purpose. For example, it was God's plan for Jacob and his family to go to Egypt during a seven-year famine. Four hundred years later, it was God's time for Israel to leave Egypt and go to their Promised Land. Throughout the Bible, we read statements like: *"When the time was fulfilled . . ."* That simply means that God is not going backward in time, but forward. He is not repeating the old stories over again, but He is doing new things in every generation.

In the ministry also, each generation will face its own unique opportunities, challenges and difficulties in serving God. You must see yourself as part of His present timetable.

God specifically chose and prepared you for your own time. The same was true for Abraham, Moses, Daniel, Judson and all the others who were called to serve before us. The Bible says that King David, *"after he had served the purpose of God in his own generation, fell asleep"* (Acts 13:36).

According to His specific plan, God chose when each of His servants would be born and in which generation they should serve. Accordingly He prepared, gifted and empowered them to be able to fulfill His purposes.

My dear sister, this means you, too, are specifically chosen by God and prepared for this present generation. You lack nothing that He is not able and willing to supply to fulfill His purpose through you. Don't wish you could have served God in the first century or in the time of Hudson Taylor or 50 years ago. You are most effective and gifted for this time in which you live!

God does not compare you with anyone, or your calling with someone else's. He didn't call you to be the Apostle Paul or Amy Carmichael or Sister Mary. He already has one of them. God wants you to be *you* to serve your generation. Your calling is intentionally different, and so are your talents, skills, upbringing, language, education and everything about you. You bring the most honor to God and bear the most fruit for His kingdom if you do what He created, gifted and called you to be.

But doesn't Paul say to follow his example? Yes, he does, but he doesn't mean we should wear his style of sandals or try to be shipwrecked in order to be as holy and dedicated as he was. He only asks us to imitate his faith, service, commitment to Jesus and faithfulness until death—in the context of our own calling and in our own generation.

God's grace is just as sufficient for us to live and serve Him in the 21st century as it was in the first! Paul was so strong and fearless in his ministry that we can't imagine he ever felt weak like we do. Please read 2 Corinthians 12:7–10 and you will be surprised at how much he was in need of God's grace. Jesus told him, *"My grace is sufficient for you, for power is perfected in weakness"* (v. 9).

The weakness Paul mentioned and prayed three times about was most probably a physical problem that made his life and ministry more difficult. It was something beyond his control—and something God permitted to continue. There were many other things beyond Paul's control as well: hatred and persecution from the Jews and Gentiles, imprisonments, beatings, the stoning, the storm and shipwreck, dangers on the road, false brothers, prison guards, the kings and rulers who questioned him, the Roman soldiers who escorted him to Italy, the soldier he was chained to and the Roman emperor who decided over his life and death.

Were these things not major hindrances or "weaknesses" for his ministry? For all these adversities, Paul needed God's grace to be sufficient and Christ's power to take over. And it was so. As a result, in spite of all these "weaknesses," Paul was able to keep the faith and finish the course.

God will do the very same for you. His grace will be sufficient for your specific calling and your 21st-century trials and weaknesses. Therefore, you must not be afraid of what God wants to do with your life, the difficulties you will encounter, the sacrifices you are asked to make and the victories you are called to win. When you are the weakest in yourself, then His grace will be totally sufficient to carry you through, and Christ's power will take over and accomplish the impossible. And then, in the sight of everybody, all glory will go to Jesus.

My dear sister, may you serve the Lord with great joy.

In Christ's love,

Gisela

28

THE GREATEST REASON
TO CELEBRATE

DECEMBER 2011

Dear Sister,

It's almost Christmas, my favorite celebration of the year. I have so many wonderful memories of celebrating this holiday growing up, and later with my husband and children, and now with my grandchildren. Perhaps you don't have the same Christmas traditions as I have, but I hope you will make Christmas a very special day in your home and in your church.

I would like to share with you a few thoughts about why Christmas is the greatest reason for God's people to celebrate with great joy and a thankful heart.

Mankind had no hope left after sin
separated them from their Creator.
Adam and Eve had disobeyed God
and had to leave the Garden of Eden.
Sin had cut their and their descendants'
relationship with God.
There was no way back.

They lived in terrible darkness.
From this time on, mankind was
subject to the consequences of sin:
spiritual darkness, sickness and death.
The further they drifted away from the Living God,
the darker and more corrupt their lives became.
Idolatry, injustice, oppression, hatred, greed, dishonesty,
slavery, bloodshed and war marked the path of humanity.

Satan had power over them.
When mankind chose to disobey God,
Satan gained power over them.
He afflicted them with every kind of evil—
deception, suffering, addiction, bondage
and even demon possession.

They could not save themselves.
People throughout the centuries
tried to find forgiveness of sin
and to free themselves from their
sinful nature and Satan's power, but they failed.
There was no escape.

They would be eternally separated from God.
The tragedy was that their separation
from God would not end with death.
They would go into eternity without their sins forgiven,
and they would end up in hell together
with Satan and his demons.

In the midst of all this, God promised to send them a Savior.
God, however, did not forget us, because He loved us.
He promised Adam and Eve and
all their descendants that one day
He would send us a Savior who would take our sin away

and restore us back to our Heavenly Father.
He repeated this promise through many prophets
so we would have hope.

For thousands of years, mankind
was waiting for this Savior to come.
All those who put their faith in God's promise
were eagerly waiting and praying for our Savior to come.
They trusted God's Word that the Savior
would take the sin of all mankind away,
starting from Adam and Eve up to the last person who
would ever be born in this world.

Finally, 2,000 years ago, our Savior came to this earth.
God sent Him as a little baby.
He is God's greatest gift to you and me.
God loved us so much to give us His only Son
to die for our sin:
*"For God so loved the world, that He gave His only begotten Son,
that whoever believes in Him should not perish,
but have eternal life"* (John 3:16).

Now we can have salvation by believing in Jesus.
All our sins are forgiven.
Satan's power over our life is broken.
All our bondage is gone.
Our relationship with our Creator is restored.
We become children of God.
We will go to heaven when we die.
We will live forever in God's presence.

All this is the meaning of Christmas!
Christmas made all the difference for mankind.
That's why we celebrate.

When we celebrate Christmas:
We thank God for Jesus our Savior.
We proclaim to the world His coming.
We celebrate God's amazing love.

Christmas is the very best time to tell others about Jesus.
People who don't know Jesus
wonder why we are so joyful at Christmas.
They are curious why we sing Christmas carols,
put up stars and give gifts to each other and to the poor.
They will be eager to listen to the Christmas story
and learn about God's love for them.
Let's tell them!

Let's pray together for all the Christmas programs and outreaches of our churches and the Women's Fellowships. Let's believe that thousands of people will come to know Jesus as their Savior as a result.

My dear sister, I wish you God's blessing and joy for this wonderful Christmas season and for the new year. May God's love become real to you as you reflect on the gift of our Savior.

Your sister in Christ,

Gisela

29

TAKE YOUR PLACE

Dear Sister,

T his is already the second month of the new year. I trust that you are excited about what God will do with and through your life this year. After all, He chose you to serve Him.

As I write this letter, my family is in India; they went for the leaders' meeting in January and the Kerala convention in February. This time I did not go with them. I still need to gain more strength before I travel overseas, but I am confident that I will be able to travel later on this year.

In this letter, I want to write about how important you are for God's kingdom and His plan for this world.

The Lord Jesus died for the sin of every person ever born on this earth: *"For God so loved the world, that He gave His only begotten Son, that whoever believes in Him should not perish, but have eternal life"* (John 3:16).

Jesus told His disciples to take the Gospel to all nations: *"Go therefore and make disciples of all the nations"*

(Matthew 28:19). They went and preached the Gospel in Israel, the Middle East, Europe and Asia.

He empowered His messengers with the Holy Spirit: *"But you shall receive power when the Holy Spirit has come upon you; and you shall be My witnesses both in Jerusalem, and in all Judea and Samaria, and even to the remotest part of the earth"* (Acts 1:8). The power the disciples received enabled them to preach the Gospel along with signs and miracles and to be bold witnesses in spite of opposition, persecution and martyrdom.

They all are gone! All the heroes of faith we read about in the Bible are dead: Abraham, Isaac, Jacob, Moses, David, Elijah . . . as well as the apostles and the disciples of the first century. So are the saints, reformers, great preachers and missionaries of the last 1,900 years: St. Augustine, Martin Luther, John Wesley, Hudson Taylor, Adoniram Judson and Amy Carmichael. And some of the great men and women of the 20th century are very close to leaving us: Billy Graham, for example, is 95.

What does it mean that all these great men and women of God have gone to be with the Lord?

It means we are the only ones God has left on this earth to reach this generation! Please take some time and think deeply about this. God is actually counting on you and me to reach the lost millions of our 21st century with the Gospel before they die. *We are it!*

It means we need to take our place. There is a definite task God wants us to fulfill in His plan, whether we are in full-time ministry or not. If that were not so, we would not have been born in this century.

But what if you are not ready? Perhaps you look at yourself and you feel small, unqualified, fearful and weak in your walk with God and in your witness. You barely make it yourself as a Christian and can't imagine how you could possibly disciple and teach others how to have victory over sin, overcome temptation, have a consistent walk with God, love others as God loves them, exercise faith and be faithful in all things.

It is very true—you cannot lead and help others in what you yourself have not succeeded. Only what you have become through the work of the Holy Spirit is life, which you can pass on to others. If you are not ready to take your place in God's plan, don't make excuses. Get serious today about getting prepared and ready.

It means we need to arm ourselves with the same things these heroes of faith and the apostles had: God's Word, a Christlike character, faith, power, love, faithfulness and endurance.

1. Know God's Word. There is no shortcut to knowing God's Word other than to study, meditate on and practice it. *"This book of the law shall not depart from your mouth, but you shall meditate on it day and night, so that you may be careful to do according to all that is written in it"* (Joshua 1:8).

2. Seek to become more like Jesus. It is God's will that we take on the character of Christ. This starts by renewing our mind through what God's Word teaches (see Romans 12:2), receiving correction and allowing God to mold us into the image of Christ (see Romans 8:29).

3. Develop faith that can receive from God. Faith comes by hearing God's Word and allowing it to take root in our hearts (see Romans 10:17). Our faith grows not by theory, but by opportunities to practice. Keep this in mind when you encounter situations for which you have no solutions.

4. Be filled with the power of the Holy Spirit (see Acts 1:8). It's not for a few privileged Christians, but for all who believe in Jesus. *"You shall receive the gift of the Holy Spirit. For the promise is for you and your children, and for all who are far off, as many as the Lord our God shall call to Himself"* (Acts 2:38–39). Jesus told us that all we need to do is ask and we will receive (see Luke 11:9–13).

5. Grow in love until you can love like Jesus. We experienced God's love because it was poured out within our hearts (see Romans 5:5). Divine love is part of the fruit of the Spirit who lives in us (see Galatians 5:22). That fruit grows in our hearts when we stay connected to Jesus and His life flows through us (see John 15:5).

6. Become faithful in all things—even until death (see 1 Timothy 3:11; Revelation 2:10). Faithfulness is part of the fruit of the Spirit (see Galatians 5:22). It takes time to develop and a commitment to abide in Jesus. Practice by being faithful in small things: being on time, keeping your word, doing your best when you perform a task, speaking without pretense and being honest in even the smallest things.

7. Develop endurance. Endurance is gained through tests and trials we go through. *"Consider it all joy, my brethren, when you encounter various trials, knowing that the testing of your faith produces endurance"* (James 1:2–3).

My dear sister, perhaps you noticed that getting ready to be used by God does not come cheaply or by accident. It comes by giving ourselves over to Him fully, without any plans to walk off when the training gets hard.

If we don't take our place in God's plan, we will lose our generation. God has no other plan than using you and me. Let us pray for one another that in this year of 2012 we will rise up, pay the price of becoming useful to God and take our place in His plan.

I love you in Jesus,

Gisela

30

Expert Help for Our Prayers

Dear Sister,

How are you doing in your personal life and in your ministry? I wish I could visit you and learn what's on your heart. Maybe you are full of joy over the good things the Lord has done for you, or perhaps you feel discouraged because of the struggles you are going through.

God knows every detail of your life, and He wants to encourage you daily with His Word. In this letter, I would like to share with you some scriptures about prayer that should make you glad every time you think about them.

The Bible exhorts us to pray continually and about everything:

Pray without ceasing (1 Thessalonians 5:17).

Be anxious for nothing, but in everything by prayer and supplication with thanksgiving let your requests be made known to God (Philippians 4:6).

It also says that we must pray in faith; otherwise, we will not receive anything:

> *But let him ask in faith without any doubting, for the one who doubts is like the surf of the sea driven and tossed by the wind. For let not that man expect that he will receive anything from the Lord* (James 1:6–7).

However, there are times we don't know how to pray for a difficult situation. For example:

- A son has gone astray and lives in rebellion to God and his parents, and they don't know how to rescue him.

- A husband quits working, drinks and mistreats his wife and children. He doesn't care about the tears and suffering of his family and won't accept any advice.

- An old grandmother is near death, and her family has no idea if God wants to take her home or raise her up.

- A young woman is treated poorly by her in-laws, and she is discouraged and hurt and doesn't know how to change the situation.

- We face opposition and problems in our ministry, and we are unable to stop the harassment.

Yes, we pray for things like these in faith, asking God to intervene and to do a miracle—but only in a general way. So often we can't pray specifically because our knowledge about the situation is limited. Also, we have no idea how God wants to deal with it.

Did you know God already has provided someone to pray the right prayer on our behalf?

In the same way the Spirit also helps our weakness; for we do not know how to pray as we should, but the Spirit Himself intercedes for us with groanings too deep for words; and He who searches the hearts knows what the mind of the Spirit is, because He intercedes for the saints according to the will of God (Romans 8:26–27).

This scripture means: When we got saved, the Holy Spirit came to live in us. He knows the difficult situations we face and the hurt and sorrow we feel. He also understands the limitations of our prayers and knows the will of God for each situation we encounter. So when we pray, He strengthens our weak prayers by adding His prayer to ours. He does this by interceding for us and our problem according to the specific will of God.

This is good news for us, because there is a promise in the Bible that says:

This is the confidence which we have before Him, that, if we ask anything according to His will, He hears us. And if we know that He hears us in whatever we ask, we know that we have the requests which we have asked from Him (1 John 5:14–15).

There is someone else who always prays for us:

Christ Jesus is He who died, yes, rather who was raised, who is at the right hand of God, who also intercedes for us (Romans 8:34).

He is able to save forever those who draw near to God through Him, since He always lives to make intercession for them (Hebrews 7:25).

After Jesus went to heaven and took His place at the right hand of God, He didn't forget us and our struggles. Even right now, He continues to pray for us.

We are so blessed that both the Holy Spirit and Jesus intercede for us. It's like our Heavenly Father gives us a double assurance that our needs and prayers are presented before Him in a perfect way and that He will surely answer us according to His perfect will.

Because we have such wonderful and expert help for our prayers, let us pray faithfully and with courage for the needs of others as well as for our own.

Today, let us pray together:

- For our recent Bible college graduates who have gone to their mission fields. Ask the Lord to watch over their lives and open doors for them to share the Gospel.
- For the new class of our Sisters of Compassion that started a few weeks ago. Ask the Lord to prepare them for their ministry among the poor and needy.

My dear sister, may God's love and grace be with you always.

With love and prayers,

Gisela

31

GROWING DEEPER

Dear Sister,

On June 4, we had the joy of welcoming Hannah, our fourth grandchild, to our family and to this world. Our daughter, Sarah, her husband, Danny, and little David came to stay with us before Hannah was born. We are deeply grateful to God that Sarah and Hannah are doing well. Hannah is so sweet and beautiful, and her brother David (3½ years old), cousin Esther (4) and cousin Jonah (2½) love her a lot. David likes to hold his little sister, sing songs to her and show her his picture books.

By the time you get this letter, I will be leaving for India. It's my first trip overseas since I had my operation a year ago. Thank you for praying for me. God answered, and I recovered and gained enough strength to be able to travel again. I am looking forward to seeing our Women's Fellowship leaders and being with them for our training seminar in August.

In this letter, I would like to share with you a few thoughts from the closing of a letter the Apostle Peter wrote to believers:

". . . but grow in the grace and knowledge of our Lord and Savior Jesus Christ" (2 Peter 3:18).

The apostle desired for these Christians to grow much deeper in their relationship with Jesus than they already had. We look to these first-century Christians as our examples and heroes of faith, and we wish to become like them. They loved Jesus, were filled with the Holy Spirit, fearlessly proclaimed Christ, had amazing faith, experienced incredible miracles and were willing to suffer and die for the Lord. If these Christians still needed to grow, what about us?

We often think and act as if we have already become all God expects us to be. Perhaps we have been Christians for 10 or 20 years and know enough of God's Word to teach others. We may have experienced answers to our prayers and are successful in our ministry. And when we go to church or a conference, we hear nothing that we didn't already know. If you are in this category, the Apostle Peter's exhortation is for you: *"Grow."*

We are to grow in two specific areas: *". . . in the grace and knowledge of our Lord and Savior Jesus Christ."*

Grow in the grace of Jesus: Grace is favor we don't deserve. It is rooted in God's amazing love for us, the depth of which we can only begin to understand when we look at the price He paid at the cross for our redemption.

Jesus introduced us to the grace of God when He came to earth and died for our sin (see Romans 5:2). We are saved by grace, are kept by grace and will go to heaven by grace. Everything we receive from God comes to us by grace, including our calling to serve Him. All we are and all we accomplish for the Lord on this earth is by grace alone (see 1 Corinthians 15:10).

If you want to grow in the grace of Jesus, you must:

- Walk in humility: *"God . . . gives grace to the humble"* (James 4:6).
- Receive God's mercy and grace for your life on earth (see Hebrews 4:16).
- Allow God to place you in situations where you must depend on His grace to get through (see 2 Corinthians 12:9).
- Extend grace to others.

Grow in the knowledge of Jesus: This scripture doesn't tell us to grow in knowing *about* Jesus but in knowing Him. We can know all the Old Testament prophecies and New Testament facts and teachings about Jesus and still know Him only a little, or not at all. The only way we can really get to know Jesus is to spend time with Him on a very personal level. We need to walk with Him, talk with Him and be with Him wherever He is—in good times, in ministry and in suffering.

Physically, this was only possible for the disciples and those who lived in the time of Jesus. We can't go back in time to be with Jesus while He was on earth. So how can we be with Him? Jesus told His disciples, *"I am with you always, even to the end of the age,"* before He went to heaven (Matthew 28:20). So even if we cannot see Him, Jesus is with us. If we choose to spend time with Him, we have the opportunity to get to know Him better each day of our life.

Paul became a Christian after Jesus had already gone to heaven. In his letter to the Philippians, he told us what he was doing to grow in the knowledge of Jesus:

I count all things to be loss in view of the surpassing value of knowing Christ Jesus my Lord . . . that I may know Him, and the power of His resurrection and the fellowship of His sufferings, being conformed to His death (Philippians 3:8, 10).

This is what Paul meant: "To know Jesus is my greatest desire in life and my only focus. It is worth it for me to suffer and to sacrifice everything I am and all I have in this world. I am willing for God to take me to places where I am in need of experiencing His resurrection power, to places of suffering and to the cross where I face death with Jesus. All Jesus went through I am willing to go through with Him, so I may know Him intimately."

If you want to grow in the knowledge of Jesus, you must:

- Be aware of His presence with you.
- Live consciously with Him throughout the day.
- Enjoy His fellowship and love for you.
- Talk with Him about everything and listen to His answers, just like you would with a friend who walks beside you.
- Spend daily time in prayer and meditation on His Word.
- Be willing to let Him lead you through places and circumstances in your life that will teach you to rely on Him, stretch your faith and increase your trust in Him to take care of you.
- Allow Him to let you taste a little of the rejection and suffering He faced for you, so you will get a glimpse of how deeply He loves you.

My dear sister, it is my prayer that you desire to grow in the grace and knowledge of Jesus.

—————— ❦ ——————

Let us pray together for our Women's Fellowship leaders' training in August:

- For God's protection for all the sisters who will be traveling.
- That the training will encourage and help the sisters become more effective in their leadership.
- That God will help our sisters to make plans for the Women's Fellowship programs that are on His heart.

May the joy of the Lord fill your heart and may His grace be with you.

Your sister in Christ,

Gisela

32

UNDERSTANDING OTHERS

Dear Sister,

A lot has happened since I wrote my last letter to you. I traveled to India in July and came back at the end of August—without any problems. I praise God that He restored my health and strength, and I am grateful to you for praying for me.

In August we had our Women's Fellowship leaders' seminar in Kerala, and it was good to see the sisters again. I was encouraged by their reports and their commitment to see the WF program grow.

During the seminar, Dr. Daniel, our son-in-law, taught two sessions: preventing the spread of disease and women's health issues. We want to teach these important lessons, along with others, in all our local Women's Fellowships, so Sister Jeena is organizing a special training seminar for January 2013. Two sisters will attend from each district where we have churches, and they will then travel to all the WF groups in their district to teach the lessons. It will be a great blessing for our churches as well as for the ladies from these communities, whom we will invite to attend the classes. Please pray for Dr. Daniel and his team as they prepare the needed teaching material and do the training.

Since I returned home, in addition to my normal writing assignments, I have taught in six women's retreats in different parts of the country. Though this kept me quite busy, it was a blessing to share God's Word with so many ladies from churches that love and pray for our ministry in Asia.

In this letter, I would like to share with you a few thoughts on how to better understand others.

People come from so many diverse backgrounds and experiences. Their looks, lifestyles, customs, ways of thinking and values may be so different from ours. Yet as believers, we are supposed to accept, help and love them as Jesus would. And especially when they are born again, we are one with them in the Body of Christ—for eternity.

How can we even start to relate to them? Listen to them carefully, so you will get to know what's in their hearts. Learn about them without judging them and love them in spite of their differences.

Actually, Jesus made understanding people very simple. He gave us two rules to follow:

1. *"However you want people to treat you, so treat them"* (Matthew 7:12).

2. *"You shall love your neighbor as yourself"* (Matthew 22:39).

These verses mean that:

- I am created very similar to others, even if I look different, speak another language and come from a different background and educational level.

- What I feel, desire and value, they also feel, desire and value.

- What hurts me hurts them too, and what makes me glad makes them glad also.

Look at yourself and think about what hurts you:

- When my leader, teammates, school friends and church members prefer others and ignore me.

- When they laugh at me because I am skinny, fat or have a disability.

- When they make fun of me and publicly put me down.

- When they don't take me seriously because I am less educated than they are.

- When they gossip about me or talk behind my back.

- When they take advantage of my willingness to work hard.

- When they exclude me from their fun times.

- When they always give me the dirtiest jobs because I am from a lower class of society.

- When they never thank me for anything I do.

- When they remind me often about the mistakes I made in the past.

- When they never say anything appreciative after I do something well.

- When they take credit for my hard work or good ideas.
- When they give gifts to each other, but never to me.
- When they criticize me constantly and tell me that I will surely fail.
- When they ignore my efforts to learn a new skill.
- When they never mention my name when my team receives recognition for a job well done.
- When they never ask for my opinion or suggestion on a matter.

Jesus says: Don't do these things to others—they feel just like you would! It hurts them deeply, hinders them from succeeding and destroys them.

Look at yourself and think how you wish others would treat you:

- I wish they would listen to me when I say or share something.
- I wish they would value my opinion, suggestions and ideas.
- I wish they would take me seriously.
- I wish they would give me an opportunity to do something significant.
- I wish they would encourage me when I am struggling.
- I wish they would keep the promises they made to me.
- I wish they would talk positively about me to my leaders.

- I wish they would acknowledge the good work I did.
- I wish they would have patience with me while I learn a new skill.
- I wish they would love and accept me for who I am.
- I wish they would appreciate my work and tell me so.
- I wish they would build up my confidence by telling me that I will succeed.
- I wish they would assist me when I need help with a task.

Jesus says: Do these things to others—they feel just like you would! It lifts them up, gives them courage, helps them succeed and enables them to reach their potential.

My dear sister, I hope these thoughts will help you to understand and love others just as Jesus commanded us.

Let us pray together for:

- All the upcoming Christmas programs in our churches and Women's Fellowship groups, that through them many people will come to know the love of God.
- The WF training seminar on health issues in January.

May the Lord bless you and keep you walking close to Himself.

In Jesus,

Gisela

33

I AM WITH YOU ALWAYS

Dear Sister,

Happy New Year! I came to India last month, and my husband and I celebrated Christmas with Sarah, Danny and their children, David and Hannah. It was a lot of fun to be with them. Daniel, Erika and their children, Esther and Jonah, returned to the United States the beginning of December, and we missed them at Christmas. We look forward to all being together in the same place at the same time.

I will be here for our Women's Fellowship training seminar on health issues in January and for the Kerala Believers Church convention in February.

Just a few days ago, we all entered a new year. I imagine that most of us attended a Watch Night service at church and received a little promise card with a Bible verse for the new year. I always look forward to getting one, and I keep it in my Bible so I can read it often and think about God's faithfulness.

Jesus gave us one of the greatest promises we have in the Bible for our life here on earth. Just before He returned to His Father in heaven, He told His disciples and us, *"I am with you always, even to the end of the age"* (Matthew 28:20).

Jesus made this promise to us because He knows the uncertainties and fears we encounter. He lived on this earth for 33 years in our human form. He saw and experienced all the things we go through: joys and disappointments, celebrations and grief, successes and losses, expectations and unfulfilled dreams, friendships and betrayals, love and hate, hope and fear, freedom and oppression. Because He lived our life, we are assured that He understands us and has compassion on us.

The Scripture tells us how deeply Jesus felt our pain and the struggles we go through. He was moved with compassion when He saw the multitudes who had no one to lead them. He had mercy on all those who came to Him with sicknesses and in bondage, and He healed and set them free. He even touched the leper no one else would touch, felt compassion for the grieving widow and raised her son from the dead, embraced and blessed the little children His disciples didn't regard as important, prayed that Peter's faith would not fail and wept over Jerusalem and the judgment this city was going to face.

Jesus' promise to be with us always does not mean that we will not face any difficulties in life. It is a false idea that believers are spared from all the troubles the rest of mankind suffers. Yes, God carefully watches over His children and protects them from the Evil One. But because we live in a fallen world, all of us will face normal human problems, hurt, sickness, old age, death and grief. And as believers, we will also encounter rejection and persecution because of our faith in Christ. However, the difference is that Jesus has promised to be right there with us when we go through these things.

I encourage you to meditate on these promises God has made to His people to walk with them through their trials:

Do not fear, for I have redeemed you; I have called you by name; you are Mine! When you pass through the waters, **I will be with you;** *and through the rivers, they will not overflow you. When you walk through the fire, you will not be scorched, nor will the flame burn you. For I am the Lord your God, the Holy One of Israel, your Savior* (Isaiah 43:1–3).

Even though I walk through the valley of the shadow of death, I fear no evil; **for Thou art with me** (Psalm 23:4).

This means: We are not alone when our child is sick, when we face financial struggles, when we fail a school exam, when someone we love hurts our feelings, when we need to go to the hospital for an operation, when a family member dies, when others reject us, when we disappoint ourselves and God.

His promise to be with us always is an invitation to cast our burdens on Him:

Come to Me, all who are weary and heavy-laden, and I will give you rest (Matthew 11:28).

Casting all your anxiety upon Him, because He cares for you (1 Peter 5:7).

His promise to be with us always is an invitation to put our faith in Him. Think about this: The God who spoke the universe into existence is right there with you in your problems. He understands your pain, has compassion on you and asks you to cast your burdens on Him. Not only that,

He also invites you to put your faith in Him because He is able to still the storm, heal the sick, cleanse the leper, give sight to the blind, cause the lame to walk, raise the dead, free the oppressed, change hearts, save sinners, comfort the broken-hearted and make all things new. In the midst of our struggles, we have great hope and confidence, *"for all things are possible with God"* (Mark 10:27).

His promise to be with us always assures us that He leads us in a perfect way, even if we don't understand His far greater plan and purpose and even if He answers our prayers differently than we expected. We can trust Him fully. He never makes a single mistake. David spoke of the Lord as *"the God who girds me with strength, and makes my way blameless"* (Psalm 18:32). I have this scripture in a German translation on my wall. It says: *"God arms me with strength and leads me in a way that is without reproach."* I often read this verse when I could not understand what was happening in my life. It gave me the assurance that God leads me in a perfect way, without mistake.

No matter what we encounter, Jesus will never withdraw His promise to be with us always. Dear sister, this truth should calm our hearts and keep us from fear as we walk through each day of 2013. Let us place our hand into the hand of Jesus and trust Him with all our heart. Nothing will happen in 2013 that He does not know about and for which His love and power are not sufficient to see us through.

———— ❀ ————

Let us pray together that we will honor Jesus with our life in 2013:

- That each of us will trust Jesus fully, regardless of what we may encounter.
- That we will faithfully live for Him in the place He has assigned for us.
- That He will give us open doors to share the Gospel with those who don't know Him.
- That God will renew our burden for the unreached and fill us afresh with His Spirit to be His witnesses.

May the Lord bless you and encourage you with His Word every day of this new year.

With love and prayers,

Gisela

34

REMEMBER HOW MUCH HE LOVED US

Dear Sister,

I came home from India in the middle of February, and life has been busy ever since. In March, we had an international leaders meeting in the United States and a conference for our friends, and both were a great blessing.

Our January Women's Fellowship health care seminar in India went very well. Dr. Daniel, our son-in-law, and Sister Idalene (a nurse) taught and trained our sisters, who came from every region. Now all the teaching material is being translated into various languages, and our regional sisters are preparing for the upcoming training of our district sisters.

After our district sisters study the lessons, they will go and teach them to the women in the villages of their district. No doubt the teaching will be a great help for these women and a wonderful opportunity to introduce them to the love of Christ. With the many preparations necessary, we expect to be able to start the actual teaching in the villages by the month of July.

Last month, along with millions of other Christians, we remembered Jesus' suffering on the cross, and we celebrated His resurrection on Easter. I trust you realized afresh how much Jesus loves you. It will greatly strengthen your faith and walk with the Lord if you often reflect on how His love led Him to die for your sin.

Jesus decided to become your redeemer before the world existed. God knew ahead of time that Adam, and the whole human race along with him, would fall in sin. Therefore, He put a plan of salvation in place before He created the earth. The Apostle Peter wrote about this event: *"For He [Christ] was foreknown before the foundation of the world"* (1 Peter 1:20). That means His love for you predates creation.

Jesus could have changed His mind after living among sinful men. For 33 years He was surrounded by people's sin, bondage, sickness, corruption, greed, selfishness, rebellion, hatred, violence, oppression, abuse, deception, ungratefulness, spiritual darkness and hardness of heart. Jesus could have been fed up with their bent toward evil, their self-righteousness and their arrogance toward God. Yet He never lost His love or compassion for them. They were God's lost sheep, and He had come to find them.

He had a choice to say "no" in the Garden of Gethsemane. Jesus fully realized what it would mean for Him to accept the cup the Father was asking Him to drink. The cup contained not only the extreme physical suffering of scourging and crucifixion, but also the utmost emotional pain of being betrayed and forsaken by His closest friends and then being rejected as the Messiah, humiliated, mocked, spit upon, falsely accused of blasphemy and condemned to death by the religious leaders.

It also included that He, who had never sinned, would have to face the unimaginable spiritual agony when the sin of the whole world would be charged to His account and laid on Him. He would have to endure the wrath of God for billions of people and bear their full punishment. And in the end He would die like a sinner, separated from God the Father. Jesus fully understood how great this darkness would be, and as a result, while agonizing in prayer, His sweat became like drops of blood. Yet He said "yes" to the Father's will for our sake. He loved us more than all the glory of heaven and His own life.

Jesus could have ended His suffering at any time. He could have simply walked away or ascended to heaven in the middle of the trial, the beating and the scourging—and definitely before they nailed Him to the cross. He could have annihilated His tormentors with one breath or struck them with blindness and leprosy by speaking one word. Yet the word He spoke on their behalf was not a curse, but a prayer: *"Father, forgive them; for they do not know what they are doing"* (Luke 23:34). Jesus bore the suffering so we could be redeemed by His blood and healed by His stripes.

He had the power to come down from the cross. While Jesus hung on the cross, the chief priests and elders were mocking Him, saying, *"If You are the Son of God, come down from the cross. . . . He saved others; He cannot save Himself. He is the*

King of Israel; let Him now come down from the cross, and we shall believe in Him" (Matthew 27:40, 42). They considered Him helpless and weak, unable to do this miracle and prove He was the Messiah.

The truth is, He had the power to come down from the cross, but He chose to stay for you and me. What held Him there were not the nails, but His love for us! He stayed on the cross in order to pay the full price necessary for our redemption, until He could cry out, *"It is finished!"* (John 19:30).

You are loved by God for all eternity. There is nothing that can cause Him to love you less or withdraw His love for you. The Apostle Paul wrote:

> *For I am convinced that neither death, nor life, nor angels, nor principalities, nor things present, nor things to come, nor powers, nor height, nor depth, nor any other created thing, shall be able to separate us from the love of God, which is in Christ Jesus our Lord* (Romans 8:38–39).

Now my dear sister, walk daily in the knowledge of His amazing love. It will cause you to rejoice and be glad, even when people reject you and you feel lonely and misunderstood.

— ❖ —

Please pray with us for the Women's Fellowship health care teaching:

- For the translation of the health care lessons into different languages.
- For the upcoming training of the sisters from the district level.
- For all the plans and preparation to implement the project in the villages.
- For Sister Jeena and her team, who lead and coordinate the program.
- For the name of Jesus to be lifted up through this new ministry.

May the love of Jesus fill your heart as you live for Him and serve Him.

Your sister in Christ,

Gisela

35

DON'T PASS IT ON

Dear Sister,

I t's been a while since I wrote to you. In June our Women's Fellowship sisters started teaching the health care lessons in 17 states of India. The reports we've received so far are very encouraging, and the women who participate are grateful for the things they've learned. Let's keep this new program in our prayers daily.

Today I would like to share with you a few thoughts from a letter the Apostle Paul wrote to the Romans: *"But put on the Lord Jesus Christ, and make no provision for the flesh in regard to its lusts"*(Romans 13:14).

We often are satisfied with the fact that our sins are forgiven and we are going to heaven. And indeed, we should rejoice for all eternity over God's grace toward us. However, there is far more to God's plan for our lives than going to heaven. What God has in mind for us is to *"put on the Lord Jesus Christ,"* which means we are to become transformed into His likeness in all areas of our lives. His love, kindness, gentleness, holiness, integrity and servant's heart should replace our old character.

What are the consequences when we fail to be transformed into Christ's likeness?

- We are a misrepresentation of Christ to this world.
- God, His Word and the Church will be dishonored by our words and actions.
- We are a hindrance to others receiving Jesus.
- We miss out on living a victorious and fruitful Christian life.
- We pass on what we don't overcome.

All of these consequences are serious. In this letter, we will look at the last one: *We pass on what we don't overcome.*

We may not take seriously our lack of integrity and holiness, inherited bents and destructive habits. We may call them weaknesses instead of sins, and we may have many excuses for them. For example: "It's part of our normal culture." "My whole family has this habit." "I inherited this weakness from my father." We live with our weaknesses for so long that we defend them instead of condemning them.

We believe that our private sins, bents, weaknesses and destructive habits don't hurt anyone. God's Word tells us that this is not true. Even if we try to keep them a secret, what we are on the inside will influence those around us. Most of all, the practice of our weaknesses will set a far more powerful example for our children than all our correct teaching. It will also influence all our relationships as well as the people we lead and disciple in our ministry.

There is a spiritual dimension to all of this: When God revealed His name to Moses, He said:

The Lord God . . . who keeps lovingkindness for thousands, who forgives iniquity, transgression and sin; yet He will by no means leave the guilty unpunished, visiting the iniquity of fathers on the children and on the grandchildren to the third and fourth generations (Exodus 34:6–7).

We may not understand how spiritual laws works, but we all know families in which stealing, dishonesty, laziness, violent anger, gossip, jealousy or addictions can be traced back for several generations. Somehow these unrepented-of and tolerated bents and weaknesses of the flesh have consequences. They provide an open door for the Enemy to keep on destroying lives beyond our own.

Abraham had a weakness he passed on to the next three generations—lying. We greatly respect Abraham as the father of faith, and we are asked to follow his example. However, there was a time in Abraham's earlier life when he resorted to lying, and it obviously influenced his future descendants to practice the same. Twice he lied about Sarah being his wife. At the same time, he thought his dishonesty was a smart move to save his life.

Isaac his son did the very same thing when he lied about Rebecca being his wife. Jacob, Isaac's son, became a master of deception, dishonesty and lying. Jacob's sons were dishonest in their shepherding duties, and they lied to their father for years about what had happened to Joseph, whom they had sold as a slave.

Joseph broke this family bent toward dishonesty.
Perhaps what he saw and suffered from his brothers made him hate dishonesty and lies. How did he do it? As a young man in Egypt, he made a decision to not do anything that would dishonor his God. That included not only rejecting the offer of Potiphar's wife, but also being honest and upright in all his service as a slave, prisoner and prime minister. Joseph recognized that God is truth and that he too must choose to walk in truth to honor God. With this decision, he stopped the family bent toward dishonesty and enabled God's lovingkindness and blessing to flow to his own life, the children of Israel and thousands of others.

We must take a good look at our lives and decide that we will no longer tolerate and excuse our *private sins, weaknesses, family bents* and *destructive habits.* Instead, we must determine to overcome them—so we will not pass them on.

God has given us everything we need to overcome every bondage and weakness in our lives:

- The blood of Jesus that cleanses us from all sins and breaks every bondage.
- The Word of God that instructs us how to live a life that is pleasing to God.
- The Holy Spirit, who empowers us to overcome all things.
- His love and grace that never fail.

Our part in overcoming is to:

- Repent and truly turn from our sins, inherited bents, weaknesses and destructive habits.
- Daily say "no" to the desires of our flesh and obey the instructions of God's Word instead.

- Cooperate with the work of the Holy Spirit in our lives.
- Trust in God's grace and promises for our victory.

When we overcome, we enable God's blessing to flow to us, our children, grandchildren, great-grandchildren and thousands of others. Dear sister, it's worth living under God's blessings instead of the consequences of our family bents and weaknesses.

Please join us in prayer for:

- God to use our sisters who are traveling and teaching the health care lessons.
- The Lord to bless the Women's Fellowship conventions that will take place over the next few months.
- Our willingness to live a life that honors Jesus.

May the Lord keep you close to Himself.

Your sister in Christ,

Gisela

36

TRAVEL TO NORTH INDIA
AND NEPAL

DECEMBER 2013

Dear Sister,

I wish you and all your loved ones a wonderful Christmas and God's blessing for the coming year. May God's love and peace fill your heart as you live for the King of kings.

I came to India in October, and I will be here until the end of January. Our whole family will be together in Kerala for Christmas, and we look forward to spending time together with our children and grandchildren.

During the last part of November, Sister Jeena (our main Women's Fellowship leader), Sarah (my daughter), little Hannah (my 18-month-old granddaughter) and I traveled together to Chandigarh in Punjab, India, for our Women's Fellowship convention. We had a lot of fun, and Hannah entertained us along the way. Her brother David, age 5, couldn't come with us because he had to go to school. He stayed with his father, who volunteered to take care of him, so Sarah and Hannah could go with us on the mission trip.

When our train from Delhi arrived in Chandigarh, our leaders took us to our seminary, where our seminary staff, students and 275 Women's Fellowship sisters had gathered together to welcome us. We enjoyed watching our students perform a traditional Punjabi dance. They danced with all their might along with drums and bells. It was great!

The next day, our three-day Women's Fellowship program began, and we shared lessons from God's Word (along with practical applications) and Women's Fellowship reports and stories with pictures from many different parts of India and other countries. Sister Jeena also met with all our Women's Fellowship leaders to discuss ongoing programs and procedures. In addition, the sisters had report and discussion times, group prayer and lots of fellowship along with very tasty Punjabi food. Our leaders and staff in Punjab blessed us and all our sisters with their love, care and support. Hannah especially enjoyed playing with Pastor Martin's two sweet daughters.

After this, Sister Jeena and I traveled on to Nepal for another Women's Fellowship convention. Sarah and Hannah returned to Kerala, because Hannah had come down with a fever and cold. I had also caught a cold, and my voice had become very "small" and scratchy and I was coughing a lot.

When we arrived in Nepal, we were surprised and welcomed by our leaders and their wives. In fact, at every place we went, we felt like we came "home" to our wonderful close family.

The next afternoon was the inauguration of our convention. Our more than 400 churches were able to send "only" 500 delegates, because that was all the space available in our seminary facility. Even as it was, 80 sisters were housed in each dormitory—two assigned to each bed. They were so happy to be there that they didn't mind their long and difficult travel through the mountain regions, sleeping in the unheated seminary building or sitting all day in a tent for the meetings. In fact, for them, the climate was quite comfortable and "warm" for this time of the year.

Sister Jeena and I, on the other hand, very much appreciated the heating in the hotel where we stayed at night, and we wore all the warm clothes and shawls we brought with us during the meetings! In addition, during the colder morning and evening hours, our dear caring leaders put a large portable heater in front of us in the tent or on stage behind us to keep us going. The Lord was very good, and my voice improved enough to last through all the sessions.

We were so blessed by our Nepali sisters. They listened so carefully to all the teaching sessions, even though they were doubly long because of translation, and they made many personal decisions to practically apply what they heard.

We missed Sarah and Hannah during our Nepal trip. I taught the lesson Sarah had shared in Punjab since it was such a relevant theme for young busy mothers. However, her teaching was far better than mine because she spoke from her own present life experience.

On the last evening, our sisters put on a cultural program. It was fun to see the joy and celebration of their faith in Jesus expressed in songs and dance. Surely heaven must have enjoyed watching it as well.

We were very grateful for the support of our Women's Fellowship convention given by our respected bishops Narayan and Gopal, along with other pastors, as well as their involvement. They not only attended the sessions, but they also blessed us and our sisters with their teaching, encouragement, exhortation and prayer for those in need. Many of our brothers and pastors, including Pastor Manja, cooked the meals for our sisters. What a testimony that was of the love of Christ our believers have for one another.

During our trip back to Kerala, Sister Jeena caught my cold, and her suitcase didn't arrive for two days after we reached home.

It is our desire and prayer to be able to visit many more Women's Fellowship conventions in the future and spend time with our dear sisters. We were planning to travel to Siliguri, West Bengal, in October, but the convention was canceled because of a severe outbreak of dengue fever.

I invite you to join us in prayer:

- For all the sisters who attended the Women's Fellowship conventions, that they will follow through with the personal decisions they made.
- That many people will be touched by the love of Christ through the Christmas programs and outreaches of our churches and local Women's Fellowships, and will come to know the Savior.
- For our hearts to be thankful this Christmas that our Heavenly Father sent us Jesus our Redeemer.

It is my joy and privilege to serve Jesus together with you.

In Christ's love,

Gisela

If this book has been a blessing to you, please send us
an email at gfabooks@gfa.org.

Or write to us at the address below.

Thank you.

GFA Books
1800 Golden Trail Court
Carrollton, TX 75010

OTHER BOOKS BY GISELA YOHANNAN

BROKEN FOR A PURPOSE

Drawing from her own walk with the Lord, Gisela Yohannan shares how to find strength in God's presence and overcome seasons of testing so that Christ's life flows through you.

CONSIDER YOUR CALL

It is God's desire that we understand the joy and seriousness of our call to serve Him. In this book, Gisela Yohannan encourages us to run the race in such a way that we may win the prize.

DEAR SISTER

You will find hope and encouragement in this compilation of letters written by Gisela Yohannan over a seven-year period. She writes of the Lord's faithfulness through the events in her life and ministry—and how you can experience the promise of a new beginning as you walk with Jesus.

Order online at *www.gfa.org*

SHARE CHRIST WITH WOMEN IN ASIA

Sponsor a woman national missionary and deliver hope to some of the darkest places of Asia.

FOR ONLY $30 A MONTH, you'll make an eternal impact in the lives of mothers, grandmothers, widows and children.

To Sponsor GO TO **WWW.GFA.ORG/WOMEN**

or call us at your nearest GFA office

or fill out the form below and mail to the nearest GFA office.

❏ Starting now, I will prayerfully help support _____ **woman** national missionary(ies) at $30† each per month = $_____ a month.

You'll receive a photo and testimony of each missionary you help sponsor.

❏ Please send me more information about how to help sponsor a national missionary.

Please circle: Mr. Mrs. Miss Rev.

Name

Address

City   State/Province

Zip/Postal Code   Country   Phone (   )

Email   **HB43-RLMW**

Gospel for Asia sends 100 percent of your missionary support to the mission field. Nothing is taken out for administrative expenses.

†AUS $40, CAN $30, NZ $40, UK £20, ZA R150.

HOOKER&BROWN

HOOKER
&BROWN
A NOVEL BY JERRY AULD

BRINDLE
&GLASS

Library and Archives Canada Cataloguing in Publication
Auld, Jerry, 1968
Hooker & Brown : a novel / Jerry Auld.

ISBN 978-1-897142-40-0

I. Title. II. Title: Hooker and Brown.

PS8601.U43H66 2009   C813'.6   C2009-902909-

Editor: Lynne van Luven
Copyeditor: Heather Sangster, Strong Finish
Proofreader: Sarah Weber
Cover image: rcaucino, istockphoto.com
Author photo: Tjerk Bartlema

Brindle & Glass is pleased to acknowledge the financial support for its publishing program from the Government of Canada through the Book Publishing Industry Development Program (BPIDP), Canada Council for the Arts, and the province of British Columbia through the British Columbia Arts Council and the Book Publishing Tax Credit.

Mixed Sources
Cert no. SW-COC-001271
FSC

The interior pages of this book have been printed on 100% post-consumer recycled paper, processed chlorine free, and printed with vegetable-based inks.

Brindle & Glass Publishing
www.brindleandglass.com

1 2 3 4 5 12 11 10 09

PRINTED AND BOUND IN CANADA

To Bob,
for telling the story, and insisting that it be told again.

And to David, Dave, Art, Norm, and Jim
for breaking the trail.

Clouds as Tall as Mountains

Everyone comes to the mountains for a different reason. Certainly I didn't come looking for the highest peaks that never existed.

But what have I been searching for? These last years were so busy, yet now I'm not sure why I pursued a degree. That feeling of shocked dissociation kept me silent on the drive to the mountains. And even they look new and sharp, unlike what I remember. From Calgary, at night, in the depths of the university library, or when the mountains were obscured by clouds, I'd imagined the peaks that should stand there: towering crags, splintered and soaring. I thought this was normal, everyone must do it. Now I'm wondering. I seem to have forgotten the reason that made me study in the first place. When we drove through the Stoney Indian Reserve, I remembered a Navajo chant popular in the poster shops on campus:

Everything forgotten returns to the circling winds.

The only thing I know for certain is that underneath everything is rock: solid, hard stone. Oceans and cities and forests can disguise this; even in the mountains we can lose sight of it. I grew up here, I've always seen the peaks, standing on the horizon, fading to a dark blue as the sky pales, blotted by the night. But I need to remember this.

Now I'm in the Front Ranges at the eastern edge of the Canadian Rockies, standing on the hot boulders at the base of a steep crag, playing out the rope as the Lion, above, reaches for a hold with heavy chalked fingers. I call him the Lion because it reminds me of who he is. It's better than his real name. I watch him and hope I'll be able to follow. The sun is warm on my bare legs. We climb together today on our way to work tomorrow. He's got me a summer job on the Kananaskis Park trail crew.

We're above an emerald lake, ringed with a dusky pine carpet that, with the foreshortening of elevation, looks like a bed of nails some guru may lie down upon. A river issues here, filing back the limey fingers of stone. In the distance rests the flatness of the prairie, the end of the Great Plains. I can see the smudge of Calgary, the sliver of light reflecting from the tall library tower where only hours ago I slipped my final paper under a featureless door. I met the Lion on that campus, years ago. Closer spreads the town of Canmore, as if it has been washed up against the range and left to dry, like a fossilized jellyfish. The road winds into Kananaskis Park, following the path of least resistance, and where the trees have been torn up, the earth reveals the same stone as the crags.

A clank like a broken bell. The Lion grunts and I look up to see him hammer a piton into a crack and clip the rope to it through a carabiner and sling. His hips shimmy with a hula of climbing gear, sparkling in the afternoon sun.

On the drive up I'd barely managed to explain my own changing circumstance, let alone ask him about his accident last year. When we reached the base of the route and looked out over the valley, the Lion said, "These trees must be like weeds to you geologists." The Lion is always saying things like that, trying to catch my goat. He was hunched over a disembowelled pack of bright rope loops and climbing gear, chewing some food he'd found. We haven't seen much of each other the past two years while I finished my studies. His truck sits below on the side of the road, next to a highway sign that swings in the wind like a raven croaking a warning.

Now he's above, pulling up past a shelf. His shoulders heave, and he moves with more skill than I remember. In the last two years he has climbed and improved while my hands have softened on the edges of library racks.

When he pauses I call up, "How do you feel?"

"Chicken," he says. He shakes his helmet. "No headspace."

The first climb of the season: always a blind date.

The Lion digs at a horizontal crack of loose chips. Can I trust him, or is our friendship like this limestone, hard and solid-looking but friable, having a tendency to shatter? Handholds here are notoriously portable.

The rope jigs and teases like a fishing line as he pulls out of sight. A pause, not short. Then he calls down that he's secure.

I pull the rope from my belay device and feel the butterflies inhabiting my guts. The rope rises as if charmed until it comes tight on my harness.

I step up and feel the rock. It's warm, rough, passive, and inviolable. Everything I want in a lover. I pull my fingertips down on an edge, step up on a nub, and feel my other leg swing heavy. I push up, scraping my free foot onto purchase, already forgetting my map of the holds. Getting started is the key. I tell myself not to pull too hard, to trust my feet and stand on my legs, on my skeleton, but the motion seems foreign, translated.

After unclipping the first piton, I'm looking up from under the lip of my helmet for the next moves. I reach high and wide, finding small ledges but not committing my strength and weight to them. Backing off. The rope hangs patient. My fingertips feel so soft that the abrasive smear of a hold seems too painful to carry me. Winter fingers. My tips mash into pockets and as easily they roll out, like putty as if I can't scrape the rock. My shoes slip and skid, relearning balance. Trust, I say to them. I've done this before, but it was years ago. Now I see a hold and instinctively dart to it, then disdain it. I reach above the shelf but find nothing. Just smooth stone, washed with years of water over its sloping deck. What the Lion made easy is indecipherable. I wish I could create a hold. I feel like I'm flipping through an exam for a multiple-choice section that isn't there. My breath dusts the rock. With my wrists cocked back, my knees start to stutter.

I'm a riot of questions. *How did he lead this? How good is his anchor? Should I do a master's or get a job downtown?* I flutter over the rope, seeking any purchase. It didn't use to be like this. I don't want to fall and test the rope, not on the first hard part. I force myself to commit. Push on a toe, scrape fingernails, palm an edge. A body-memory shifts free from the mental sediment. I move up with baby steps, feeling better.

At the anchor I clip in; my hand shakes. It takes will to let go, to set my feet and lean back in my harness, staring at the thin rope that holds me there. I should have checked the harness again: the vision of the webbing blowing open in a plume of chalk is too immediate. I am aware of gravity, pulling behind me as it scrutinizes each act for negligence, for opportunity.

Pressed against the Lion, I feel the heat of his shoulder, the heavy muscle, the flex of his thigh. He shifts and hands me the gear: brass nuts on wires for slotting into cracks, metal camming devices for expanding into pockets, all attached by gated carabiners and slings of bright nylon loops. Through the smell of dust and his breath and my sweat and the spruce below, he smiles.

The extra gear weights my harness. The hammer especially seems like an unwilling slave; its iron was mined, smelted, forged, and then returned here to beat spikes into the stone fissures. The Lion plasters a creased route map against the rock. In pencil he has marked the ledges, cracks, and possible anchors. The climb goes straight up and then flares left under a bulge, forming a pinching crack. The paper flutters. I wish it had more detail, that it was a book of secrets that would take an eternity to read.

"That'll be fun," I say, looking up, trying for conviction.

4

I shake my head, rasp my helmet brim on the rock, and start up on my pitch. The crack is vertical, and my fingers dig because I don't believe that the friction of my feet will stick to the flat surface. I pull down on a jammed finger and feel pain. I weight it even more to move; the pain means it's too tight to slip. Two moves later I dig a chip from a hold and fling it, the flecks of mica sparkling. My knuckles are starting to bleed. The throb is reassuring. I have the negotiation underway now, we're bruising each other: neither the route nor I will leave unchanged.

I gaze down at the Lion. He looks back, unblinking. But the boulders below appear far and hard. I don't have any protection in yet. If I drop, the Lion's anchor may not hold and I could rip both of us off the cliff. It's called a factor-two fall—directly onto the anchor without anything to slow me. In my structural metals class, I once read that bridge workers were taught, if they fell, to throw their rivet hammers down, to break the water tension. But from here, nothing will break the cruelty of the earth below.

Each movement up strengthens the sense of gravity. Every time I look to place a piece of protection I drain strength from my arms, yet every move up increases my height and the exponential force of a fall. The Lion mutters. I start to panic, looking for a crack that could hold a piton or a wire-nut while my forearms burn. I snarl and try to will my hands to hold, but the numbness is creeping. The limestone is tan, not dulled grey by rainfall, so I must be right under the overhang. There's quartz laced across the rock, little nubbins my fingers are too clumsy to use. A crack constricts. Fumbling with my rack I snag a brass nut and snug it in, clipping the rope in a lurching grab. It won't break a fall: the rope movement could lift and displace it, I still have to move, but the nut fills my hold. Fear is consuming the exposure of my mind, flaring to white, curling the edges.

A slow curtain of shame blunts my fear. I slam my fingers into a pocket and shimmy up by my feet. The long lip of the traverse crack is at eye level. It forms a shadow as I reach. I'm close enough to lick it, my mouth dry and chalky as the stone. The sharp edge cuts into my palm and I want to impale it there, into my bone, to shoulder up and drop in an elbow and rest.

The Lion cries sharply, something indistinct, probably a comment about my bad form. I walk my feet up on outstretched arms. There is nowhere to stick any gear. The groove is deep and runs in gaps under the curving bulge. I start to move, quickly now, desperate. As soon as the crack narrows, enabling me to place a cam, I do, yanking hard to test it, my feet slipping.

I reach into the crack. It's cold inside, and slippery. Something in the dark backs up as my pale fingers push in. I jam my fist, daring anything within.

I should know how the gap formed, but it's like blanking on a test. Other thoughts come instead: like how the Lion's partner died last year in a crevasse.

The rope drag becomes heavy as I pull sidewise. Each step to the left means that if I slip I'll drop and swing, grating along the surface, probably pulling my protection. My legs quiver. The gap leads slowly upwards.

I scrape the rock white with a brass nut as I fumble it into a constriction. Normally, that colour would mean something, tell me the composition of the rock, but now I have no memory.

Arms numb, I move without regard. Just up, along the crack, as long as it will take me. All I can see is the next metre; maybe that's all I've ever seen. Now I want it to keep going, angling up to the vertical, continuing this essential movement where to stop is to die—and where there is no room to reflect. Just keep going. past exhaustion, past decisions.

Finally, I reach the top. I grab the slings anchored there. The Lion grunts again and I ignore him. I secure myself and prepare to belay. My forearms are dense as clubs. My mind is humming. I pull in the rope, wondering if the wind just started.

Soon the Lion appears, edging and traversing, fast and involved. He tests everything, checking slings and the effectiveness of the placements. For a fleeting moment, his eyes are visible, deep brown like tunnels. When he pulls up beside me, it's not his physical body I sense but his intention coming close.

After I secure him, time becomes slow and expansive, so that anything is possible. We hang there with all the time in the world. His arms are lacerated. He points. My legs are the same, as though I've dragged them through barbed wire.

"Horseflies," he says, disgusted. I hadn't even noticed.

I turn to look out, across the valley. In the early summer's warmth, the snow collecting on the eastern crags bleeds black water stains like a claw has mauled their stony faces. The lake below reflects nothing in its milky haze. The sweep of the peaks is bigger than I'd imagined, so big it becomes a headache. I feel as though I've never seen any of it before.

▪ After each descent I return to the maps. Not always consciously.

At the dinner table I flip through a guidebook. In my room I spread a trail topo on my bed. I'm always folding a sketched route into a plastic pouch for my pack.

In such gestures I find my bearings, ground myself. No matter how fantastic it feels to climb up a sheer wall, then drop back down, as if I've slipped its notice, the map puts my experience into perspective. It takes away my fear, my awe, my hammering heart. The maps replace those unreliable perceptions with a symbol: circled, checked off, understood.

On the first days of the job, the Lion hikes beside me and shows me the ropes. Trail crew isn't rocket science; it's more endurance than finesse, so physical that my mind can play all day while my body works. But first there's a blizzard of maps and names and references: trailheads and nicknames, road numbers and radio call signs. Mine is L69. The Lion is L71. I know from the trucker movies of my teenage years that 10-4 means "Okay." Now I learn others, like 10-20—"What's your location?"

One of our first jobs is to work with a helicopter flying materials to bridge sites and flying out the full "honey barrels" from the outhouses. In a small field, the helicopter hovers above me. I can see the pilot looking down from her bubbled side window. The whole thing is a whirling dervish of energy. Not so much the chopper, but the beating blades make air and trees around us vibrate, make my muscles shake. I never imagined the sound would be so loud or the wind so forceful.

"L69. Helicopter. You got to move that ruminant, over." The pilot's voice comes over the radio, calm as a dinner conversation. I have no idea what she means. She repeats her request. I don't move for fear of moving the wrong way. Finally the Lion runs over and grabs my arm. The helicopter lands right where I stood.

"Ruminant," he explains, "means a deer. That's you: deer in the headlights. You got to keep moving." Within an hour the radio has spread my new nickname. That first week everyone seems to be asking with a laugh, "What's your twenty, Rumi?"

The next day the Lion and I walk the fire road around Upper Kananaskis Lake, a rocky jumble of sharp limestone that he hates because of its monotony. He's showing me how to kick rocks off the trail without breaking stride or bruising toes. We do this so the rocks don't trip hikers or wear down the tread, creating grooves that pool water and start erosion. But when the trail turns into exposed bedrock, there is nothing to do but hike and reflect and listen to the radio chatter.

I met the Lion in my first year at university, in a philosophy class. Philosophy was a humanities option for me but a major for him. He got excited by the Greeks when we started climbing together, then evolved to the existentialism of Kierkegaard and Sartre. The last time I saw him he was still raving about them, his thoughts coming in short breaths of exertion. "They really got it. Nothing is but what we feel. My life is a stage. There's no script. We have to be the writer. And the actor. The first asking, Who am I? The second interpreting the answer. I'm going to live here.

Among these peaks. Like a guru. And dream myself. The most meaningful life."

But now he talks of Plato, the ultimate Idealist. The regression in the Lion is striking.

I like the name "the Lion." Like mountain lion. Reading about minerals as a boy, I realized their names meant something. I remember easily how gypsum, which is mined here in the park, means "to cook" in Greek and how it's found near hot springs, or how feldspar is German for "field" and "rock without iron." When we played cowboys as kids, my friends and I gave one another long, descriptive animal names like we imagined the natives had. The habit remains; I name all my acquaintances by their characteristics, sometimes rock, sometimes animal.

"This road must turn you on," the Lion says, once again baiting.

I usually get one reaction when people hear I studied geology: they look around for rocks as if they've just noticed them. Mostly this search leads to nothing, but sometimes, usually men, will point.

"What's that?"

"Gravel," I report.

"And that?"

"Sand."

Then they look at me as if I'm an impostor. If I say it's silicon mixed with pyrite and quartz, they tilt their heads like dogs. Other times, they look around for a rock to present to me. The Lion spends the first days on the trails making me laugh with his impression of a geologist, frothing and gibbering, trying to gather every rock in sight, running stooped, dropping his armload with each new find. I'm too shy to tease back.

The Lion comes from the west coast, from the Fraser River Valley farms, a hundred kilometres from saltwater even as Greater Vancouver creeps closer like a spring tide. He says his family has been there for generations. He is broad-shouldered, lithe, enormously strong. Around his bull neck he wears the only indication of his coastal heritage: a seashell necklace, a band of white rings, pierced and threaded.

Shells are made from calcium, an element essential for cellular life. Large deposits are found in the basins of ancient seabeds, representing eons of tiny shells drifting down on top of one another, crushing together. But what I know that most people don't is that calcium is a metal, harder than lead, yet sliceable by a knife. It's an earth metal, rarely found pure because it reacts with other minerals to form living structures. Here's another favourite habit: equating people with minerals. The Lion is calcium. With his heavy bones and vigour for work, the comparison seems obvious.

"How do people react when they discover you're a geologist?" the Lion asks as we walk down the fire road. I keep shifting my pack, getting used to the weight. The large fire axe, the pulaski, hanging between my shoulder blades, is ridiculous. And this title is new for me too; it fits awkwardly. For too long I've just been a student.

"It's different now," I say. "People look at me like I have some deviant sexual behaviour. Like we go to Geologists Anonymous meetings to say, 'I like rocks.' Maybe they think I stand in front of marble statues, fantasizing over the thin veins."

I remember when I did my interview with my soon-to-be trail boss, the Ant, who looked suspicious about my education.

"What about you?" I ask. "A philosophy major?"

The Lion smiles. "Philosophers don't get those looks. People are so surprised to meet a philosopher that they keep quiet, like they're wondering how unstable you are. Like we go to Philosophers Anonymous and announce, 'I am unbalanced.' Most of the time I notice people waiting for me to say something profound. Usually I make up nonsense and then look at them seriously. The best is when they nod after a moment."

The Lion kicks rocks off the back of his heel or the side of his boot, a quick snap as he passes. I've asked before why he'd studied philosophy. It seemed somehow not solid enough for him. He told me that as a kid watching action movies he used to wonder about all the people getting killed in the background. The movie just rolled along, forgetting them. He watched the extras and wondered about what a surprise that would be; you get up one day and then—wham—dead. Didn't see it coming. He always wondered if we could ever wake up and know it was the day we would die.

That explanation reminds me of that time in university when a girlfriend of his told me that he'd seen a kid in his elementary class get hit by a car. The car sped off; the kid died at the hospital. The Lion had picked up the boy's hockey stick from the blood on the street.

I'd asked the Lion about it one night after leaving the pub, when the mood had turned fearless and people were drifting to their dorms. We stood under a streetlight in the vast, empty parking lot. He told me what happened, but it was his impression of the events that stuck: he said the schoolyard had swarmed like a field of ants when one of them gets stepped on. He looked then as though the arc-sodium lights could shine right through him.

At the end of every day that first week we reviewed the trails and techniques.

"It looks easy, but it matters," he says. "Work diligently."

That's what I like about him. That's why we're friends. He has this clear view on what's important, this determination to make his life happen without regrets, without waiting for approval. Though I suspect he has regrets. Sometimes he seems not to listen. His education is not in demand. He's out here without the pressure of choices. Unlike myself.

▪ Toward the end of the first week, even though I'm dead tired, the Lion convinces me to attend an interpretative play. These interpreters come from all over Canada. They have sparse audiences at the start of the season, so they need encouragement, the Lion claims. I ask what it's about and the Lion shrugs. The park management hires them to make the wilderness more accessible to the tourists.

We sit in the stands and watch a slender woman jangle the bells in her jester's hat and stretch her grease-painted arms.

A long time ago, before our grandfathers, before the continents were divided by the oceans, there was a kingdom over this land, spanning sea to sea. This is the Borges fable.

The Interpreter leans forward and points in a long arc over the audience's heads. The firelight illuminates her outstretched hand with bright authority. Some of the children turn to look over their small, blanket-wrapped shoulders.

The powerful king had a magic mirror that told him the future. He surrounded it with towers so he could look down on it at any time. One day, he saw his sons distressed, each holding small and mouldering maps. He foresaw the battle to divide his kingdom and ordered his cartographers to make a single map of the land.

The Interpreter's even voice and French accent make her sound royal. Early-season visitors are scattered before her on concentric benches. The stage is packed earth. Recessed lighting gives the feel of a small room, the dark night provides the walls. The visitors huddle close and hunch forward, their children clustered at their feet.

She wears a shirt with multicoloured stripes. Billowy pants exaggerate her motions. On her left a solemn man wears the robes of a scribe and on her right another has the grim face and armour of a general. The scribe holds a heavy book while the soldier leans on a spear. The firelight glints off the aluminum foil of his armour.

I sit with the Lion on the cold back benches. He has his feet up, his worn boots wrapped in duct tape. His shell necklace is bright against his tanned neck, his teeth white in the lights. He seems enthralled with the performance, but during pauses he leans over to ask small questions.

"Do you know all the trails yet?" he whispers.

"I think so." I keep my eyes on the interpretive show.

And the commissioners sought out the greatest map-makers in the kingdom and they worked hard over their boards of ink and parchment, reading the latest legends and reports from the king's armies. They drew a map that showed the known world, and the greater portion was that which the king ruled.

"As of tomorrow you're on your own. If you have any trouble you'll have to radio me. Chances are you won't get me because of the mountains. Try to remember which peaks have signal repeaters and aim your antenna toward one."

But the king rejected their work, saying "This is the mirror of magicians who want me to see what they value. I want to see my territory as it is, and not be told of borders, which are just the line where your fear becomes larger than your knowledge."

"For any trail, do you know where to go, where to park, and how long it will take?"

"If you tell me a trail, I'll find it," I say.

And so the commissioners sought out the papermakers, and the surveyors, and they spent years completing a map of the kingdom.

"I'm just asking because the Ant will push you. We don't always have time to check the map."

In order to complete it, by royal decree, every person in the kingdom would detail his or her surroundings.

"I've studied the maps for two weeks now, how many trails can there be?" I hiss.

"You'll be surprised."

The final map was so detailed that every rock and house and tree was on it.

"Everything's on the map."

"Not everything," he whispers.

The king had grown old, but when he saw the map, he was pleased and commanded that it be shared across his kingdom. It spread to all the corners of his land like a blanket. It covered the fields and the towns and the royal capital.

"Why do you call him the Ant?"

The Lion laughs. "'Cause he can lift six times his own weight. He once hiked sixty kilometres in one workday. Eight hours. That's a lot of expectation coming down on us."

But it was impossible to keep current. For as a house was built, for every child born, for every fire or plowed field, the map had to be updated.

"Are you going to get new boots?" I ask. "Those are falling apart."

"They'll last one more season. I spent my budget on climbing gear."

The effort to keep the map updated began to take all the resources of the kingdom, and so the empire started its inevitable decline.

The Interpreter sweeps around the stage in garish melodrama, never at rest, punctuating her sentences with deep glances at the sparse audience. I feel small compared to the vast dark park beyond the stage lights. There are only the two of us this year to maintain the trails.

"Last year we never got to everything. He hates to leave anything unfinished," the Lion says.

When the king died, his sons divided the kingdom amongst themselves. They thought it would be easy. They cut the parchment along the lines of the provinces. But the paper started to roll up and twist and slowly began to fall apart.

"Budget's been cut again, but the standards haven't changed. I remember last year. I hiked my tail off," he says.

The people said that they could see the disintegration of the empire as they slowly watched the map fade.

"That's why you have to know the trails. We'll be going non-stop as soon as the passes are free of snow."

"The sky's clearing. Could be a nice day tomorrow," I say.

You can still see that old kingdom through pieces of the map that are left. They are just small, wind-torn pieces at the farthest reaches of the forest. And tattered scraps still remain on the highest peaks, frozen in time under the snow . . .

"You never can tell," the Lion says. "C'mon. Friday tomorrow, and we have a long one."

■ The next day I hike with the thump of rain on my cap and a light pack because I'm wearing all my gear. The forest mists open and close around me like a school of fish. Only the sub-peaks of the ridges are visible, as if the mountains are dissolved in solution, isolated hints of the elaborate fortresses above.

I keep glancing at the map to see if the land is as amazing as I imagine. The blisters and aches of the first week have faded, and my boots look as though I've been hiking for years. The radio fizzles occasionally from the top pocket of my pack, the tools in the small garbage bag in my gloved fist hardly rattle, and the pulaski no longer feels uncomfortable.

The forest lulls me. I haven't even thought about the decision I know I have to make in the autumn. I'm just dawdling at a signpost between two clear choices; there's no hurry, I've got all summer. The mountains show the thrust of the rocks, their passage and their faults. It's a good place to select the best route in life.

At a section of wind-felled trees, I pull my park-issued red flip pad to note the work to be done. The graphite of the pencil smears on the damp pages. Graphite is the softest mineral of all. It's elemental carbon, and under different circumstances it could have become diamond, the hardest mineral. One is opaque and soft, the other hard and transparent. I like the potential of one to become the other. I've always had an affinity for carbon.

My trail leads to a hill crest. I look warily at the clouds for the flicker of lightning, which can be fatal on an open ridgeline, and search the undergrowth for signs of bear and other wildlife. The Ant mentioned that this forest had burned completely in the 1930s, the fire igniting the coal seams that broached the ground. Apparently the coal still smoulders deep underground, the combustion kept in check by the lack of oxygen. The Ant claims to be able to see the smoke through the snow. During a hot, dry summer, which the Ant predicts this will be, the smouldering may reach the surface and spark. With the forest unburnt for seventy-odd years, it's highly flammable. I asked him what I should do if it caught fire.

"Run," he said.

From the ridge top, I turn slowly. I want to record the contours in my memory, but the mountains are always changing. The clouds pour from the west like the breaking foam of a great sea. To the north is clearer. The peaks have the colour of wartime photos: greys, whites, dark navies, umber browns. They pose in position like a flotilla, painted in camouflage, the clouds catching on summits like plumes from boilers.

Before the geology, before my studies, before the explanations, I felt an innocent wonder at scenes like this. Something had happened here, something big. The earth had ripped itself up and pushed high into the air, rumbling and breaking. That energy still seems to vibrate, but I've lost my wonder, forgotten somewhere in the avalanche of books and terminology and math.

In the shattered blocks of the ridge crest, several pits gape open. My favourite professor maintained that Blackfoot, Cree, and Kootenay natives climbed most of these peaks first, before the Europeans. During their vision quests, they would sit in a pit, covered with logs and skins so there was no light, and remain like that at the top of a mountain for four days without food or water. But the pits I'm standing beside on the ridge are too small for people. At their bottoms, the rock is glassy like obsidian, a volcanic stone that doesn't occur here. The icy wind evaporates my heat. I watch the churning atmosphere to the west and radio my position to the Lion as the clouds start to flicker internally. This is Nature's warning; once the clouds have cleansed themselves of any positive charge, they will attempt to resolve their imbalance with the ground in the form of electrical bolts.

Through the static I ask the Lion about the pits and jab a toe at the strange stone. I hear the anxiety behind his words. He says I'm standing where the lightning has channelled so much power that it has blown the rock open and melted the stone to glass. I'm thinking that something in the ridge must be attractive. A deposit of ironstone?

I know I need to get off the crest as fast as possible. But just then, something appears across the valley in the clouds and rivets me: a smudge that remains immobile when all else is swirling. It expands into a ridge, shredding the clouds. It's straight and steep, impossibly close, rising hundreds of metres above me. It seems like a battleship prow surging above an icy swell. I'm transfixed, like it's the handhold I dream of when climbing, huge and hard. I'm still learning the park geography, but I'm certain nothing that large should stand so close. The snow plastered on the black rock hangs suspended like a secret veil that hides some heroic, more perfect, realm. The summit appears, cold and forbidding, where something blown on the winds might catch. The view lasts only seconds. I take a bearing before the clouds seal.

I turn and rush down, jumping with an energy that comes from the mists around me. What could the peak be? Only quartzite or dolomite can make cliffs that steep, but those formations are farther west. The rain comes harder, and I run with my tools down the slippery trail, panting up to my truck in the gloom. I drive with rubbery arms and finally come to the compound and the empty asphalt lot.

■ I want to run to the maps and solve the mystery, but I'll have to deal with my co-workers first. I've met some as staff arrives for the season, and no encounter is without long introductions. Friday night should be full of new humans. I walk from the truck down the shining gravel, under the dripping spruce, through the peaty smells of moss and bark to the mellow glow of the windows. The cookhouse is a squat log building, overlooking a field of shadowy meadowsweet and bog bean. Behind it are cabins, dark behind the moist trees, each divided into four rooms: our quarters. Back in the 1970s, when the province poured money into the parks, a trail crew of thirty men lived in the cabins. Now the parking lot is nearly empty; the cabins are used by the sparse population of seasonal rangers, trail crew, and interpreters.

The Lion looks up and smiles as I enter the kitchen. "That's a relief! Back from Elysian?"

The kitchen is separated from the wide living area by a door frame that has never held hinges, let alone a door. Compared to the dusk of the living room, the brightness here is startling.

"That ridge was scary. It's called Elysian?"

"No. Elysian Fields, from mythology. Where the virtuous souls would find eternal peace," he says, chopping lettuce. "The name means someone struck by lightning because Zeus was the god of lightning. It means you were blessed."

At university, I had many nights to recall our climbing adventures. I tended to remember the Lion in emergency or in darkness: under a serac, suffering rockfall, in a blizzard, or reflected against the inky winter windows of humid huts. Yet in every memory he was smiling.

"I've got bread in the oven and a salad on the way. Your turn to cook dinner tonight," he says. He seems unaffected by the hard day of rain and cold.

"How many?" I ask.

"Only four."

"How come?"

"People found out you're cooking," the Lion says. He's carefree, perhaps secure in his store of philosophy. He'd expounded on enough theories when we'd first started climbing together that I know his foundations are deep. Which is why his preference now for the simplicity of Plato is all the more curious. We started on the bouldering walls in the basement of the physical sciences building, improving at the same rate, and we never let classes or girls get between us. Except once. But that green-eyed girl belongs to a different time.

Now, in the kitchen, his hand produces a grey stone.

"Check this out. Nature doesn't usually have straight edges, but this rock's almost a cube."

"Quartzite," I recognize. "Harder than steel. Not much of that here." It reminds me of the mountain I've just seen. The mountain that shouldn't be.

In the walk-in fridge I select the ingredients for pasta. Most shelves are empty, as the fridge is large enough to hold stores for thirty people. I hate it: cavernous, white, and cold, like a glacial crevasse under a seal of snow, a tomb. I wonder what the Lion feels when he's in here.

"More cutbacks." The Lion shrugs at a black-haired woman standing by the counter. "We only have the two trucks and the tools from last year. We'll make do."

She smiles back. "They cut your boot allowance too?"

"You look different without the jester's hat," I say.

She is Québécoise, tall and quiet with muddy brown eyes, pale skin, and long hair twisted into a plait. It whips like a tail as she turns her head and gives a curtsy. "Thank *you* for coming to my show last night. Soon it will be *so* packed that you will hardly find a place in the stands. And this little interpreter will be able to do *nothing* to help you." Her arms sweep without regard to shelves or knives, and she mocks a sad face.

"How did you know about that fable of the king's map, and why would you tell it?"

"Well, those kids need to trust themselves and not just follow the paved trails. And I should know about it more than you, since it was based on an Argentine legend. And Spanish is closer to French. But honestly, you know, I just *read* about it in our ex-*ten*-sive files. Anything that will make the people *gasp* in wonder."

The Lion points to the living area. In a dark corner are shelves of books. I fill a copper pot with a gush of water. I want to keep talking to her.

"Pass me the box of spaghetti?" I ask the Interpreter. "On the left."

But she's facing me and turns toward the fridge.

"No, the other left."

She cocks her hip and gives a warning look.

"The north wall," I try again.

She waves that down. "I have *no* idea. Point."

As she drops the box on the counter, I ask, "Do you really not know which way is north?"

"*You* need to know. In my job everything is relative; things are right or left, ahead or behind."

I'm surprised. "I always see things in relation to themselves: north or south, east or west of each other. The advantage in the compass points is that nothing moves. You give directions and they're always clear. North is north no matter which way you face."

"But who are you facing? Where are you in this picture?" she asks, almost quivering, her hands on her hips, just waiting to fly at the slightest release. "Who are you giving directions to, a stone? People move. Who carries a compass?"

"Why do highway signs mark the junctions as a north-south highway, or the eastbound road?"

"That's *not* true. I see signs all the time saying, 'Next right,' 'Turn left.'" Her hands wave like an air traffic controller's. "Imagine if we had to drive on the north side of the road and not the right side. Cat-*as*-trophe! I'm never driving with you."

She stalks out, and the Lion suppresses a grin.

"Dramatic, eh?" I say.

"You're going to learn a lot of different things on this job, my friend. If you thought this was just about hiking . . ." He shakes his head.

I prepare vegetables. Even the varnished grain that flows in oval shapes around knots in the wood reminds me of contour lines on a map. I pin the slippery tomatoes from BC and slide a knife through their skin and watch the seeds spread on the board. The black olives from Ontario absorb the light, rolling off in squat rings. The onions from Québec crunch into half-moon whorls and sting my eyes. The pasta, Alberta wheat, smooth and dry, splashes into the pot.

I'm on the verge of a tremendous discovery.

The Lion comes over. "I love the smells. I'm a walking stomach on this job. I've rediscovered food: textures, tastes, mixtures. This job could turn me into a chef." With each phrase he poaches a bit of vegetable for his mouth.

I set the sauce to simmer and walk to the big wall map of the park in the living area. There is no rush. I've been savouring the discovery. Except for the nagging question how such an impressive mountain could be undiscovered.

I run my hand along the huge map. The mountains are amoebas of contour lines, but the ridges give no resistance. I find my trail, go up the crest, and trace out along my bearing. The valley is empty. My eyes dart back, search again; I hold my breath. My gaze ranges the map as if distance is nothing, my fingers slipping on the smooth paper, looking for something sharp.

I hear the sauce boil and return to the bright normality of the kitchen. I feel as though I'm in love, weightless. This must be the way the early geologists felt when they'd found something new and important. The image of stone raking the winds high above haunts me. But another fact nags: maps don't lie.

The Interpreter returns. I tell her what I've seen and what I can't find.

"Oh?" she says, hands stopped. "A grand peak. I *love* how these mountains surprise us."

"But it isn't possible. Everything's been discovered."

"Yes, but what if? What if there was a mountain hidden? A place among them that has never been seen?" Her eyes flash and she speaks as if she's tasting her words.

I return to the living area to confront the giant wall map, this time with a broomstick. I slap its wooden shaft against the map, pivoting from my ridge crest, watching for any peak to appear under its sweep. Nothing matches my experience. Maybe the compass needle was thrown off by whatever was attracting the lightning to that high ridge?

"Find what you're looking for?"

The question comes half-interested, as if from an end-of-shift waiter. It shocks me back from the silence of my imagined heights. A tall man, slender, wearing a windbreaker and pack slung with braided rope.

"Just searching the mountains."

"They haven't changed."

"Of course. I just don't know them all."

"And now you do?"

"I know their names at least." I glance at his fingernails, smudged with chalk, his forearm sleek with muscle and already tanned. "You been up today?" My chin indicates anything outside.

He nods. "The rock was cold. We climbed under roofs to keep the rain off."

"What routes?" I'm trying to conjure the guidebook pages.

He shrugs. "We were just climbing what looked interesting."

I introduce myself. The Ranger reaches to shake without moving his feet. "I'm here for the summer. Or at least until I hear better. Until then, I'm here. You should put that broom on the floor if you're going to be of use," he says, laughing.

I turn to the map, following the broomstick. Down in the far corner my heart catches. A massive peak, five valleys over from my ridge. But that's Mount Assiniboine, the highest in the southern Rockies. I wonder what effect of clouds made it seem to loom over me.

The Ranger dumps his pack on a couch and tromps into the kitchen. My inspiration flattens like a spread-out map. Everyone knows Assiniboine. It's celebrated in tourist brochures and guidebooks. The Matterhorn of the Rockies. I'm deflated: my prize is already known to everyone.

The Lion passes, carrying milk and butter. I tell him what I saw, what it turned out to be, how it made me feel. "The unknown always trumps the highest," he says.

The Interpreter walks by with an aluminum bowl filled with crumpled lettuce. "You sure lost your enthusiasm quickly."

The Ranger overhears me say Assiniboine and declares loudly as he brings utensils to the table. "Wouldn't go near that if I were you."

The Interpreter's eyes follow him closely.

"Assiniboine's aspects are all cross-loaded. The snow's adhesion is weak. The prevailing slopes are dangerous for human-triggered slab avalanches up to class three. There's even natural point-releases from cornice failure. People have been killed."

The Interpreter looks confused.

"Stay off the snow," summarizes the Lion.

"And always be sure of your ropes," says the Ranger, pointedly, back to the Lion.

I serve the salad, watching the Lion and the Ranger. There's a tension between them. I wonder what the Ranger knows about the Lion's accident last winter. This valley is one huge caldron; we've all been picked from different shelves to see what kind of sauce we'll make.

■ At first impression, the Ranger is the clean-cut kid you knew in school who had hobbies and was never at the centre of things, just quietly competent. Years later, you're surprised to learn he's become a cop. Afterwards you realize that's not so surprising.

He's tall but spare, a good physique for a climber. Even though he resides in the staff cabins, he has a pickup with a covered bed. Inside is a shelf built over milk crates full of camping gear, and on top is a mattress and his dog: a husky crossed with something. The Ranger's from Ontario, near Kingston, the Thousand Islands between the Great Lakes and the St. Lawrence Seaway that leads out through Québec into the Atlantic. I associate him with zinc because he has a heavy brass compass in his shirt pocket. It's scratched on the case and polished at the edges. Brass is made from copper blended with zinc, and those transition metals are mined in huge pits north of Lake Huron in the Sudbury crater. I wonder what brings him all the way out to the mountains.

He thinks the Lion is Buddhist and mocks him for it. The Ranger seems to disparage any ideas that come from the east. Maybe he wants to forget where he comes from.

"Immigrant," the Ant says about the Ranger. "An import from the east." This shocks me because the Ant isn't jingoistic.

"This is him, this job. If he fails, he goes back east, a deportee. So he won't fail. Work himself to the bone before that. Never underestimate the immigrant."

I had seen the Ranger almost every day up until then, in his blue-grey uniform, wearing some sort of helmet or hat or cap, a sandy curl of hair behind his ear, always too busy to answer my questions. Instead he would ask me something I was interested in, then move off without waiting for an answer. I think about his compass, heavy above his heart, polished from moving through the day. Zinc is believed to aid healing, but too much can be toxic.

"So where're all the others?" asks the Ranger after we've eaten the salad.

"Down in Canmore. It's specials night and there's a good band," says the Interpreter. "But how could we miss this: the discovery of Assiniboine?"

The Ranger smirks. "Gonna go climb it?"

The Interpreter is smiling mischievously. I slump back.

"Only fools rush in. That face can get covered in verglas," says the Ranger. He describes the layer of ice that coats the rocks when water vapour in the air freezes. He tells stories of friends finishing routes where the last easy pitch took all night because each step meant melting through the ice with their fingers before they could move higher.

The Interpreter's eyes are large, the Lion is unimpressed. The Ranger leans forward.

"It tends to form this time of year, when the westerly is heavy with moisture and the air masses over the Front Ranges. The snow is more like freezing rain."

"Have you been up there?" the Lion asks suddenly.

The Ranger nods and turns back to me, smiling. "And I wasn't the first, obviously. That honour goes to Sir James Outram, who climbed it more than a hundred years ago. So don't go flat-heading out there looking for some first ascent."

I try to salvage my position. "I was just imagining what it would have been like back then: to see the mountains before anyone else, unnamed, unclimbed. I'm used to photos with the route mapped on it. But seeing a mountain so . . . feral was . . . inspiring. I wanted to drop everything."

"Sounds like Hooker and Brown," says the Ranger.

The Lion makes a low whistle.

"What is that?" asks the Interpreter.

I've never heard of them but don't want to concede that. The Ranger isn't local.

"No? I thought you were from these parts," says the Ranger to me. "Hooker and Brown were two massive peaks reported to be straddling the fur trade route to the Pacific."

He gives no ground, waiting to be asked their height.

"Reported to be seventeen thousand feet," he answers.

I'm incredulous. The Interpreter shrugs.

"That's higher than anything in the Canadian Rockies," the Lion whispers to her.

"Mount Robson's the highest," I say. "And she's only fourteen and change."

"You said the fur trade. When *was* this? Exactly?" asks the Interpreter.

"Two hundred years ago. At the height of the trade, when the yearly brigade would travel over the passes. It would take them four months to do the crossing."

"Why didn't they just go to the Hudson Bay? They could have caught a ship there," the Interpreter says.

"Couldn't," the Lion says. "Very few rivers actually go east. Most go north to the Arctic, or south into the Mississippi drainage. Everything else was owned by the Hudson's Bay Company, with exclusive rights to anything that drained into it. By law, courtesy of the King."

"The only way for rivals, like the North West Company and their great explorer, David Thompson, was to hike up and over the mountains. There was a big search for a pass through the Rockies," adds the Ranger. "They established the route through Athabasca Pass."

I sit uneasily. This is my backyard, I should know these stories. I grew up in Calgary. Maybe that's why I dislike the Ranger; I'm still carrying that Wild West mindset. I hate being lorded over by anyone with a uniform; I hate that there are rules to follow and I only grudgingly respect authority. I resent the police attitude of guilt before innocence. The culture of my youth hasn't helped: the cops wore pressed navy uniforms, drove cars that were always clean. In a time of fading disco, punk rock, and teenage angst they seemed made of preformed plastic, their faces all moustaches and aviator glasses.

This may be why I trust maps—they provide an authority I can manage. Calgary was growing in my teens, accelerating outward like an exploding star. We needed a map to find our way to parties because so many communities were new. As a kid I lived at the edge of the city, almost on the prairie, but by the time I went to university my community was considered old, even inner city. This change didn't sit well with my pioneer self-image. Moving to the mountains was a clean solution.

Back at the table the Interpreter asks the Ranger if he's been to Athabasca Pass. I notice he defers, claiming to have only looked up the valley to where the mountains should be.

"There's hardly a trail left, and it's very boggy. There's not been a fire up there for a hundred years. But just so you don't get any crazy ideas," he says to me, "they've already been searched for by the great mountaineers: Arthur Coleman, James Outram, and Norman Collie. Guys who are all forgotten now, but they were the ones who opened up the mountains for the rest of us. They were looking for the two mysterious peaks, and in the process they discovered the Columbia Icefield and everything in between."

"I do not know these men," says the Interpreter.

I can't help her; I feel as if I've just heard a family secret from a stranger. I'm suspicious about the Ranger's claim that these men opened up the Rockies, when climbers could just follow the fur trade trails to the Pass. But he insists that the old trails had been forgotten, a hundred years after the railway revealed the Rockies to an exploration-fevered Europe.

"This was even before Alberta became a province. Canada was very young." He looks hesitantly at the Interpreter as he mentions the country's name. I watch her reaction as well, wondering if she's politically supportive of a separate French province, but she's so engrossed that her hands lie still on her lap. I get the impression that he's providing all this information as he would to a tourist, divulging his studies without sources, a self-declared expert. "Hooker and Brown appeared on all the atlases, but the surrounding valleys, rivers, and trails have slowly been erased. The maps of the day showed a huge empty whiteness with two peaks standing alone."

"They'd just have to look at earlier maps then."

"No one could find them. Maps that had been used by the brigades were guarded as secrets by the fur companies. That trade had declined and they no longer needed to cross the mountains. Remember, the west coast was like another continent back then, easier to get to by sailing around South America than by hiking across the mountains. This big spine of the continent had been glimpsed and then just as quickly forgotten. There weren't many public maps, and what was available was copies of copies."

"Same as now," says the Lion.

"Something must have been the original."

"That's where it becomes a mystery. Hooker and Brown don't appear on Thompson's map."

That rings a bell. "But didn't David Thompson cross the mountains first?" I ask.

"No, that was Mackenzie. But Thompson found a pass to trade

through. One that worked. He was the first to cross Athabasca Pass, which runs between Mounts Hooker and Brown."

Thompson didn't mark the two giants on his great map of the northwest, which was the benchmark for accuracy and the basis for all charts for the next century. Maybe he crossed in a blizzard, figures the Ranger. I finish my pasta, push my plate away.

"But it's obvious when you're rounding a large mountain: the larger the mountain, the larger the base," I argue.

"Could be a plateau you're going around," says the Lion from his quiet end of the table.

"And you don't have bad weather all the time," I continue, ignoring him. "Especially when you're finding your way through unknown wilderness and travelling slowly."

"When I first came here I saw nothing but clouds. I did not even realize that their tops were the snowy peaks until they did not move." The Interpreter laughs, cupping her mouth.

We join in. "We've had a stormy spring. But nothing is that tall around here."

"True. But Hooker and Brown were there, next to the highest in the Rockies, Mount Robson, which hadn't been discovered at that point. Nor had most of the other high ones. A hundred years ago big mountains were not just possible but undiscovered. Two hundred years ago Thompson wasn't interested in high peaks. Mapmakers are concerned with their objectives, not an impartial view of the land."

"But how *did* the mountains get on the maps?" asks the Interpreter.

"And why didn't anyone question it? Even asking why a pass would go between the two highest mountains? Why wouldn't it go wide around?" I say. "Because they just weren't there."

"Stop knocking down the walls!" says the Interpreter. "You would turn a chateau into a chalet. I think it is romantic. Two mysterious mountains!"

The Ranger grins. "And to answer your question, think of the

Chilkoot Trail up in the Yukon. It was a high pass but used during the gold rush because it was the shortest route. And besides, the easiest way into a castle is through the gate, even though that's where the walls are the tallest and the towers the strongest."

"I could never go there," says the Interpreter. "Not because of bears, since they are harmless if you think like them. But because of forest fires. They do not think when they eat."

I sit back and try to imagine a map that can't be while the Ranger and the Interpreter clear the dishes. "The only problem," the Ranger concludes, "was that when they finally found the Pass after years of searching, there was no trace of the giant mountains. It would be like going to Nepal and finding the Everest valley with no mountains of significance."

■ The Lion waits outside after I turn off the lights. He is a diffuse shape against the trees. Out of habit I search for the North Star.

"You got whipped in there. And for a moment I thought she liked you," he says with a laugh.

I shrug. "She's not my type. I study rocks. She's into the romantic illusions of peaks."

"When have you ever cared about type? You're more impulsive than a racoon on a trash can. What exactly is your type, anyway?" he says. "And, hey, you haven't always figured people perfectly."

I want to deny that. "I like peaks I can climb. I want facts, not tales."

The stars spill out. I can't find the pole star amid the black cutouts of spruce.

"Oh, sure. As soon as you saw him interested in her you started in. A morsel to fight over."

"She's beautiful, yes, but not a morsel." I know he's baiting me; I know he doesn't think of people as morsels. But I don't like his tone. It was a dark night like this one, back on campus, when we'd made our pact not to chase the same girl. A much colder night. I push my hands into my pockets.

"I was just pointing out the holes in his claim," I say. "Lot of help you were."

"Yeah."

"She's new here. I wanted to clear the distinction between story and truth," I add.

"A story always trumps fact. Our imagination is too dramatic to settle for the truth."

"Come on. What's that got to do with mountains thousands of feet taller than could be?"

"Just that folks are determined to go after dreams. The flimsier they are, the more they chase them."

"Flimsy is right! Seventeen-thousand-foot mountains?"

"They couldn't have known any better. Most of these parts were still very wild."

"Yes. But simple rational thought?"

"Is always better in hindsight. You're judging based on your knowledge. Perhaps they wanted them to exist. Columbus thought he had found the western passage to India because he believed it to be there. He knew nothing of America."

"But these guys knew enough to know better."

"Maybe. What's funny is you're no different. You were ready to drop everything to explore a new peak." His heel crunches the walkway gravel. "And you live in a time where you know a mountain the size of Assiniboine couldn't exist without being mapped."

I stand under the dripping spruce. I think about what my type of girl might be, try to envision her. It's a simple question. I think I knew, a long time ago, but it's a shock, now, to find that I don't really know.

■ Over the next weeks I drop books from the Interpreter's library into plastic bags to read at lunch on sharply cold passes or under gnarled trees. At night I can stretch out the covers and my spine and read quickly, no wind tearing at the pages or muffled movements nearby to distract. But it's only on the trail that I can really hear the words of the first explorers: Arthur Coleman's *The Canadian Rockies: New and Old Trails*, James Outram's *In the Heart of the Canadian Rockies*, and Norman Collie's *Climbs and Exploration in the Canadian Rockies*.

Those writers relayed a passion born of the awe for the land. But they were also steeped in the mindset of superiority of the industrial Edwardian–Victorian age, when Earth was meant to be explored and its secrets discovered. Any mystery had a solution if one reasoned enough. And with so many mysteries there was no thought that we might exhaust them, any more than that the multitude of buffalo could disappear from the plains. They write with pride about shooting as many mountain goats as they could while passing.

The mountains barred them from the coast trade: looming dangerous, necessary to conquer. The unknown still existed, the blank spots on the maps bigger than the charted areas. Each journal page stepped further into a world in which neither writer nor reader knew what would appear next. I realize for the first time how much I've taken for granted.

One morning, passing the lakeside on my way to the farther trails, I see the Interpreter at the top of the tourist viewpoint, gazing down at the water. I wonder how to draw her in.

■ The TV is dark. Racks of videos sleep in their worn sleeves. The Interpreter waves to her boisterous colleagues and settles down on one of the couches with a novel. The Lion turns in.

I return a book to the library and pull another from the shelf. I do this in full view of the Interpreter but conceal my choice.

"What did you choose?" she asks.

"A history of the Rockies, first explorers and all."

"Still looking for Hooker and Brown?"

"Still trying to figure out where they came from," I say.

"And have you *deduced* it yet?"

"There's all these little stories, some really interesting. I can't believe I've never heard of them. There's a whole history that happened right here."

"I always dreamed of the backcountry, ever since I was little. You have heard of *Les Maudites*? It is a story my grandmama would tell me whenever I got mad and swore." She giggles. "I did that sometimes. Raising the roof to get my way."

"I can't imagine."

"You have heard it, I am sure. *Les Maudites* means the damned. Some say the poor men are woodcutters, but I always like to imagine them as voyageurs. What is romantic about cutting down trees? But the voyageurs paddled across the whole land."

She smiles as if hearing it again from her grandmother.

"The voyageurs are far in the west, deep in the forests, pulled up on the side of a river, a very long way from home. It is the eve of the New Year and they are all lonely, thinking of their women and warm homes back east. They sit around the fire and one of them, called Baptiste, says, 'I would give my soul to see my woman tonight.' And some of the others agree, and some don't and go off to sleep. Then the devil appears in the fire and says to them, 'I can enchant your canoe to take you home in an hour, but you must be back before dawn, never fly over a church, or touch a crucifix, or speak the name of the Lord in vain. Otherwise your souls belong to me.' Seven others and Baptiste agree and climb into their canoe—and up it rises and flies them dripping into the east. They carefully paddle around church steeples below them like the sharp rocks in a big river. They land outside their houses in old Québec, below the Citadel, and their women are overjoyed. They drink and eat all night, as men do. But then it is close to dawn and the men remember the conditions of the Devil. They say their goodbyes but find Baptiste drunk and sleeping under a table. So they gag and bind him so that he won't swear unconsciously, and they board their canoe and start back. But the cold air wakes Baptiste, who is furious to be bound in the bottom of the canoe. He works loose the gag and yells, 'Mon Dieu, why have you tied me up?' At the mention of God, the canoe drops down, and the men are never seen again."

"Spooky."

"Ouais. My grandmama would tell this to keep me from swearing, since all the profanity in Québec has to do with the church. I always got quiet after the story, not because I believed it, but because I imagined being one of those who stayed behind, waking up the next cold morning beside the endless river, knowing that some of the men had gone home."

"Men who never returned."

"Yes, and who were damned. But would that make the longing any less? That is what I would wonder for hours. I often dreamed of going far into the woods, beside a river, maybe as far as I could go, maybe to the very source of the river, just to see what I would long for so deeply that I would be prepared to sell my soul. Even just for one night."

The lights are low, the windows inky.

"Is Baptiste a popular name?" I ask when the spell fades.

"Not now," she says. "Maybe then."

"Because there was a Baptiste in David Thompson's party too."

"I am too tired to read. Why do you not tell me about these stories?"

I read a passage from David Thompson's journal, when he is about to reach Athabasca Pass for the first time.

Janʳʸ 8ᵗʰ 1811 A fine day, partly Cloudy, wind SE in the Evening, & Night a Gale. Much Ice left in the Mountains & they are abᵗ 1M ascender—but not above 2000 ft high, & the highest not exceeding 3000 ft. Broke my Snow Shoes. DuNord beat a dog senseless—& the Sled we made got broke & was with the Dog thrown aside.

She doesn't like that reference to dogs. I tell her that it seems to be the harshness of the land, of that place in time. Thompson wrote it without judgment.

Thompson found the Athabasca Pass because the Peigan Indians were blocking other passes, preventing guns from reaching their rivals, the Kootenay of the interior. He gave it a name, put it on his map.

"Wait." She waves. "First dogs are beaten. Now an arms race. That's not interesting."

"What isn't?"

"The facts."

"But that's what happened."

"But that's not *why*. I want to know what Thompson was feeling. What drove him out there."

I consider that. "Okay," I say, finally.

"Tell it like a story," she says, settling back. "I love stories. My grandmama told them all the time. Especially when I was uncontrollable or scared. I *always* stop for a story."

I wonder wildly how to start. My favourite professor at university made classes interesting by telling the material in the form of stories. In the narratives, the adventurers seemed to have seen the route through the mountains not as a map but as a series of empty spaces that transformed into landmarks, each reflected with names they chose from their circumstance.

David Thompson was born in England. At fourteen his mother sends him to Canada for an apprenticeship with the Hudson's Bay Company. He stands on the docks at Southampton to board the *Prince Rupert* and never sees his mother again. He's good at math and learns surveying after he breaks his leg. He limps ever after, but despite that leaves the Hudson Bay Company to become a partner with the Nor'-Westers, a rival fur trading company. He travels eighty thousand kilometres and maps most of the northwest territory of Canada. The Nor-'Westers can't take any furs from areas that drain into Hudson Bay, so they have to work closely with the natives, explore inland, and find a way over the mountains to get their furs out via the Pacific. Thompson's dream is to find that Great River of the West.

She's not convinced. My telling is too disjointed, too impersonal. I need to make it more intriguing if I'm to impress her. I clear my throat, try again:

▲ David Thompson crosses the Rockies at Howse Pass in 1807 with Kootenay guides. The Peigan are distracted by Lewis and Clark returning through the Montana Rockies. By 1810, the Peigan close Howse Pass, so Thompson hires the ten best men he can find at Fort Edmonton and an Iroquois guide named Thomas. The Iroquois is from around the Great Lakes, but his tribe is being pushed west by colonization. The voyageurs are French Canadian. Everyone is moving west. In January 1811, Thompson moves up the Whirlpool River, where two Snake Indians claim there is a pass marked by a pool that drains on both sides.

Thompson, short and stocky, limps in his snowshoes. He finds Thomas in a glade. To Thompson it looks as if the guide is listening to voices within a great chapel.

"It is almost sun-height," the Iroquois says.

"I'll wait here and make a fix. When the others arrive, keep them moving."

"Their dogs are going slow."

"It's not the dogs, it's the men."

Thompson pours quicksilver into a pan and sets a hinged pane of glass above it. It is almost noon. The glass acts like a prism over the quicksilver, forming an artificial horizon at which he can point his sextant. Thompson has been snow-blinded in his right eye. He pushes his black hair away from his ruddy face and holds the sextant to his left eye, adjusting the swing along the arc until the sun appears in the mirror.

The sun descends toward its reflection as it rises in the sky above him. He thinks of moments when he's noticed the sun at its height: a flash of his mother's face on the docks, the boardroom of the North West Company of traders at Fort Kaministiquia, four years previous, when he was made a partner with orders to open trade with the coastal Indians. His thoughts drift up the rivers to the various forts in which he's wintered. He ponders his wife, Charlotte, and his four children at Fort Augustus. Surely Fanny must be taking some of the tasks at hand with the smaller children, she'd be nine, almost ten. He smiles slightly to think of his son Sam, almost seven, who must be having the time of his life on the sled with the bells.

The sun slows, hesitates, stops. He marks the time on the watch. It is set to Greenwich Mean Time. London time. The difference between noon there and here tells him exactly how far he has travelled. He checks his compass.

This Thompson, the one the Kootenay call Koo-koo-sint, the stargazer, is gifted by the Great Spirit to always know where he is, thinks the Iroquois.

Baptiste the hunter stands in a fog of his breath. The long barrel of the gun is wrapped in leather so it doesn't freeze to his skin. Baptiste has brilliant green eyes that pierce the trees.

"I was hoping for this Mammoth that all the men are so afeared. Would've liked a shot at one of those," he says to Thompson. His lips split in bright cracks.

"Snow's too heavy to hunt in, man. We can scarce haul what we have."

Baptiste laughs. "No need to carry it. I just want a shot."

Not all men are like Baptiste. Fear gathers heavy like a buffalo robe in these lands.

They make a platform of logs for a fire, and men and dogs sleep around it. Before morning, the fire has melted itself down to a pit and as their legs start to slide into it, they wake.

The men leave, and the valley goes back to the way it was. The days stretch. What has changed? Why does it look different? Only this: it has been seen, it has been named, and the time until men return is now being measured.

She smiles, but I want a better ending. I need to create the moment and transport her there. I'm starting to hear the voices between the words of the stated history, like light trapped behind imperfect crystals. I tell her that David Thompson started a yearly brigade that travelled without roads or maps.

There's a line of men snowshoeing up a steep glade. Their furs would rot if it wasn't so cold. The creaking of leather and the groaning of some glacier above them boxes their words. Oaths are muttered about the hoof prints that circled their camp when they woke. Half the men warn of their demise, others curse that superstition. A procession of hunted men.

"I saw a shape that ne'er reflected the lustre of sun," whispers one.

"Your rheumy eyes. How can you see something unseen?" scolds the Trader, the leader and the only educated man among them.

"Some shades are so by the absence of light—"

"You're snow-blinded again."

"—others exhale the blackness of the pit."

The slope hunches back. The clouds above are thin as their breath. The men freeze. The stars are gone. Against the sky, on either side, faint rising arcs. They soar to points, like the crests of folded wings. Starlight flutters in a nimbus on their edges.

"Wha' the devil?" A voyageur's voice, high in the strangling air.

Incandescent mercury spreads along the invisible vertical border, a heaven above them, bursting and fading. The Trader's eyes gleam. "It canna be him. He of the Abyss does not raise such towers."

The day rises and the brigade pushes through the snow. They do not need the peaks or the sky. They are following the river, leaving the branches that pool from the descended fingers of a shattered glacier, and turning always to the fork that leads deeper into the forest.

The men wear slatted cloth wrapped around their eyes, coated now with crystals from their breath, a kaleidoscope of colour. When the clouds move, they do not notice at first that the highest do not. They are the purest, sharp and dazzling. Only in a rent of blue do the men realize they are looking at summits of untrodden snow. They stop, each remembering tales of fairies and prophets, of the impossible, from their forgotten youths.

The dogs, who have never known proverbs, flounder and nip, without understanding.

She takes a while to adjust to me stopping. Then, "Why a traitor?"

I'm mellowed by the force of the story. None of these words came from the books. The essence did, sure, but I feel like someone in the past is talking through me.

"No. Trader. A fur trade route," I say.

She wants more. I tell her, next came David Douglas, a botanist with the Royal Horticultural Society of London. A gardener who, through hard work, managed to get posted to the uncharted New World to gather and classify new species. He meant to prove himself by collecting thousands of samples. His most famous is the Douglas fir, which grows everywhere in these mountains. But he also named the forgotten Hooker and Brown.

"Take me there," she says.

"Let's see. Where did he begin? This would have been at the end of winter, in Scotland, up on the hill above the Firth of Clyde, on the university grounds."

"The Firth of what?"

"The estuary where Glasgow is. *Firth* is Lowland Scots for a really big river. Stop interrupting."

"Can you do a Scottish accent? I like that accent."

"No."

"Aren't most of the people in the fur trade Scottish?"

"Yes. Douglas, Drummond, Simpson, they were all Scottish."

"Then you'd better learn."

I tell her of a place cold and foggy.

The year is 1823. David Douglas is twenty-five and sits behind the frosted windows of a small office. It's very late, and his lanterns sputter. The night watchmen change.

"Take no mind," says the retiring watchman to his still-sleepy colleague. "Mr. Douglas has been late every night for months now."

"What cause has he?"

"He's studying. Not just plants, but the stars and animals and maths and such."

"What does a lowland gardener need of maths?"

"Have ye not heard? Dr. Hooker has had the society send young Douglas to America to collect for the University Garden."

"America? What? A gardener, son of a mason? What's he done to deserve that? Stolen from the registrar or looked at Hooker's daughter, I imagine."

"Oh, I declare, that Dr. Hooker has plans for him, he does."

"But he is not at the Pass," says the Interpreter.

"Not yet. But this seems important. It might tell us about what happened."

"Mmm." She stretches and pulls a blanket off the couch. She smiles slightly and doesn't open her eyes. "Tell me about the Pass."

I watch the soft shadows pool in the plains of her neck. Her skin is much smoother than the rock I've been studying for the last five years. I'm opening up to the well of stories from all the reading I've done. "Okay. Douglas travels to the eastern sea-board of the States and has a very successful trip collecting. He's sent back, this time to the west coast of what was then not even provinces or countries, but simply forts on rivers. Meanwhile, the fur brigade is making its way over the mountains each year. In autumn 1824, the lieutenant-governor of the Hudson's Bay Company himself travels through the Pass. Even though it had been thirteen years since Thompson, it was still very wild and large parties were needed . . ."

> ▲ A party of Iroquois voyageurs moves quickly up to the round pool at the height of land. They keep in a tight, disciplined group, hauling in a steady line.
>
> "Hold!"

The group reforms like mercury into a cluster beside the ice-covered pool. Lieutenant-Governor George Simpson is a man used to being obeyed.

"Gentlemen, we stand at the apex of a continent, within a defile of these barricading mountains, the only opening that allows our trade to flourish. This tiny pond indeed feeds the Pacific and the Arctic oceans. Such humble beginnings aspiring to such greatness, as a pond does to an ocean, surely deserve a distinguishing title: for it is the spirit of all endeavour and business. If we have the same aim, how can our enterprise fail? We trust ours to the guidance of the Board of Directors. So I shall name this pond the Committee's Punch Bowl, in honour of our lords. Bring forth the rum."

An indifferent murmur becomes a cheer and then erupts. A presentation of tin mugs.

"Gentlemen," Simpson cries. "To the Committee."

Each little circle of rum reflects the drinker's face, surprising them all after months on the trail, their future as desired and implacable as the rum.

"And that's how the little pool at Athabasca Pass got its name."

"Describe this pool," she asks quietly, her dark eyes reflecting the reading lamp.

"It's small, set like a bowl, perfectly round. Lying between two huge mountains. Why?"

"All of them travelled through during winter, when it was covered. No one saw it in summer?"

"No. They didn't travel then. Not until Coleman, seventy years later. Why?"

"Nothing," she says, looking away, her hands forgotten.

I walk out of the backcountry. There's no boundary, just needle-blanketed trails, a gradual firmness underfoot, the asphalt appearing under drifts of old leaves.

I've been looking for "moose-moss," something the Ant

claims grows in a symbiotic cycle and hangs yellowish green off the aspen buds. The aspen grows higher, letting the moss catch the light and keeping it above the rodents. When the moose eat it in the spring, their hooves aerate the roots of the trees and their droppings fertilize new aspens. So far I've seen no sign.

But with the asphalt, there are human signs: a calendar on a discarded cigarette package sleeve, a faded bread bag from someone's lunch, chipped yellow paint on a parking curb. I emerge through a tangle of dead branches into a parking lot. The sense of space is distinct from the forest: half empty, single purpose, still. Workers have dug the bitumen from huge pits and hauled it here, mixed it with crushed gravel, heated, rolled, and smoothed it. The pavement exists foreign and unyielding, scattered with flakes of quartz and lime from hiking boots and car tires and winter sanding trucks.

This trailhead is by the confectionery. I spot the Interpreter making notes on her aluminum clipboard and wave, then sit on the curb to eat lunch. The radio clears its throat beside me. Under the hot sun the asphalt sparkles. After a while I realize that this is a symbiotic system too: the pavement needs potash, and potash requires metal to build the trucks that transport it, and oil to run them, and mines and wells to begin the process, and roads to bring the asphalt. The roads allow more cars, more people to visit. More visitors need more roads, more parking, more metal for cars, more oil, more roads for trucks, more places to park them. Someone, a long time ago, decided to push a trail into the edge of this park, before it was even a park. Small decisions create momentum.

The Ranger drives in, parks, and crunches over in big boots too heavy for hiking. He stands, eating his chicken sandwich from a foil wrap. The tourists are excited and mill like children, a little lost, but realizing a dream. The dream is not childish to them. I wonder when I let my dreams go. When her group files into the restaurant, the Interpreter comes to join us.

"Another dent," says the Interpreter, raising her clipboard.

It has the insignia of the Echo Valley Provincial Park in the Qu'Appelle Valley. "I love it, all shiny and modern, but it seems so easily scratched. Back home in Sainte-Foy, the big bridges were made a hundred years ago and are still used. No dents. These mountains always make me think of the big stone houses on the Grande Allée running down to the old fort in Québec City, or the Pont de Québec across the St. Lawrence, or the trestle spanning the river to Cap Rouge."

"Aluminum is the lightest metal," I say. "The shiniest. It's even softer pure."

The Ranger grunts, balling his foil and flicking it toward the garbage. He misses and the little ball of metallic edges rolls near my foot. He is already looking at a group of kids at the edge of the forest who are yelling and throwing their pop cans at something in the branches.

"There's recycling bins right there," he says, shaking his head. He walks heavily toward them.

I wiggle my toe toward the shiny ball on the asphalt. Tiny triangles fold sharply along the crystalline shear: what we see in the macro comes from the microscopic. "That's worth more than the cans. It has more aluminum in it, yet it's always just thrown away," I tell the Interpreter. "Aluminum is the third most common element in the earth, most common metal overall."

"You are full of facts," she says. She's aluminum, I figure.

"It resists corrosion, it's a good conductor. But it's rarely found pure because it's so reactive."

Her hands stop, come away slightly from the clipboard.

The Ranger wanders back, secure in his authority. He stands listening behind sunglasses.

"You should recycle that," I say, gesturing toward the tinfoil ball.

"You're the trail crew. You pick up trash," he says, grinning.

His hands are tanned dark. The tan lines on my wrist stop where my work gloves normally start. "It's not trash."

"And it's not valuable," he says. "One tiny crushed-up ball. Imagine all the metal in the cars here, in the power lines, or the rails that go clear back to Québec."

"Aluminum used to be worth more than gold," I say.

"You're full of crap," says the Ranger, not sure.

"Seriously. Six hundred years ago at the English court, guests ate with gold utensils, except the most honoured, who got aluminum."

"So? They came, they ate, they got Alzheimer's, and they forgot about it," says the Ranger. He kicks the little ball under the garbage can and walks back to his truck, hitching his belt and pulling free his radio.

"Clear up that brush, hey?" he calls back, joking, pointing to the trailhead.

The radio crackles, the Lion requesting me: "L69, L71. What's your twenty, Rumi?"

The Interpreter sits, lightly touching her clipboard, bright in the sun, looking for a reflection.

■ After work the next day, I climb with the Interpreter on the short cliffs near the compound. I thought it would be a date but then find out the other two will be joining us as soon as they're off work. I climb angrily at first, wondering how my expectation and my message got misinterpreted. Eventually I relax: right now it's just the two of us, and I climb well. I'm getting strong, and now the exposure doesn't faze me and my feet seem sticky. I secure myself to an anchor on a small ledge where the route ends. I watch her long, tanned arms as I belay her up. She smiles when she reaches me, exhilarated. I tie her in, then stack the rope for descending, having her hold the midpoint while I thread it through the anchor chain.

I'm not sure how it's happened, but as I pull the rope through my hands a snag catches my attention: a small tear in the woven mantle. Maybe a rat chewed it while I watched her climb. She looks at me. The rope is useless—without the mantle the flexible inner fibres could be damaged and snap under our weight. She wonders about throwing it away when we're down. But that's the future. Until then, we're here. We both know we can't trust the rope.

The drop is real and the route doesn't look easy anymore, the rock smooth and sloping. I double-check the slings and anchor. She is pressed at my side, and I can feel the warmth drain from her shoulder. A deep trembling begins.

"The others are coming here as well. They can bring up another rope."

She stares at the coloured thread hanging useless.

"They won't be long. We're perfectly safe," I say. I think of my radio on its charging bed back at the cookhouse.

She's transfixed by the space. "Tell me something," she whispers.

I repeat that we're safe, but really I'm falling flat. We're stuck here. Together.

She straightens, looks out across the valley. "Tell me about that little pool again. You never told me about David Douglas."

I test the slings gently, trying to shift myself away from the ledge. Maybe *ledge* is misleading. A ledge to most people is something to sleep on; this one is only about right for our heels. So many guidebook descriptions are ambiguous, this being only one example. But how else to describe a mountain of ridges, shelves, buttresses, arêtes, gendarmes, and peaks? I've read lots of anecdotes about how people react in bad situations, how rescuers talk people down by asking about simple, familiar, or comforting topics. A story doesn't seem so crazy. We're both looking into the distance to fend off the suck of air at our toes, like the pull of tidewater. The hard part is imagining another place when this one has such a hold on my stomach. "Well," I say. "He was behind the others. He'd only just arrived in Fort Vancouver, near present-day

Portland, Oregon, at the mouth of the Columbia River, a few months before."

I feel the tremble in her relax slightly. I struggle to hear the thread of the story, the voices of history that want to speak through me.

"Tell me," she whispers in my ear.

⟁ David Douglas, newly arrived, squares his frail shoulders, recalls Hooker's directions, walks across the salon. The heavy floorboards creak beneath the carpets with his approach.

"Pardon the intrusion. You are Thomas Drummond, I presume?"

The small group exchange glances. Thomas Drummond, eminent botanist and the first European naturalist to venture onto the North American continent, turns to the newcomer.

"David Douglas. I've been sent by the Royal Horticultural Society to collect. Honoured."

"I've been notified that the Society was sending someone," Drummond replies. "We met in the wilderness. You studied under Sir Robert Preston and Dr. Hooker, no?"

"Yes. John Lindley of the Society oversaw my final preparations."

"Ah, good. Sounds like you're ready. But mind, past ninety miles upstream the country's wild and rugged, and you'll need to go farther afield to hunt something new. You'll need a strong constitution. This is absolutely not a Scottish garden."

"So then Douglas crossed the Pass and saw the giant mountains?" she asks.

I can't see the Ranger or the Lion yet; they may be some time.

"Not quite. Drummond crosses over first, right after New Year's in 1827, with a military man, a lieutenant by the name of Simpson. *Not* the Lieutenant-Governor Simpson, but a different man."

Imagining the cold then is better than thinking about the air below us now.

"Lieutenant Simpson!" calls Thomas Drummond as he strides over the crusted snow toward the round pond, where a small fire is set on a platform of branches. A lean man with a heavy moustache looks up. Only his eyes are visible under the fur and leather.

"We don't need to stop; there's no shelter." It's clear and sharp in the frozen air.

"But this is the height of land, no?" asks Simpson.

Drummond squats beside him, frowning. "Yes. What of it?"

"Well, sir, this is the latest in proven scientific measurement. I have in my possession a chart that, based on a standard atmosphere, will deduce the altitude of this pass simply by reading the temperature at which water boils."

"Astonishing. Is it because the rarefied air has a lower pressure?"

"Aye. The vaporization pressure is reached sooner with less resistance. Look! There we go. One hundred and ninety degrees Fahrenheit. That would make this Athabasca Pass . . . not less than eleven thousand feet."

Drummond stares hard. The catalogue of specimens and their descriptions of adaptation at such a height could change his career. "We'll camp here."

"So they know it is high," the Interpreter says.

"Eleven thousand feet is higher than most mountains around here."

We call as the Lion and the Ranger walk into the clearing, trying to indicate our predicament. They gaze up at us, then at each other. They set up below and the Ranger starts. The Interpreter looks over.

"Would they not measure from sea level? I am confused. Are there two Lieutenant Simpsons?"

"Apparently. But now Douglas crosses the mountains, a month later, in the spring."

David Douglas stands on the snowshoe trail in the silence of the pass. The others have gone ahead, bent unseeing under their ninety-pound loads.

He catches his breath, stunned by the variety of tree species here where the mountains crest. He's wondering if he should return to Europe by walking via Alaska and Siberia, and try to establish a connection between conifer seeds to prove that the North American natives originated in Asia.

Douglas lowers his pack at the edge of the frozen tarn, noting the algae visible beneath the sheath of ice on the rocks. Everywhere he turns! I've stumbled into God's pantry on this trip, he thinks. The Horticultural Society will have no higher honour to give; they'll have to invent something. And this is just one high pass; how many thousands more could there be?

He squints. The snows have been damaging the eyes of everyone in the party, and Douglas is no longer the crack shot he once was. To the east rises a wall of black stone overhung with broken seracs, but to the west a series of rock bands, deep in snow, leads to a flying ridgeline above the trees. From there he'll see everything. He leaves the trail and starts up.

Hours later, the long, snowy ridge stretches ahead of his snowshoes, falling away on both sides to glaciers. The surrounding peaks and valleys are endless, wavering in the thin air. The top is not so far. Beneath the wind are the first faint stirrings of the summit's siren song. Douglas writes later,

"The view from the summit is of too aweful a cast to afford pleasure. Nothing can be seen in any direction, as far as the eye can reach, except mountains towering above each other, rugged beyond description."

Returning to the trail at nightfall, he looks back at the peak. He's descending the height of the continent. The high place he once trembled in is already a fond memory.

"He was so far from home," she says.

"They travelled months by canoe across the prairie," I explain. "Douglas finally wound up at Hudson Bay, at York Factory, the largest of the fur processing forts, awaiting the spring breakup so he could go home after three years away. All the explorers came together there."

The Ranger's blue helmet moves below, coming quickly. When I shift, a pebble dislodges and glances off the rock. He flinches and looks up sideways. I have a few moments left.

▴ Douglas is talking to George Simpson, the lieutenant-governor of the Hudson's Bay Company, just arrived from Montréal. They've been discussing David Thompson's charts.

"Mr. Douglas, I presume? Spare an autograph?"

Douglas turns at the half-remembered voice and squints at the speaker.

"Mr. Drummond!" Douglas cries. It is an amiable reunion, with no recriminations.

Thomas Drummond clasps Douglas's hand. "We've heard of your travels for some time now. None of us can quite comprehend the sheer volume and quality of your exertions. I am proud to be in the same profession. Having crossed Athabasca Pass myself only last year, I'm humbled to hear you gathered species I hadn't glimpsed. Lieutenant Simpson measured the pass, mind you, and found it no less than eleven thousand feet above sea level. I'm certain your samples from such an altitude will turn botany on its ear!"

Douglas smiles a slow satisfaction, the spread of warmth on his face like a brandy. "Honoured, sir. I found *Pinus banksiana* at the pass. And climbed the one I christened Mount Brown, after our patron in Glasgow. I figure it's another five thousand feet in elevation."

"So high? Those two peaks of yours are the highest in North America!"

The Ranger pulls up, ignores the sling I stretch to him, clips his own system to the anchor. He moves in a rapid efficiency of hands and gear.

"You okay?" he asks the Interpreter. "I'm going to lower you off."

Only when she is nearing the ground does he look coolly at me.

■ I work with the Ant under a brilliant spring sky, pulling the summer signs out of a murky slat shed and preparing to hike them up the trails and replace the winter signage. I dig the thin metal squares from their stacks and sort them on a flatbed wagon.

He tells me about the time before the park was established, how the mining companies had elevations showing the way to the mines but little else.

"The fishing charts," he claims, "were better. At least they had the lakes marked correctly, although the mountains around were just added for effect."

"I found mistakes too," I say. "Up by the prison camp there's a bridge that doesn't exist."

"Never did," he says, looking at me seriously. "That used to be an internment camp during the war. Minimum security; they didn't get many escape attempts. The water at the river is very real and deep. No bridge; easier to catch people that way."

Bars of moted sunlight pierce the vinegar layers of mildew, but the shed remains dark. I brush compressed webs from the old directions.

"These signs," the Ant says, "place them only at head height. The winter ones are raised on account of snow. Two ways to make a sign stand out: raise it or lower the surroundings."

"How far away do you think you could see a mountain that was more than a kilometre higher than anything else?" I ask.

"Maybe not at all. It's not just height. The signpost has to be clear."

"Height is clarity when we look for mountains."

"Mount Assiniboine," he says. "Tallest around by a long shot and we can't even see its snow cap."

"That's because we're in this shed," I say.

"No, because the shed is in the way."

"You can see Assiniboine from lots of trails."

"But you can't climb it," the Ant points out.

"Why?"

"No time off. These signs won't replace themselves."

I bend to the task, gloves slipping on the thin metal. The Ant's reputation for hard work always intimidates. As I sort spare posts, it strikes me that although the glaciers that filled these valleys melted and gouged out the canyons and lakes, some almost a kilometre deep, the mountains stayed the same, poking up through the ice. I tell this to the Ant.

"Who's to say that they weren't covered deep in ice too?" says the Ant.

"The valley, sure. But the tops of the peaks? How could they get so much ice? Summits are not exactly the broadest platforms."

"No need to be. Snow doesn't form out of thin air."

"No, you need vapour and dust. Something for the crystals to form around," I say.

"Ever seen rime on the trees at a high pass after a freezing rain? They get all frosted with huge icicles standing on them?"

"Yeah."

"If a tree can grow ice, why not a mountain?"

My forearm has a dust-tan up to the pale white band just under the cuff of my work gloves.

"Jus' speculating." His Ant-like eyes fix on me. "You gonna work or try an escape?"

I sit on the platform at the old station at Laggan while the Lion takes the Ranger off to the park office to settle a disagreement over elk–wolf interactions. Their footfalls fade. I hear the Lion say, "Amazing, eh? We drive four hundred kilometres just so that we can climb on quartzite." Then they're gone, leaving the Interpreter and me to laze with arms numb from climbing all day behind the lake. I'm pleased to have time alone with her, but she's looking at the end of the platform. We sit with our backs against the old logs that have been painted so many times there's no grain visible—just big, round tubes that could be made from plastic. It takes some squirming to get my shoulder blades in the right groove.

"Sometimes I think they do not like each other, and other times I think they do," says the Interpreter.

"Rangers are happiest when the rest of us think like them."

"I think he is an orphan, or at least does not know his parents. Just like a lot of the voyageurs. That can make you stick to rules." She turns her chin to me. She wonders if something happened with the Lion to make the Ranger so judgmental.

The shade becomes cold. I didn't intend to think about the Lion's partner. Not under the sun. Not around her. "An accident. Last year." I say. I want to change the subject. The rails heliograph under the hot sun and shine bright at the vanishing point. I tell her of David Thompson—she's not interested in reading the factual histories and prefers my embellishments—but she admits confusion.

"There are too many with the same name. Thomas, Thompsons, Davids, and Simpsons."

"Maybe that's what happened," I say, moving out beside her in the sun.

"Everyone got mixed up?"

"There weren't that many people crossing in those days. People passing on the trail, on the ships back to Europe, on the portages, hunkered down over the winters. Maybe it was like a giant version of that game telephone, where somebody says something, it gets passed along, and by the time it gets back to the originator it's totally different."

"When you say telephone I miss my family back home," she says.

She's come a long way to be here. Maybe her great-grandfather was a voyageur who saw the mountains and returned to speak of them. We lie in the sun and wait for the others to come back. The smell of chalk mixed with rock-dust and sweat, of musky creosote in the hot air, the steel rails thicketed by juniper and chokecherry. I think about the Lion's late partner and feel relieved to be alive. The Interpreter says she likes the smell of the rails. It reminds her of lightning trapped in metal, flashing across Canada in a moment, then reflecting back again, bouncing between the oceans.

"It's the iron and manganese oxidizing that makes it smell like copper," I say.

"I prefer the way I tell it better."

"Oh. Okay."

"I like the rails, ever since I was a little girl. I would look at them to a point in the distance and wonder how the train stayed on them. I tried to imagine where they went."

"They just keep going. When I was a kid, I once hiked to where they turned a corner. I was terrified my parents wouldn't let me, so I walked as fast as I could before they could call me back. The cross-ties were never the right distance for my steps, but no matter how fast I hurried, the rails just curved away."

"They go right to my home. Those rails. Right. There," she says, pointing emphatically at her feet. "They go all the way to my hometown and through it and out to the coast on the Atlantic another five hundred kilometres. And they never touch once or grow farther apart. I love thinking they connect me to that. If I touch them, I am touching where I come from. It makes me sad to think they never touch each other, though, travelling all across this huge land, never getting closer."

Will I ever connect with her, even sitting beside her?

"Maybe people felt like that when the railroad was first built," I say. "You know, back in Toronto or Montréal, they'd ask, What's at the other end? What does this connect me to?"

"If they knew it came to such a beautiful place, they would have bought a ticket."

The grey peaks still hold streaks of snow. The sun is so direct that their slopes have become shimmering surfaces. I can't tell where the bowls are except where old snow provides definition. The colourless sky is only blue close to the peaks.

"This station was one of the most important places in the early days. For most of the people who came, this was their first stop."

"Well, they have a hotel here. The brunch on Sunday is to die for," she says. "But now it seems cheap. Drive up, walk through a crowd, take a picture, leave in traffic. Destiny is not a mass-produced fortune cookie. It must be individual to be true."

The tall poplars and trembling aspens cast cool spots on our slowly browning skin.

"Where are you at in your search for the mountains?" she asks, indicating my books.

"Toronto." I pull Arthur Coleman's *The Canadian Rockies: New and Old Trails* from the bottom of my rucksack. Books seem the only way to explore the past.

"These tracks go to Toronto," she says with her eyes closed. "What is there?"

"A professor."

"Looking for the little Punch Bowl?"

She wants to hear about going to the Pass in summer, when there's no obscuring snow on the pond. She lays her head on her pack and adjusts her hat. I tell her about Arthur Philemon Coleman, a professor of geology at the University of Toronto at the start of the twentieth century. Mountains were important to geologists because they could see the strata openly. Coleman's interest was in determining how the mountains had formed.

She raises her hand. "As a story, please."

"Coleman came west. In 1885, Calgary was a town of a thousand people. The tip of the railway had passed Laggan and was descending into the Columbia Trench. That slowly moving point was called The End. This would be winter. Late winter in Toronto, bleak and very cold. The air coming off Lake Ontario is frigid. There are no big parking lots, as the car hasn't been invented yet. That happened next year, courtesy of Karl Benz."

"Oh, Mercedes-Benz!"

"Shush," I say, and I fall into the clouds and tell her,

Professor Coleman tugs absently on his short beard and looks at the maps in his lecture hall. He lights his pipe, listening to the last students in the hallway. On the wall is a comparative diagram of the mountains on each continent, showing a series of increasing heights. There is Africa, culminating with Kilimanjaro. Europe with Mont Blanc and Elbrus crowding far right. Then Asia, with Mount Ararat and Everest. And finally North America, crowned by Hooker and Brown.

Next to this is a Geography of the Dominion of Canada, a coloured relief map from the forty-ninth parallel to the Arctic. One hundred years after David Thompson the entire northwest is blank, from Hudson Bay to the Arctic coast and the northern stretch of the Pacific. Only a few thin, squiggly lines: the rivers of Mackenzie's, Fraser's, and Thompson's explorations. Even now, with the railway nearing its completion to seal the political fact of Canada, the geological information is pouring in—descriptions of rocks, fossil beds, hot springs, strata.

Perhaps enough to determine the age of these Rocky Mountains and prove the Contraction Theory. This hypothesis, favoured among the faculty, suggests the planet was once a molten ball. In the process of cooling, the surface cracked and folded on itself. If this is correct, then all mountain ranges should be the same age. Coleman wants that evidence, but something else calls his attention. Above the mapped areas, north of the railway surveys, standing alone in the midst of white space, are the peaks of Hooker and Brown.

Coleman finds no references for these two mountains in any of the publications. They appear on all the maps but without description or drawing. Why hadn't Stanford Fleming's provincial surveyors mentioned them? Why hadn't Paul Kane included them in his paintings of grand peaks when he crossed in 1845? Coleman later wrote:

"A high peak is always seductive, but a mountain with a mystery is doubly so . . . I studied the atlas and saw . . . the highest points in the Rockies, and I longed to visit them."

"So he goes hiking on the university's pay? Nice job."

"Seems so. He made eight trips, most looking for Hooker and Brown. The fur companies had come and gone, and like a glacier withdrawing, the landmarks had been scoured from the maps, the rivers rerouted, and left behind like erratic boulders on a plain were two enormous peaks, always out of sight. The way there was lost. It took the railroad in 1885 to change that."

"What happened then?"

"Mountaineering had become a craze in Europe, and now there was an entire continent worth of mountains, unclimbed, unnamed, unknown. The Himalayas were being explored as well. And Africa. And the poles still hadn't been found. There was a lot to explore and a lot of competition among the climbers who could afford to travel widely."

"But there were no maps. So what did Coleman do?"

"He read everything he could find." Coleman and I are connecting. He earned a PhD in his thirties, rushed to the mountains before the railway was even complete, went to the end of the line, and wandered out into the wilderness—an impulse that strikes me as boyish and uncomplicated. That's the life I want.

▲ In an elegant, dark-panelled study, made mellow by the aimless flood of Saturday-morning light, Professor Coleman reads through David Thompson's narrative. Coleman had been dismayed at Thompson's lack of interest in elevations, then reminds himself it was an earlier time, with different priorities. He follows the journey up to the pass and notes with satisfaction the reference to the elevation as eleven thousand feet, credited to Lieutenant Simpson. This was a clear consensus, an indication of fact, and it carried no less an authority than that of Lieutenant-Governor George Simpson. Imagine a pass rising two miles above the sea, supporting mile-high peaks. Coleman wrote about it later:

"Lifting my head above the final ridge of rock, a strong wind coming from space laid hands on me and thrust me back.

This powerful, invisible current, sweeping across the continent at 8,500 feet above the sea, leaving the stagnant air of the valleys untouched, seemed to typify the vast, mysterious forces influencing the world beyond the touch of our senses."

"Was Simpson the lieutenant or the governor? This is where I get confused," she says, rolling away from the sun.

"Both. Same name. Different men."

"So one makes a mistake on the elevation—the one who is really no one. And because he has the same name as the governor, the one who was someone, everyone thinks the measurement must be true."

■ The Ant is so wiry that his grin is creased on his face. He needles me about my fitness.

"Young bucks," he says. "They make out like rabbits. Amazing you've any strength left."

When I protest, he makes an incredulous face.

"Oh? Who's that interpreter you're chasing? The one with the hair straight as arrows?"

That surprises me. "You've seen her hair down?" I'm perhaps a bit too interested.

"Lead pencils," he says. "Think you licked a few too many." He stifles a grin, amused at my eagerness. "Down to the small of her back, in a fanning point. Light as the feathers on an arrow."

"What do you know about her?"

"You see?" he says. "One-track mind. I don't hire interpreters, just sex-obsessed trail crew."

I insist he must have heard something. Eventually he relents.

"Look, she's worked at a lot of parks. Ontario, Manitoba, even Saskatchewan. She's moving west, season to season, park to park. She's a friendly sort, everyone likes her. She got involved with a warden I know at the Qu'Appelle Valley park. Seems she likes the guides."

■ I've settled into my routine. I meet the Lion in the early chill each day on the compound between the maintenance sheds and the ranger headquarters, and the Ant gives us our assignments. I never ask what the next day will bring, partly because I don't want the Ant to assign me the worst job and partly because I like living without a set schedule. The mountains and forest are calming. On the long trails some forgotten issues rise to the surface.

I finally ask the Lion about his accident last winter. In a monotone, he tells me about holding the rope as his friend died, just out of sight. His partner was leading their rope across a glacier when a snow bridge gave way. The Lion says his partner simply disappeared: a pull on the rope that nearly broke the Lion's back, arched his hips forward like a bow, then plowed him into the crust. The Lion arrested the rope, stopped the fall, then dropped his pack to gather gear to make an anchor so he could set pulleys and lift out his partner. But then, whatever his partner rested on collapsed, and he fell again, and the Lion was dragged, only metres away from his pack, pinned there for three days by the weight of his partner, hanging.

With no sound to wake him, he sat on the glacier, numbed to a stupor in the constant ocean-echo of the wind. Then the rope would slip and he'd wonder if he'd slept. Alert, he'd look around. Had anything changed? He'd check if he was still alive. The tension on the rope at his pelvis and the locking pain in his knees never lessened. He couldn't feel his back.

The silver line of the horizon bulged, unable to settle into its confines, like mercury tension. The sun glanced off the ice; his eyes rasped with snow blindness, like a fine dust. He tried to keep his eyes open, tried to keep looking. He could smell the burnt skin on his face. He knew his lips were blood red and swollen, and he despaired at the feel of his tongue. Sweat collected behind his collar, but he was no more able to open his jacket than to close it at night. His hands were frozen on the rope, braking it.

He prayed for the skies to stay clear, even though it meant

the afternoon sun heated everything into a desert and the snow softened and he started sliding. The rope inched closer to the crevasse despite the lack of sound from the black slash in the snow. He kept telling himself to try again, to flip to a crawl, to snare the pack. But every shift he made lost him ground, the pack behind him, bright slings like intestines spilling. Just there.

Sometimes, after looking too long, the horizon changed. Then he gazed down a vast white wall, his legs dug into the sugar-crud snow to keep from falling off the precipice. Other times the jagged shadow of the crevasse seemed to be above him, the head of a huge tack whose iron-hard pin was the rope shot into his guts, fixing him there against a white wax board. A slowly flapping insect, caught.

I think about his story on my hikes and wonder how much of his philosophy he burned through sitting there on the ice. He's changed, as if he needs to believe there's something permanent out there, something to cling to. The existentialists thought that our consciousness is only there while we are alive, and while we are, we're responsible for our actions. Once we're dead, we cease to exist. But Plato believed in a world of ideas that never changed. At least Plato would die and return to the idea of a perfect man. I can see why the Greek would appeal to the Lion now.

Sometimes I find myself questioning his actions. I know I'm not the only one. The climbing community is small and word gets around. The next night, when the Lion is in Canmore for groceries, the Ranger tells me point-blank that he thinks the Lion was poorly prepared: "He should have cared less about what happens when we die and more about preventing that death."

■ I watch the peaks. Black Prince is a good name for a mountain. Awe is born from wariness of power. I walk cautiously on the path that crests the hill. In a jagged meadow stands a fire tower.

When the Ant gave me my assignment that morning, the Lion

smirked. We stood in the large shed with the corrugated barn doors open. The mechanics who run the heavy equipment waved grimy hands and turned to their coffee, complaining, oblivious to their surroundings. Their navy coveralls blotched with oily melanomas, fingernails bleached white from working around carbon monoxide. The Ant looked at me.

"Fire Lookout," he says. "People say she's mad."

"Mad about what?"

"Not mad-angry. Mad-crazy," said the Lion.

"All alone for six months. Mind gets a little squirrelly shut in like that."

I hike past the warning signs posted on the road and then through the clearing, like a child crossing a graveyard on a dare. Then the Fire Lookout calls and invites me up. For just a second I consider running. But I turn back, cross the grassy mean, and climb the steel-grid stairs to the surrounding balcony. The Lookout brings tea in battered metal mugs.

"Black Prince is the wrong name. Mountains shouldn't be named after battleships," she says. She's slender but not frail, has grey hair tied up in a bun, long crow's feet in old leather, very clear grey eyes. She walks to me carefully, not from age, I think, but like a prisoner in a small cell; I wonder how often she leaves the tower and how far she ever walks in a straight line.

"Some aren't so bad," I respond. "Mount Indefatigable. Mount Invincible. Mount Warspite."

"The question is whether the characteristics match the mountain. Just because the men that first passed through here did so after the battle of Jutland doesn't mean they could christen the peaks with a history that had nothing to do with this place." Her voice is an airy old teacher trying to force the significance of her lesson.

"But it had everything to do with those men. Jutland was the greatest sea battle ever," I say.

"Until a bigger one happens. One boy dies in a foreign war and you have to name a billion-year-old rock after him? Who wants to be the first to die after the last mountain is named?"

"What names would you have chosen?"

"Not battleships," she says. "Why name a mountain after a sunken wreck? Those hunks of iron will corrode, but names stick like reputations in a small town. Who'll care in a generation?"

"You seem angry."

"Of course! I sit here for six months reminded of some ship or old guy long eclipsed. I feel the mountain's true nature has been overshadowed by the characteristics of its namesake."

"Can a name change all that about a mountain?" I ask, wondering what the Ant would say if he caught me resting. Assiniboine stands clear to the northwest, a ruler pondering the cracks on the floor of her throne room. Dirt sticks in the teeth of my boots, hanging high above the ground.

"Names are our guides to reality. If they're not accurate, we get lost," she says.

How lost is she? I wonder how hard I should push, then ask, "So that's your deal, eh? Get dropped off with six months' supply and leave everything behind?"

She laughs back. "Oh, my boy. You would be surprised what we think we leave behind." She wags her mug. "You give up *vino* for *veritas,* but the sum of our vices remains constant."

I turn to the view that she sees every day. She's looking at me across her nose.

"Assiniboine looks lonely, all by itself up there," I say.

"She sees the world. That's enough. One can't be in the valleys and the peaks both."

"She's called after the tribe, the Assiniboine, the stone-boilers, after their method of cooking."

"That wasn't her original name. The first missionary thought the mountain's clouds looked like steam from a teepee. This is my third season; I still don't know her well enough to name."

"But we do need names. That's what anchors our language."

"Ever consider that language is just a set of symbols that

represents real things?" The Lookout places her hand on my forearm as she says this. It's warm, gentle, inviting.

I stare at her, wondering at her life, at what decisions brought her here. "Sure, but I know this trail. I don't have time to describe it every time I talk about it."

"You don't *take* the time. Language is modified by the lazy."

"That's insane. Are you for or against names?" I'm shocked at my accusation, a casual hyperbole of language. I try to recover. "Language is shorthand for experience."

I'm nervous, questioning if she just made an advance on me. Maybe I'm misinterpreting; I don't always read people right. If only there were maps for that.

"Relax," she says. "Enjoy my tea. Names are a reference, but they say little about the owner. We only need them to talk about someone absent. When is that ever in their best interest?"

"You think maps lead us to poor decisions? But they're our agreement on the truth."

"So truth is democratically elected? Maps are made by the conquerors." She stares at me.

"When you spot a fire, be sure to let us know," I say. I'm wondering if she is mad. Mad-crazy, not just mad-alone. I'm uncomfortable with having to watch my words so closely.

"If there was a fire in this valley, do you know what would be left?"

I shrug, finishing my tea, and reach for my pack.

"If everything was reduced to ash, and if you piled it all up, what would you have?" she asks.

"A lot of carbon," I admit, reluctant.

"And if you packed it together?"

"Eventually coal. Anthracite coal, actually. Very little water. It burns so much hotter than the lignite coal from the Dakotas that the old steam engines used to blow up in Canmore."

"Hard to keep firemen around if they keep blowing themselves up." She laughs.

"There was a real demand for them as the trains passed the Dakotas."

"Tell me, if you took all that coal and squeezed it more?"

I relent. "Graphite. You'd need a lot of weight."

"Say you had it, and kept squeezing," asks the Lookout.

"Eventually you'd get diamond."

"How big?"

I blink, look out at the vast valleys filled with trees. Millions of trees.

She extends her hand. In the palm, a small gold ring with a diamond from a long-ago marriage, or one in hibernation, or one that ended in disaster. Why is she here? I don't know, don't ask.

"Just think," she says. "You could carry this whole park around on your finger."

I rise and pass back my mug, hoist my pack and axe. I spot the lines of books on shelves above the windows. "Ah, you do have friends up here."

She glances over her shoulder as I start down. "You know what I like?"

I'm wary again. Madness, by definition, is unpredictable.

"We don't know each other's names," she says, white forearms pressed on the black rail.

As I walk down the trail, I scrutinize each bush and needled tree. It feels as if everything has sprung from a sparkling diamond, released from confinement, and is now blossoming. Sprung from water and minerals and the power of the sun.

▨ Friday evening of the first long weekend of the summer, and the headlights of cars headed into the campgrounds stretch back along the valley. I look at the maps. They don't show the cars, or the weather, or the night. On the maps it's always high noon, roads empty.

I'm young and fit and a bundle of hungers and hormones

looking for an outlet. I walk eagerly to invite the Interpreter for something ambitious, a summit perhaps. The dim cookhouse holds only the Lion, standing at the counter surrounded by open containers of food from which he eats without ceremony.

"Hiking thirty-five a day, my lunch lasts until ten. I'm still losing weight."

I join him in constructing sandwiches. I've been thinking of the view of Assiniboine from the Lookout's tower and remembering how it once grabbed me. Only it's Hooker and Brown that seem to inspire me now.

"We *are* going climbing this weekend," he insists.

"Sure. Where are the others?"

"Most of the interpreters have gone into Canmore. Big band tonight. The Ranger has taken your favourite one climbing for the weekend."

I stop constructing. "Where?"

"Assiniboine. I told him you'd take care of his dog." He laughs.

I'm stunned. I sputter, "What? The one that's supposed to be half wolf?"

"Ever hear of one that was half something else and owned by a single mountain man?"

I stare at the chunks of mangled food.

"I guess he had a better story," says the Lion. "You got all weekend to get a new one."

"I thought I wasn't doing badly. There's more to Hooker and Brown the more I read about it."

"What always intrigued me is that Coleman had figured the mountains didn't exist. Yet years later Norman Collie decided to forego Assiniboine—which was right there: proven, virgin, and a few days' hike away—to look for a pair of peaks that were months away and miles above. Something that would take years. Assiniboine would have taken a week and made him famous."

"Let's not talk about Assiniboine," I say.

He stops. Finally I return his look. "I don't get you, man," he says. "Why don't you just ask her out. Enough foreplay, already." He shakes his heavy head. "You know what? I think you're just in it for the chase. If the Ranger didn't like her so much, neither would you."

"Not true."

"Maybe it's her hair then. All those big black curls falling every which way . . ."

"She had it out of the braid?" I've been imagining it straight, like the Ant said.

"Yeah, man, what a mass! It must weigh a ton. Nice, actually. Changes her face and everything. Look, forget it, Rumi. How about Mount Gordon?"

I've read that from there, Norman Collie's party had looked north and seen a massive peak in the distance, at the very edge of their horizon. "I want to see what Collie saw," I say.

"Yeah. Just north of the rail lines, several days' travel for them—three hours for us. It's right at the apex of the Wapta Icefields. Something done in a day if we went light and used skis on the glacier," says the Lion.

I can't dispel Hooker and Brown. I've never seen a photo, but I keep imagining them enormous, distant, hazy. Underneath the story is some mystery, smouldering and waiting, gone to ground with the occasional whiff, like a fire that burns deep in the coal seams.

▲ ▲

Touch It—You're Here

High above the dark waters of Bow Lake, the wind splinters triangular shards of wind slab off my ski tips. My bindings creak in the whispered language of snow. I wipe the sweat from my eyes, look up the dazzling glacier, and hope the weather holds so we can see what Norman Collie saw when his party made the first ascent of Mount Gordon. Especially since the sight shifted his attention away from Assiniboine to the south and onto the possibility of peaks far to the north.

Spindrift blows on the surface of the glacier, as if we're moving across cloud banks. This gives me the sensation of coming free from the ground. The horizon line of snow and sky bobs slowly and my gaze wavers across the expanse without rest; an albatross searching a mastless ocean.

The Lion and I ski up the glacier's long headwall. We've hiked around Bow Lake and up the long canyon carved by the draining ice, and now we near the top of the bulging, snow-covered glacier itself. At last we stand on the rim of the Wapta bowl, looking at a circle of peaks. The snow that collects in the bowl weighs the ice, pushing it outward between the rock spires.

In a whiteout there would be no bearings.

"Gordon doesn't look like much," I say, looking south. It's just a bump.

"There's no trees, no scale," says the Lion.

"Are you sure that's it?" I ask. "This map shows contours, but it can't be that high."

"It is. There's just nothing to compare it to."

I move off the path of the headwall and the winds drop. The sun glares, baking my face. Mount Gordon rises until I can feel the massive tide of bedrock surging up beneath the ice. The basin is kilometres across, our trail a thread on the snow.

Finally, the Lion starts to lead up a long ramp. We can see down the Yoho Valley and its long, glacier-carved basin. As the slope falls away toward the Yoho, it fractures into hundreds of crevasses, dark beneath white lips. Some are big enough to eat a school bus without chewing.

"You will rescue me, of course," says the Lion in a gentleman's tone. "If it's no trouble for you."

I remember the story of Norman Collie's trip up here. Strange how the Lion can joke so readily about an infamous accident.

"What are they waving about? That spur can't be higher than our summit."

The Swiss guide squints up from his pack. "I see four. There were five."

"Oh, Good Lord, let's go." The remaining party races recklessly across the flat summit ridge.

"It's Thompson," Norman Collie says, "but I can barely see him. I think he's upside down."

They can see the sole of a boot wiggle slightly, sixty feet below. It looks very small.

"If you could make haste and extricate me, I would be extremely grateful," calls up Charles Thompson, his Boston accent drowned in the pinching ice.

Norman Collie is the thinnest, and a bachelor. He strips to his flannel and knickerbockers. A stirrup is made. At the edge he leans back, yells down. "Hold on, Charlie, I'm on my way."

"If it's not too much trouble," says Thompson.

The summit snow is packed hard from the sun and wind, a névé that we can walk quickly upon. From here it seems the whole world is mountainous. I delay looking north, aware of my anticipation, but the draw is inescapable, and there stands Mount Forbes, the tallest on the horizon, a shark fin among the stone reefs. It draws attention like the vanishing point on a perspective.

"We *have* to climb that," the Lion says, mesmerized.

It's easy to believe there could be more, and higher, behind Forbes.

Above us a raven rustles its papery wings, croaking a demand: drop the food and back away.

"He's knows what's important," says the Lion.

To the south, Assiniboine towers above her neighbours. We stand in a direct line between her and Forbes. This was Collie's dilemma—but if Forbes was so big, and if it could hide others, and if Hooker and Brown were farther on, higher than all, the choice couldn't have been an easy one.

"When Collie stood here, Assiniboine had not yet been climbed. What would you have done?"

"Assiniboine probably. It was a bird in the hand," says the Lion, eating one of my snack bars. "One mountain is good enough, why do you need two?"

They're both three-day trips, but Forbes is there to the north and higher, less travelled, more of a prize. This is the map as I see it: Assiniboine spikes like the Matterhorn, the dominant peak south of the rail lines. I bump my fingers up the map northwards and hit the bulk of peaks clustered around the touristy enclave of Laggan. I cross the highway and follow the vertebrae of the Rockies onto the Wapta Icefields to the peaks of Balfour and Gordon. This is all parallel to the Banff–Jasper highway. Tourists stop and look at the great ice caps pushing over the ridges, but we ski up those tongues and see behind them huge bowls of snow, cupped among peaks that are less known and whose heights I can only guess at. It's a wonderland of wilderness. From those icefields I can skim to the high fin of Forbes. That's as far as we can see now, but from the maps I can dream across a series of glaciers that bring me to the real giants: Columbia and Bryce and the Twins. Then a gap. Not a pause in the mountains, but a pause in the superlative. One hundred kilometres of sharp, untouched, hostile peaks. Then the Yellowhead River, and then Mount Robson, the highest of them all.

Somewhere in between is a space of rugged stone that should have raised something groundbreaking, something noteworthy. It should be there. Norman Collie believed so. Now I'm searching.

I want to follow Norman Collie's path. Collie followed Arthur Coleman, who followed old Indian maps. Coleman found the pass but no mountains fitting the descriptions of Hooker and Brown. He named what was there in their honour—just two smaller peaks, names referencing names. Collie needed more proof, and he couldn't give up the dream of two massive mountains. He kept searching. Yet each high peak Collie climbed revealed another to the north, even higher. The high knife of Mount Forbes is what he saw from Mount Gordon. What did he see from Forbes?

"Think the Ant will give us time off to tackle Forbes?" I ask the Lion.

"Not if we ask."

I kick the shale outcropping, loose, dusty, covered in fossilized shells.

"Look at these cephalopods. This was the bottom of a shallow sea," I say.

"Lucky for us we're a billion years late."

"Which one's that?" I ask, pointing west across the Yoho glacier to a large, bowled peak.

"Mount Collie. You think it suits him?"

"It seems like him, tall, dignified. Distant."

"I wonder how it seemed before it had a name," says the Lion as we start down.

■ Every morning we mill about, packing tools and evaluating clouds, until the Ant assigns our trails. My days consist of hiking, clearing wind-felled trees, redirecting water erosion, and repairing bridges. The days we work with helicopters are the gravy. Today is gravy.

We arrive at King's Creek Canyon. As the truck stops, the Lion and I jump out, grab our packs, and sprint across the muddy lot. My steel-toed boots run like blocks and my tools make the packs bounce. The orange overalls we wear rub stiff; it's too early in the day for sweat to soften them. My focus is the thin track that leads into the canyon through willow and alder. I dart low into stringy branches splashing cold dew. My breath billows past in the crisp air, and the canyon's stained limestone walls move closer through the undergrowth.

At the side of a seething creek cling the ruins of a bridge, smashed by ice moving against it when the runoff began. Now it's stuck, buckled in strange angles, water pouring over its twisted decking. The stringer, the main supporting beam, is broken open in arm's-length splinters. Slippery green algae that have grown on all the slats wash with the stream's flood.

I hear rotor blades approaching. Less than a minute now. We both open our packs, pull out wire cables with eyelet ends.

"I'll wave the chopper in, you truss up the stringer," the Lion yells over the sound of the creek. He runs back to a small glade, sizes up the approach and the canyon walls.

I creep onto the sloping deck, trying to reach the midpoint. Whenever I weight it, the bridge begins to lean into the full force of the torrent. I lie flat and stretch, manage to drop a cable past the mid-post. I thrash the downstream water for the end while freezing spray lands on my cheek. The chopper is loud in the canyon, too close even to echo, drowning the roar of the creek. I catch the cable and pull it through.

"No! No!" yells the Lion, waving me down. I turn to question and see the sleek helicopter bank into the shadow of the canyon.

"You've only got the top part. You've got to get under! Under! Or you'll just rip the planking!"

I force my hand against the gush to wiggle the cable under the main beam. The water is so cold it feels like oil over my hand. The helicopter shifts its tail like a fish inching upstream, dangling a short wire of only two metres. I've little clearance to hook the line, and the pilot will have even less between the walls. My cable is lost in the churning wash. The water numbs; the bridge rocks violently. I look at the Lion, standing with arms out like a bird, flapping, slowly lowering the helicopter. The thrumming of the blades is deafening. The Lion yells something that's lost in the cacophony. I can't tell if he's trying to warn or encourage.

I know I have to. This wasn't part of the plan, but if I don't commit, we'll waste the helicopter's expensive time. I breathe, commit, roll off the decking, and swing into the icy water, my upper hand clinging to the topside cable. I'm up to my chest in turbulent snow melt, the cold constricting my ribs. I duck and reach for the other eyelet, sweeping blindly, then pull it to the surface and clip the ends together with a gated carabiner.

The wide rotors are a blur of pulsing sound and air. The helicopter trembles in the air, a monstrous hummingbird. I hook the ring onto the dangling short line, then stumble back, wave clear with one arm, let go, and get swept downstream into a springy alder. I watch the cable whip taut, see the snapping of nails and planks, then the bridge tears free of its sills and slowly rotates. The Lion pulls me up and we stagger down the trail. Everything is muffled. I feel drunk and wonder when that happened. The Lion has his arm under mine, pulling me through the bushes. Is he drunk as well? It reminds me of university, after the pub let out, weaving out onto campus. I haven't been this drunk in a long time and it's confusing. He's yelling in the radio.

Then the Ranger is there, lifting me, pulling my shirt off, wrapping me in a blanket. It looks warm, but I can't feel it. He's asking me what day it is. I figure his job is ridiculously easy if that's what he does all day. I want to giggle, but I feel sick. I look around for the Lion. The last time we were this bad he disappeared too, leaving me explaining to a green-eyed girl outside the student union building how *mica* is Latin for glittery. She was all glittery. But mica is almost transparent, with a low carbon exchange and almost no conductivity. Like a typical undergraduate so immersed in his studies that he can form no other metaphors, I was making a fool of myself. I told her carbon is the basis for all organic life and bonds to anything. I asked her to go climbing. But she was so non-reactive that it seemed nothing interested her. I remember she studied history. I thought she liked me, but she ended up in the car with the Lion. These details seem so important that I try to tell the Ranger about them.

The Ranger asks me questions about school and Calgary. The Ant peers over his shoulder with deep concern. I hear him say "hypothermia," but I forget what that means. The Ranger tells me how the body core gets too cold for the brain to work, but that still doesn't *mean* anything. I feel a painful heat prickling in from my skin, trying to overheat my heart. I feel as though I'm sleeping and then realize I'm wrapped and lying in a bed with the Ranger sitting beside me. He says no one acts the same, some need to tell stories, others need to hear them.

Hypothermia is mostly embarrassing afterwards. The Ant says it's like being drunk: warm and unreasonable. "You don't have to be that dedicated." He grins, relieved.

■ The Interpreter's hair is black as jet.

It comes to points on her forehead, sweeps in a lazy curl on her neck, and ropes into a braided tail. It pales her skin, blends her eyes, and twines like a Turkish column down her neck.

Jetstone comes from a river in ancient Turkey. It's a softer form of coal, a material that was once alive and existed on the

Earth in a different form: green and waving lightly under the sun, and now dense and very black, polished to a high degree.

On the weekend the Interpreter and I stand in King's Creek Canyon and face a bulging wall of limestone. I count the number of bolt anchors the guidebook says have been placed into the stone. The rope can be clipped to these pre-drilled metal loops screwed and cemented in the rock. Very safe. Last week the Ranger asked me why I trust them more than placing my own gear, especially when I don't know who drilled them into the rock. He has a point.

"The map says there is a bridge," the Interpreter says.

"We need to update that."

"Are you climbing the book or the rock?" she asks.

"I'm figuring out how much gear we need."

She turns to face me squarely, pushing a finger into my chest. "You have your nose so deep in that book I have not seen you look at the route itself."

I look up at the cliffs and try to impose the sketched lines of the map onto the rock.

The Interpreter stretches her arms behind her head. "I think we should put the book down and find the routes as they naturally form."

I let the book slowly drop. Maybe she's right. My first impulse is to look at the maps. Maybe I need to rub my nose in it and see what I can do without the guide.

"Okay, let's go," I say, throwing her the end of the rope.

I step up to the rock face, my harness dripping with carabiners and slings. The rock smells cold and sucks the sunlight down into its impassive grey. Tiny ledges and grooves and cracks appear, and I start up bracing against each, testing my balance. Holding on to the wall by the barest of tension, feeling my toughening fingertips smudge and catch against the pressure. It isn't long before I'm looking for the next bolt to ensure that I'm on course. Halfway up, a move eludes me. On a corner just above, the steel

of a bolt's ring glints against the pinkish-grey layers of the con-
glomerate rock. I scramble and puff for a larger hold above. I'm
fighting the terrain. Still I can't move up. I burn knowing she's
watching. The bolt distracts me from the rock. I try to forget it,
but it shines out like a beacon. My eyes keep coming back to it.
The desperation of inertia closes in. If I stop I'll slowly tire my
arms and hands until I fall. I need to shut the bolt out.

I close my eyes. The rock takes on a deep texture. Grooves
and lips I haven't noticed before emerge under my fingers. I
sweep slowly and begin to construct a mental map of the rock.
There is so much more here than I ever realized before. I test the
edges with my shoes and stand up, imagining the holds. Tiny
moves, but it's motion all the same. I don't care when this ends,
I'm consumed by deciphering the stone, as if its story is here in
Braille. I keep moving, eyes tight. I'm so entranced that her voice
is startling.

"You missed the bolt," she calls.

I open my eyes and see the bolt ring at my waist. I breathe in
a gust. Something is happening. I clip the rope to the bolt and
close my eyes again.

I finish and the Interpreter lowers me off and I have an odd
warmth in my head.

My experience reawakens an old memory of my first climbing
course, when the instructor had the Lion and me climb blindfolded so that we would learn to sense the rock and our balance,
and not just see the obvious line up the wall. That's when I fell in
love with climbing.

"My turn," she announces.

"Too easy. You know all the moves after watching me. You
want to find the route as it is?"

She watches me. Dangerous ground, her eyes say.

"Trust me?" I ask. The rope is already up and threaded through
the anchor, there's no risk.

"I barely know you," the Interpreter says.

I spin her wary look away and tie her bandana as a blindfold, just as instructors do.

"Now try it." I guide her by the shoulder to the rock. She's tentative, her feet now testing each tender step. I hold her as she reaches up the wall. Her arms sweep wide and fast and her balance suggests she might quit. I whisper encouragement as scores of tiny muscles in her waist vibrate under my palms.

"Relax," I say. "You know this. It's totally safe. You're on top-rope. You can't fall."

Her fingers scrabble over the surface and finally tap curiously on a small ledge, like a child exploring a relative's face. Her mouth hangs open. She extends her arm up until her cheek is flush against the cold rock. Then she swallows and steps up, scraping her feet for purchase. She mashes her soles onto spots beside more obvious footholds, guided by her natural balance.

She gasps as my hands leave and take up the rope. She looks wildly around and presses her forehead against the stone. Then she moves, slower than I've ever seen her, like a dancer who doesn't react to but actually controls the music.

After an hour she reaches the top, and I lower her. As she touches the ground, she pulls off the blindfold and seems stunned. She quietly examines her fingers. Her eyes are clear and she looks back without defences, kissing my cheek, her fingertips lightly trembling on my neck.

■ As we walk out of the canyon, everything feels more open than before. I want to order the elated riot in my mind. "Without maps there's no history, so we're the first to climb that route."

"Shut up," she says quietly. Her face is lowered, shadowing her cheeks.

After a while the buzz wears off. We sit in the dry grass at the creek edge, in the sun.

"Who were Hooker and Brown named after?" she asks. "Were they famous?"

"I don't know who Brown was. Hooker seems important." I pull a book from my pack.

"Sir William Jackson Hooker," I summarize, "was director of the world-renowned Royal Botanic Gardens at Kew, in England. Hooker was a leading man of science. As a patron to men like Douglas, Hooker was able to span the globe and bring species from all parts of the Empire. He was ultimately a collector of the superlative: the rarest, the finest, the most beautiful."

"And he got the highest mountain named after him."

"Yes. The highest. There are some letters too. Do you want to hear them?"

"Oui."

"This one is from Sir William Hooker to David Douglas, back in 1829."

> *I trust you will find enclosed a draft of the Flora Boreali-Americana that I mentioned I was publishing to showcase yours and Drummond's achievements in North America. The engraved sketch map has been commissioned and I have labelled it with the mountain names and elevations as per our conversations. I know that you are terribly busy preparing for your return to California and the Sandwich Isles, but could I implore upon you to review the maps and suggest any corrections that you identify?*

"And then Douglas wrote back."

> *I had almost forgotten to say that I have put the last impression on your map through my hands. It is very fine and will surely please you. The route of Franklin, Richardson, and Drummond is marked in RED, Parry's in BLUE, and mine in YELLOW. I must*

have the latter tint changed to green, for yellow is a most sickly hue for a culler of weeds. I cannot tell you how pleased I am to have seen the first part of your Flora Boreali-Americana before sailing, and that I am enabled to take it with me to America. The map is good and will increase the interest of the book.

"Sounds like they were friends," the Interpreter says.

"Yeah."

"What is wrong?"

"Strange, eh? Hooker is a knight, at the highest level of society. Probably rubbing shoulders with the King and Queen. But Douglas was a gardener. It just seems odd they were so informal."

"Men grow close when they work together. Look at you two on trail crew."

"But then it ends. Douglas was killed while travelling. Thomas Drummond too. Same month."

"What?" she says, alarmed, sitting up. "Both?"

"Douglas in Hawaii, then called the Sandwich Isles. Hooker gets a letter on July 12, 1834, from the Royal Horticultural Society."

It is with deep regret we learnt almost simultaneously of the loss of two pillars of the botanical field, and furthermore dear protégés and friends of yours. The death of Thomas Drummond in Havana, Cuba, and the almost simultaneous passing of David Douglas in the Sandwich Isles by such accidents and misfortune was a shock that felt itself throughout our staff. It is some testament to the skill of these men that they prevailed so long against such obvious dangers in the New World. Their passing will leave a large space in the field of Botany, but their mark on History has been noble and firmly wrought.

"Douglas supposedly fell into a wild boar trap. It wasn't empty."

"That's terrible."

"He didn't see so well after the snow blindness from crossing Athabasca Pass."

"And Drummond?"

"He was the botanist who told Douglas the height of the Pass. He died in Cuba. There's no mention of how."

"But then who was left that knew about these mountains?"

"Not many. And then . . ." I riffle the book ". . . it seems that all Douglas's records went missing. Hooker requested them from the Society. This was the response:"

> *In accordance with your request to our archives for the cited materials (Douglas, David—1827; manuscript, sketch compilation, charts, asst. notes: 182 pps.) deposited here on the late Douglas's return to England, I have supervised a search for said items but must report our embarrassment to locate any of the collections. Although our receipts clearly indicate our possession of the materials, at this time there is no trace as to their whereabouts or to whom may have borrowed them. I can assure you our humiliation is complete and I will inform you immediately on any change in this situation. I am at least comforted that Douglas's original journals are in your possession.*

"So we get the entire account from Hooker?" she asks.

"It's all in his hands. But something seems to be wrong here." I'm flipping back and forth.

"Tell me," she says, resting her head on her pack, her braid coiled.

"Listen to this. This is from the original journal of David Douglas, on June 1, 1836."

> *After breakfast at one o'clock, being, as I conceive,*

on the highest part of the route, I became desirous of ascending one of the peaks, and accordingly I set out alone on snowshoes to that on the left hand or west side, being to all appearances the highest. The labour of ascending the lower part, which is covered with pines, is great beyond description, sinking on many occasions to the middle. Halfway up vegetation ceases entirely, not so much a vestige of moss or lichen on the stones. Here I found it less laborious as I walked on the hard crust. One-third from the summit it becomes a mountain of pure ice, sealed far over by Nature's hand as a momentous work of Nature's God. . . . The view from the summit is of too awful a cast to afford pleasure. Nothing can be seen, in every direction as far as the eye can reach, except mountains towering above each other, rugged beyond description. . . . The height from its base may be about 5,500 feet; timber 2,750 feet; a few mosses and lichens 500 more; 1,000 feet of perpetual snow; the remainder, towards the top, 1,250, as I have said, glacier with a thin covering of snow on it. The ascent took me five hours; descending only one and a quarter.

"But look! It gets changed in the publication process. This is what actually gets recorded in Hooker's directives to the editor."

After breakfast, being well refreshed, I set out with the view of ascending what appeared to be the highest peak on the north or left-hand side. The height from its apparent base exceeds 6,000 feet, 17,000 feet above the level of the sea. After passing over the lower ridge of about 1,200 feet, by far the most difficult and fatiguing part, on snowshoes, there was a crust on the snow, over which I walked with the greatest of ease.

"And then when the *Companion to the Botanical Magazine*

Version Two was published, an article appears: 'A brief memoir of the life of David Douglas, with extracts from his letters.'"

> *Being well rested by one o'clock, I set out with the view of ascending what seemed to be the highest peak on the north. Its height does not seem to be less than 16,000 or 17,000 feet above the level of the sea. After passing over the lower ridge I came to about 1,200 feet of, by far, the most difficult and fatiguing walking I have ever experienced, and the utmost care was required to tread over the crust of the snow. . . . This peak, the highest yet known in the northern continent of America, I feel a sincere pleasure in naming 'Mount Brown,' in honour of R. Brown, Esq., the illustrious botanist . . . A little to the southward is one nearly the same height, rising into a sharper point. This I named 'Mount Hooker,' in honour of my early patron the Professor of Botany in the University of Glasgow.*

"So the biological information that could have indicated the pass was overestimated has been removed! Even west has been changed to north. After the magazine was published in June 1836, it was quickly forgotten. It seems the only place the altitudes ever appeared in print. You thought Hooker and Douglas were friends? Well, here's what Hooker wrote of Douglas for an obituary."

> *It was, no doubt, gratifying to be welcomed by his former associates, after so perilous yet so successful a journey, and to be flattered and caressed by new ones. . . . His company was now courted, and unfortunately for his peace of mind he could not withstand the temptation (so natural to the human heart) of appearing as one of the Lions among the learned and scientific men of London.*

The Interpreter rolls over as the sun passes behind the canyon wall.

"I think Hooker was writing that as much as a reflection of himself. He was a Lion, but he needed to publish that map or his mountain, and even himself, would be forgotten."

■ It's shiny black, kicked up by my boot. I stoop, curious.

"What's that, a rock?" asks the Ant.

"Not just a rock. Blackjack." It's resinous, oily, a perfect cleavage on one side like a knife slice.

"Blackjack?" The Ant is unimpressed.

"Common name. It's sphalerite. Zinc sulphide. Didn't think there was much metal here."

"Brass bullet casings," he says. "All around here. Training ground, legacy of the war."

We're pulling stumps out of the forest soil. The stumps are barriers to the ski grooming machines, like pylons on an enemy beach. We dig around and chop out the lateral roots, then use hand winches to break the fat tap root, sunk like an anchor chain. It's slow and hard. Even the Ant takes breaks.

"This area was wild back in the 1940s, so they used it for internment camps: German soldiers, Polish, Romanian. Even Japanese Canadian civilians. The MS camp was for POWs," he says.

"It was only minimum security for war prisoners?"

The Ant shrugs. "Where would they go? Most people don't know anything about forests."

I'd heard stories of people lost for days in this valley, walking in circles, sleeping under moss, all the while every stream leading downhill to the valley bottom and the road.

"It's the great catalyst," he says. "War opens up everything. The first folks through here came during the Great War, the First World War. Most of these mountains carry names of ships and admirals. Between the wars came prospectors, looking for gold and silver, just about anything."

I've seen some old mine tunnels and sawmills. But war fertilized: unused nitrogen from ammunition factories allowed the arid prairie to grow crops for cities. War had benefits.

"War is bad for lots of things," counters the Ant. "You could be killed."

"Sure, but not out here."

"No one thinks about the future during war. Not that war ever stopped the future from coming. It mostly just accelerates it."

"You might feel differently if you were about to be killed."

"That's a very good example of an accelerated future."

"War brought advances, like airplanes," I say.

"Airplanes, sure. But people cut roads out here without planning, and mined for everything you can imagine: coal, yes, but metals too."

I'm thinking of Ontario, under whose granite armour there are plenty of heavy metals.

"You can't have war without brass," the Ant concludes. He starts chopping. We alternate.

In between blows I say, "Metals? Here?"

"No. But that didn't stop anyone. War doesn't make good geologists, just good businessmen."

"You often find copper with lead and zinc. I just wouldn't expect it naturally here because it's igneous, formed volcanically. If you have copper, you add zinc to get brass. Or tin, to get bronze.

The Ant squints.

"Add zinc to iron and you get galvanized steel," I add.

"That right?" He points to a tree. "What's that?"

"A tree."

"What kind?"

I try to remember the simple mnemonics the Interpreter said about needles: *flat is fir, sharp is spruce.* I can't see the needles. I imagine the Lion telling me that I recognize the tree by the pattern: it's an imperfect cookie from a perfect mould. But which one? "Spruce," I guess.

"Sub-alpine fir," the Ant says, "is the correct answer." He shakes his head. "Geologists. Good with rocks. Dumb like deer. You work here, Rumi: you gotta learn some about trees."

"You work here, and you think this is a rock," I say, hefting the sphalerite. "You have to understand it: where it comes from. It's full of zinc. If you strike it in the dark, it'll make sparks. I'll tell you about rocks, you teach me about trees."

He regards me as if I'm out of line, offering him a deal of equals. He settles on his heels.

"I found out that there's no such thing as moose moss," I say accusingly.

"Yeah. I know." He grins. "But it made you open your eyes."

■ "Before we had maps, we had rhymes," says the Ant from the stern of the riverboat. The riverboat has a shallow draft to access difficult areas along lakeshores and streams.

"Careful of wind," says the Ant. "Waves don't get big here, but the boat's so light that it'll flip." He watches the shape of the clouds. "We'll be okay, that's not rain."

"How can you tell?" asks the Lion.

"Lenticulars," he says. "A new system usually rounds the upper clouds, like lenses. You'll also see feathered ones. My father used to say, 'Horses' manes and mares' tails, Sailors soon shall shorten sails.' That's how maps were in his day."

"The forecast from the rangers was fifty per cent chance of rain," I say.

"Flip a coin," says the Lion. "What an easy job."

"Ease off on the Rangers, they're on our side," scolds the Ant. "Besides, they're trained to kick the stink out of a skunk. Rely on the old ways. If I ever let you take the boat out without me, remember those rhymes. And if the barometer is rising fast, don't be going out that day."

The Lion is amused, prodding the self-serious Ant to announce more nursery rhymes. "Is there one for that too?"

"Sure. 'Long foretold, long last. Short notice, soon past. Quick rise after low. Sure sign of stronger blow.' The voyageurs who drove the fur trade up the rivers had it hard. Not like you two. They were realists, they had to be. Their memory was their best map, so colourful names for landmarks were used. You can still see this around here."

"Like where?"

"Like up the river where we're heading. Dead Horse Falls. So named for an unfortunate animal that discovered the dangerous current. Over to the south is Storm Mountain on the Divide, like a bellwether, because it gathers the first mists of a cold front. Watch it next time you're near Mist Creek. You don't forget these names, they're not just a map point."

"I remember K2," says the Lion. "That's a mountain named after a map grid."

The Ant pulls the boat away from the launch.

"That point," he says as he gestures to a spit of land with a stone tower, "is the first rangers' cabin. When they dammed the lake, it undercut the cabin, left only its chimney. Go slow, as there'll be lots of boats, but open up once you're past. Now set your bearing at the height of Hawke Island."

The boat lifts as the Lion pulls back on the throttle and I scramble through the narrow gangway between the spray windows to weight the bow down. The boat levels and starts to plane across the water, accelerating, the shore skimming. The lake doesn't seem very big now.

"Sweet spot! You feel that, when the hull starts to hydroplane?" asks the Ant with a grin. "Keep her steady on Hawke Island and watch for Point Campground to come abeam. Then make a sharp turn to port, and head directly for the point. Remember this boat is planing, so if you crank the wheel and hold it more than a second off midnight we'll end up doing a victory roll. So go fast on the action, but ease off as you turn."

The Lion throws the boat into a turn, flaring a high sheet of water. The hull wobbles as he fights the skid, then rights and picks up speed. It's a unique view: we're not under the mountains but in an arena with them rising all around.

"Now careful! You'll come around the point with twenty metres clearance, but there's deadheads that'll take our bottom clean off before we know it," he says of the old stumps from the logging days. "So forward on the throttle when you can clearly see the campground sites. That's it. Lay the bow down. The entrance to the lagoon is not that wide and only the centre is deep; that's the river channel, the banks get shallow real fast."

"Got it," says the Lion. I sit up to scan for old tree stumps under the surface. We turn the point and the bottom lurks. "We're shallow here!" I call. The Lion seems transfixed by the ghostly deadheads.

"We'll be okay," the Ant calms him. "Just keep to the middle."

I'm nervous. The stumps are murky, solid, and sharp. "What's our draft?"

"Only six inches," says the Ant without fear. The Lion steers into the lagoon. He shudders as the ominous spikes pass. The banks are low and slide into the still water. Threading a needle.

"Steady now," orders the Ant. "Aim for the inflow."

The banks become steep, overhung tufts littered with drowned trees. When the stream is two boat-lengths wide, the Ant motions shoreward. I jump and tie a bowline to a root. The Lion cuts the motor and the current swings the boat tight to the bank. The scent of wild parsley wafts over. The bank feels warm and stable.

"That's the way. No room for error. My father figured that route when the lake was first flooded, before there was a paved road."

We're here to clear some large trees up-trail. Because of the short, government-mandated work hours, we prepare to run the four kilometres, tightening our boots and packs. The Ant takes the trapper pack with the chainsaw slung in it. He tells us, "My grandfather came from England, looking for the free homesteads. But he was no farmer. Ended up out here, working on the railway and roads. His son, my father, was an immigrant too."

"How can he be when he was born here?" asks the Lion.

"Immigration," says the Ant, "is not about borders or nationality. It's a mindset—whether you belong or not. My grandfather worked himself to an early grave. A lot of them did. There was no time to sit back and enjoy citizenship. They had to prove themselves, to fit in, to earn their place. Just like you will now. I'm carrying the chainsaw, so you'll need to run with the oil and gas cans, and the handsaws. Then we'll switch on the way back. My father never stopped working hard either. They didn't get vacations or retirement. Retirement, that was their children's lives. They wanted their kids to have it easy, so they didn't have to work so hard." The Ant hoists his pack. "Ready?"

"Certainly you see the irony here?" asks the Lion as the Ant grins and starts to run. I'm just realizing that the gas can will be empty and the saw full of oil on the run back.

■ "So, Rumi, you're a geologist," the Ranger says.

He empties a load of stones for a fire ring. I'm feathering kindling with a hatchet.

"Just finished school." I hand the kindling to the Interpreter, who's building the fire nest.

"Why are you wasting your time hiking trails?" he asks, smiling. "Or is that a deer characteristic? Not being able to make a decision?"

I shrug, pick up an apricot-coloured rock, the size of my fist.

The Lion drops an armful of firewood. "This is an extension

of our studies," he says. "He's around the big rocks, and I'm like a teacher for the masses: clearing the path, setting signs, showing direction, bridging hazards. There are two ways you can go, you can quietly lead people or you can order them around."

"Or you can make them laugh," says the Interpreter.

"I might do fieldwork out here for a master's," I say.

I knock the apricot stone with the hatchet blade. The Ranger wonders why geology.

"I like the idea that these mountains were once seabeds and coral reefs and gooey mud flats with lots of plants. When I look at a mountain, it's a solid map of history."

"I see a pile of rock." He laughs, looking at the Interpreter, who smiles.

I keep tapping. "And I see the story of millions of years, right here where we stand." I'm surprised to hear myself say this, as if I've just remembered it. As a boy I imagined a cutaway of the earth below Calgary, all the layers and tunnels and secrets below. In school I lost this view, buried by terminology and seismic profiles.

"Why stare into the past when you can plan for the future?"

"I look at these mountains and think something happened here, something enormous."

"And meanwhile you're in the valley while we make history on the summits," he says.

"Because mountains are stories trapped in stone," I say. The chunk of dolomite makes a faint crack and falls open in my hand. I pass one half to the Interpreter. The apricot crust is a thin skin around the natural rock, which is almost white in its purity.

She gasps. "Oh! It is like the sky!"

The Ranger stops laughing. "Gonna dull your axe, idiot."

"This isn't quartzite. It's dolomite. Softer than steel."

The Lion walks over with another armload of split wood. He tells the Ranger of a disturbance near the old sawmill.

The Ranger shakes his head. "People see the map showing a

road and they take it, get stuck in the bog. Keep telling Visitor Services to update the guide, but every new issue is just a copy."

He hikes off to the trucks. The Lion settles in a lawn chair by the fire. I ask him what the disturbance is. He takes his time.

"What disturbance?" he asks with a slight smile. Then he gets up. "I need something."

The Interpreter and I sit alone as the fire pops and the sap starts to sizzle. She looks down at the dolomite, now glistening pale blue in the late afternoon sun, like a stone cup filled with a transparent elixir. "It is not white, it just reflects the sky. Pretend it is a magic mirror, or an enchanted pool through which you can tell me the past and future."

I remember her laughing with the Ranger and I wonder about the future.

"Why a magic mirror? Is the future so hard to see?" I ask.

"Remember the magic canoe? I am still curious to see what I would sell my soul for."

"What if you saw a destiny you hated: to return home to the land of churches."

"Ugh. That *is* my fate: settle down, have a family, a career. I want something else." She looks into the rock. "Can you see where the maps went wrong with the Committee's Punch Bowl?"

She smiles, leans back in her chair, and closes her eyes. Prepares to listen.

"No," I say. "You have to ask for it."

She squirms, a ripple of annoyance, but a curl to her mouth. "Please?" she says.

I look into the other half of the split stone and start. "Imagine it's Montréal. July. 1844."

⌂ In the sweltering office a man hunches over a table scattered with pencils and compass.

He reproduces the map in front of him, adding new information from sketches, using the new inks available from India to emphasize the trading routes important to his commissioners and to make the areas they want to keep to themselves more dangerous. All other features he simply transcribes as general symbols or reduces.

He is thinking of his supper, how he can never sleep in this heat. He does not care about the work and has never been to the west. Already the rivers and the paths have been omitted. He copies two mountains into the upper left corner of the map, just to balance the emptiness.

"We're still in Montréal. But it's five years later, in winter, and we're watching David Thompson."

David Thompson reads his journal and gazes for a long time at the fire. Through his journal he can more easily transport himself back to any campfire surrounded by mountains. The memories come rapidly. His ruddy face is still determined, but his eyes seem to melt in the fire glow. The house is quiet but not warm—tonight's log is burning down and there's not enough money to buy another. His wife and children are asleep in the next room, and Thompson works to transcribe his journals into a narrative to generate more interest in his map of the northwest.

When he reads of crossing Athabasca Pass, he is swept up in memories of cold wind, rough men, and the howls of sled dogs. In the fading firelight, he adds to his original account some official weight to give his route prominence even as the fur trade is dying:

"The altitude of this place above the level of the ocean by the boiling point of water is computed to be eleven thousand feet (Sir George Simpson)."

I stoop to stoke the fire. The evening light is almost gone, the sparks still turn dark before they wheel into the openness above. The Interpreter holds the dolomite near her face.

"Did you not tell me that one of the climbers had found the Pass and decided it was all a hoax?"

"Yes. Coleman. The geologist from Toronto. He went looking for it with his brother."

She looks deeply into the dolomite. Now it's dark blue inside its crusty cup.

"Coleman made several expeditions into the mountains when no one else had been there for a long time. In 1892, he and his brother made it to Fortress Lake, just south of Athabasca Pass."

▲ Coleman's brother sits down on the slope and rests. It's been an arduous scramble, and now, three thousand feet above the valley, they're blocked by a vertical wall. Below is a long turquoise lake.

"Magnificent" says the brother. "I'd say at least eight miles long. This could be the Punch Bowl, though so far not a lot matches the old maps."

"This isn't it," Coleman says. He pulls his felt hat off to wipe his brow.

"Well, those two Stoney Indians were right about the distance," says the brother, looking back down the tree-choked river valley. "Three sleeps and not a day more. That's more accurate than the maps we have. And we're definitely on the Continental Divide. Look at all this: huckleberries, gooseberries, even black currants. If the brush gets denser we're stuck."

"That trail could be large game just as much as Indian or an old Nor'Wester route. Look at what people remember around here—nothing! We haven't found a soul who's been up this way or knows anyone who has." Coleman stands looking at the mountains, none of which are tall enough. He rubs his chin. He can't match reality to the atlas and his expectation. The territory must be wrong. Where in creation are Hooker and Brown?

"The next year Coleman reached Athabasca Pass, after months of brutal bushwhacking."

▲ The train of soot-smeared ponies winds beside the creek. In the lead rides Arthur Coleman, a fit man of forty with an unkempt beard, heavily bandaged knee, small glasses, and a blank expression. He stops at the bank of a tiny pond, gently shaking his head.

He limps around the tarn as the ponies spread out looking for heather. The others arrive.

"This is it," Coleman calls from the other side, pushing back his shapeless felt hat.

The others crease their brows. "What? This?"

"The Punch Bowl. It's flowing out this side as well. This is the Pass."

"For Heaven's sake! It's supposed to be ten miles long!"

Coleman tugs his beard. "And Hooker and Brown were supposed to be giants! Damn it! Were people smaller back then or has everything shrunk?"

They argue about how they could miss the mountains. Their packer spits on the ground. "Is this what you've been searching for?" Nobody wants to answer him. "What about this boat we've been hauling for the past six weeks? I thought we was going to paddle around the lake? Doesn't look like it'll even fit in there, eh?"

"Appreciate you pointing that out."

They look at each other's blackened faces, at the packing cloth that used to be white, and the tiny holes burned into everything from sparking fires. Nobody sees fit to laugh.

They're all trying to keep their temper. "You were there," Coleman mutters. "South of us is Fortress Lake, and north is the Yellowhead. There's nothing but this valley in the middle. This is it." He has to admit that his dreams were wrong. He can't remember how he used to imagine the peaks. That all seems immature now.

Coleman wrote later: "We were on the Great Divide, the ridge pole of North America, but we felt no enthusiasm. Instead, we felt disillusioned."

I finish just as the Ranger walks up. He sits on the other side of the ring, his face brooding. She rolls the chunk of dolomite in her hand, the inside as dark as any other rock with the fire gone.

Later the Ranger corners me in the kitchen. "She's using you," he says.

I brush that off. Of course he'd say that. Perhaps he's the divide-and-conquer sort.

"Just so you know, she's using me too," he says.

Have I misread him? Or is this the shoot-one-of-your-own-to-show-loyalty trick? But his face is open. "She needs you to find that pool," he says. "That's it, that's all. She's obsessed with finding someone to show her what she imagines she needs."

"She's found the perfect guide," I say, meaning him.

He's shaking his head. "She doesn't follow maps, just stories."

He wants her. I try to keep that straight in my head, think about something other than his words, remind myself that zinc is kitty-corner to aluminum on the Periodic Table. But then so is carbon. I want to tell him to go packing. This gives me an image of suitcases, which reminds me of smithsonite, a mineral with a crystalline crust made from carbon and zinc.

"She thinks she needs to find this . . . *mirror* . . . to know her direction," he says. "It's a mirror: she hides from the responsibility to choose, pushing it behind her, like the curls she tries to hide behind her ears."

■ I'm assigned the rarely patrolled Mist Creek Trail.

"Your eyes." says the Ant, tapping his temple. "Keep them open. It's a long one. There'll be animals, so make lots of noise. There's a radio repeater to the north, so if you break a leg make sure it's in a north-facing clearing. Don't get bogged down clearing trees. I'd rather you get up to the pass and make a complete work list. Check the trail log and pack a replacement sign."

The Lion mimics an enthusiastic child. "Hey, boss, can I just take notes while I work too?"

The Ant swivels and looks steadily at the Lion. The Lion starts to smile defensively.

"You're prepping the honey barrels for servicing at the campgrounds."

The Lion groans. "Don't forget your nail polish," he tells me.

I check the log. There's only one entry in the last two years: "Trail indistinct."

I have the map open on the seat as I drive south. Given the situation between the Ranger and the Interpreter, the map seems refreshingly clear. I find the overgrown pullout. It's over the highest part of the park, the Highwood Pass, and the mists come down the valley as they do in the rain shadow of the Great Divide. The trees are thick fir, heavily overgrown. My pulaski clangs loudly as I pull it from the truck box. I start up a narrow trail of mossy corduroy, over torrents of cold, clear water.

I'm soaked by the time I've hiked the valley and come down from the pass. On the descent I see the long valley haunted with mist. It seems far. There's been plenty of spoor: large elk, mountain goat, and bighorn, and predators, like bear—the scat heavy in fur and small bones—but the emptiness chills the dew on my neck. The pass is a crossroads for late-season horse tours; I find the trail sign lower down in a grove of alder. The spot of the intersection has been thumbed so much that the paint has worn off, revealing a shiny absence. These days, the blank spots on the map are the places we stand, not those where we want to go. I wonder at the need to touch.

I pull the old sign, leaving a naked post. On popular trails, I've seen people standing bewildered, looking at each other, at the empty post, waiting for a sign to appear. In other places, the trailhead kiosks are covered in graffiti, as if the hikers, fearing their own transitory existence, are compelled to add themselves to the record in whatever fashion they can.

I replace the sign, which has a rivet drilled into the *You Are Here* spot. I pull out my tiny bottle of hot-pink polish a little self-consciously and paint the rivet. Nail polish is the only paint we've found is durable against the constant poking.

I strap on the old sign and thrash through the springy alder. Hours of pushing heavy branches and splashing dew has me cold and hungry and preoccupied with squelching boots. I stumble beside a meadow. A statuesque elk stands watching.

It's a buck with his five-point rack half-grown and his aquiline muzzle matted with dirt. I shuffle to find footing in the slippery bank, heart thumping in surprise and concern that he might contest his space. He's absolutely still. To the far side of the meadow, something bursts forth like an explosion of partridge, but it's low and sleek and brown-grey.

The elk bolts. My heels slip out. I sit down hard in the thicket. My axe digs its handle in but the head spears up, the old sign flips onto the grass before me in a bright square, the cold earth bleeds through my pants. My skin draws as I realize it's a wolf.

I'm almost holding my breath while the pluming nose of the elk bobs and the snout of the wolf hisses sharp blasts of mist. The canine is almost abreast the rippling flanks even as the elk builds its velocity. A feral stench of rot chokes the fresh mint of the leaves and the heady musk of the soil. It pulls me down, a low chant of death, of overwhelming will and hunger.

My mind urges the elk to accelerate and pull free from the popping jaw of the wolf. Yet in the same instant I feel the exhilaration of the chase. My fingernails claw the loam, my small human legs tremble, my heart tightens with fear and with a wild need to catch that which is pursued.

Their breath merges until the elk's exhalation is the inhalation of the wolf, becoming the only sound. In the rushing blur I can't tell them apart. For an instant there's no past and no future and it's not a question of which will prevail but simply a distribution of air that will either coalesce or draw apart. Then, in a smashing of branches, the elk springs away into the forest. The wolf pants, flattened ears, spiked fur.

The sign at my feet makes no sense. There is no wolf, or elk, or man on it, only a meaningless scribble. It shows the valley as I might use it, but that's not what's really here. I suddenly realize: if I follow the maps, that's all I'll ever find.

It's difficult to draw myself away, to remember what is me and what is not. I freeze, noticing the hackles of the wolf passing in the far bog bean. He ducks his head, lolling his tongue on a severe range of ivory peaks. Alone, minutes later, I rise, limbs heavy with coppery adrenalin.

I wonder why the wolf would try that alone. Maybe others are around, or he has used me as a distraction. Just down the trail the elk appears again in a glade. It turns, perhaps associating me with the wolf, its eyes directionless as black marbles. I realize his life is a constant reaction to being hunted. Would he be at peace if he couldn't smell wolf?

With a ponderous weave he vanishes into the forest. I try to imagine what it would be like to be always on the run, but now I can't separate the elk from the forest.

I meet the Ranger at the railway crossing. His nose is smeared white with zinc oxide against the sun. It's hot, and the schist gravel under the ties smells like iron, the ties creating an oily haze above the rails. A flash from my childhood: running to put pennies on the track before the train comes.

Not everyone sees the train tracks the way the Interpreter or I do.

"Two streaks of rust and a right-of-way," spits the Ranger, kicking the cinders at the crossing.

I slam the door of my truck. They're all the same, the parks trucks. They smell like vinyl dashboards, and the seat fabric is rough with back-road dust. Most of the chromium is chipped off. But like uniforms, they're each different in small ways. Being new, I get the one that is slow to start and accelerate. Twenty metres down the rails is a pile of grain, dumped in a squat cone.

"Black bears reported," says the Ranger. "You'll have to clean that up." The Ranger is all business, emotionally constrained by the uniform.

"I've already got my orders," I say. I heard it on the radio. The grain seeps from a broken pour-door when a train pauses. This attracts bears, which attract tourists and causes a bear-jam. Soon someone is out of his car for the perfect photo, chasing the bear into the forest.

"Do people chase tigers in Africa?" asks the Ranger, shaking his head. "It's like kids running after a burning firecracker. There's only two ways it's gonna go: bad for bear and bad for human."

I unload shovels and a wheelbarrow from my truck.

"L69, L71. What's your twenty, Rumi?" calls the Lion on the radio.

The Ranger warns some tourists away, blocks off the crossing, looks serious. The sun bakes my cap brim. I'm not allowed on the tracks until the trains are confirmed stopped. I idle by the rails, the Ranger kicks at the cinders then picks one up, juggling it carefully.

"This mica? Is that what's sparkling?"

"Think so." There are blue metallic glints in the grey-streaked rocks. What did I tell him when I was hypothermic? "It's mostly quartz."

"See, what I don't get is, how rocks like quartz make crystals you can see through."

"It's about organization," I say. "If the material is all the same type, and if it can form a lattice, the light can pass through the layers without stopping."

"That heap of grain is all the same material. I can't see through it."

"That pile has no structure. Anything will form a cone like that if the granularity is small, like sand, just like the scree aprons around the peaks. But when a rock bonds, it gets dense and holds a shape, creates walls to climb. Then it can be transparent."

The Lion crunches up the road, his shirt sweat-soaked, the long, worn handle of his pulaski sticking out the bottom of his pack, the axe-head behind his shoulder blades, bumping softly on the pack straps.

The Ranger shrugs. "When you say transparent, you don't mean clear. Just clear for a rock."

"What about glass?"

"Yeah, like glass. I've never seen a rock that was as clear as glass."

"They're called gems and are kept hidden away from people like you," says the Lion.

"Glass is just sand. Silicon. Silica heated up into crystal." This conversation reminds me of assisting freshmen in university. The 101-level course. Rocks for Jocks.

"There's plenty of sand around, so why don't we see anything like that?" asks the Ranger.

"We do, it's just broken glass. It's under the ground that you find huge crystal structures."

"How do you know nature can't produce something perfectly transparent?" asks the Lion. "How would you notice it?"

"What about a mountain of quartz?" asks the Ranger.

"Quartz has perfect cleavage," I say. "Too much would split. It's too friable."

"Who has perfect cleavage?" asks the Lion.

"To make crystal you have to pack the material. A mountain of sand makes a hill of quartz." I'm thinking of the diamond ring the Lookout held in her palm.

"Like coal," says the Ranger. "It could be a diamond but mostly ends up doing nothing. Couldn't handle the pressure of formation, eh? Just good for burning a short time."

Our clearance comes over the radio, and we bounce the wheelbarrow down the tracks to the soft organic material pouring cleanly over the steel rail.

The Lion chuckles. "Hey! Guess what? I found out that he went to school."

"The Ranger? No kidding?"

"Know what he studied? Urban Planning at Queen's. Never finished. And I heard him talking about Mount Forbes. I think he's trying to scoop us. As if there isn't enough to choose from!"

We start to shovel the grain into the wheelbarrow. With each thrust of the blade, the grain pours, filling the scoops we take away as if they never left.

■ This job makes chefs and philosophers and cops of everyone.

"There's too many climbing at the Back of the Lake," says the Ranger, who's just returned from that sport-climbing area on the cliffs behind Laggan.

That's the discussion around the table. Just like a boat with a set of fixed sails; if the Ranger gets the wind, I know exactly how he'll settle in the swell. The rest of us sit reading the open pages of magazines left scattered about.

"We got almost nothing done today," the Ranger continues. "We spent most of the day waiting for a route and keeping our place in line. When did this happen? And while we waited I watched a kid do a route I couldn't dream of doing. I think it was a 5.13." He describes a climbing grade far harder than anything I could do.

"In my day 5.9 was the limit," he says. "When did we suddenly get grades so high?"

The Lion clears his throat and tosses his magazine aside. "You know, I read an article last summer in a magazine showcasing the alpine routes at the Back of the Lake that also mentioned the great sport climbing. Call me mistaken, but I think you were one of the authors. How much did you get paid for that?"

The Ranger looks around, past me. "I never wrote about 5.13 or half of those routes." He pulls back from the table with a firm set to his mouth. When I was younger, I never saw a cop lose a fight. I don't expect now to be any different. I expect him back before long.

Later that evening, we sit around the fire pit wrapped in blankets. The reflection tans the Lion's and Interpreter's faces red.

"I don't know why he's so uptight. Maybe because he just drove four hundred kilometres for a few hours of climbing. But hey, if you advertise, they will come," says the Lion.

"That is how I came," she says.

"But it's not always the way they sell it, is it?" The Lion laughs.

"Oh yes! That was the advertisement: you could live here, in the pristine mountains. But that is wrong—you cannot live somewhere that is pristine. No one seems to count themselves."

"Well, we get used to anything if we ease into it enough. How else do you explain cities?"

I shift in my lawn chair and throw a log on the fire. The sparks pop and float up slowly until they're lost in the stars. The Interpreter's cheeks gleam; the Lion's face is shadowed.

"I do not miss it," she says. "Traffic, noise, fluorescent lighting. Not even fashion magazines."

The Lion raises his brow.

"Oh, I know," she says. "You only read those magazines that are like climbing *pornography*. Just photos of guys on big walls or skiing down big faces. Or novels. No middle ground."

"Sometimes I'm just tired. I read a picture, that's a thousand words to inspire."

"But it is not the picture doing that!" The blanket barely contains her hands. "It is you creating the story. They just sell you the seeds, but you do all the work. Why pay for that?"

"What good is money without a product to buy?"

"It is not a product, it is the fantasy that sells. That comes from you. You're buying what you already own."

"Sex sells," says the Lion, and I know he is baiting her.

"In all those magazines there is not any sex. Only in your imagination."

The Lion and I catcall her, laughing, teasing her. She is not moved.

"Sex does not sell, the mystery of it does."

The Lion chooses that moment to excuse himself to grab more beer. I hadn't noticed their bottles.

"Would you like to have a flying canoe?" she asks me.

"Sure. We could go to the Back of the Lake in moments and beat the lines."

"I don't think we would be any happier."

The Lion brings cold bottles that make my hand ache. I sip, grind my bottle into the gravel.

"We would just try to do that much more," she says. "We would get so used to flying that we would stop thinking it incredible."

A crunch on the gravel path becomes a silhouette, which illuminates the Ranger in his heavy coat. He nods all around and scrapes up a chair. The zinc sulphide on his watch hands glows faintly in the dark. He's silent, spoiling for a fight. The Interpreter doesn't pause.

"Look at our lives now. Second biggest country in the world, and I can fly across it in a few hours. Do not tell my mom that if she calls. We drive to any climb in a few hours. But how many times do you just stop and look at the traffic and think, What an amazing thing we have done? Never! Instead we think, Ugh, this will take twenty minutes to get through!"

I stretch my thirty-five-kilometre-per-day legs and enjoy the fire. "The way the Ant pushes us, I'm glad we have trucks. He might make us run to the trailheads otherwise," I say.

"Before there were roads, we might have done that," says the Lion. "Only we would pack a camp in and base ourselves out of it. Not see a fridge for a week at a time. Then someone said, 'I hate packing this stuff every day. Let's make a road and drive up.'"

"So why not a road all the way? Why hike at all?" I question.

"We save the best for last, and on foot."

"But never more than a day away."

The Interpreter leans in. "This is why technology will never save us. We get used to it too quickly and forget why we wanted it in the first place."

The Lion nods. "We need a better story than endless enhancement of convenience."

"Oh, it's not bad," says the Ranger suddenly. "Dynamic ropes, laminated skis, harnesses, ultra-light this and that, waterproof, breathable shells. Can't say technology is all bad, it can actually help if used right. Guess you could say that about your university degrees too."

The Lion waves his hand in defeat.

"What good are skis on a solar-affected aspect without steel edges?" The Ranger presses his point. I figure he's angry at the Lion for calling him out on the climbing article. "Perhaps you'd like to wear the old canvas frame packs, or just carry a putrid animal skin to hold your tools. Your jobs would be much harder if you had to wear felts and oilskins."

"You have to leave the truck to know the weight of a pack," says the Lion.

Even though I think the Lion could break the Ranger over his knee, something seems to restrain him. A residual distinction of authority, maybe.

"We do plenty. You guys open it up. We have to deploy and police it," says the Ranger.

"Why do you talk like you're educated? You say 'the aspect' of a slope instead of 'a side?'" asks the Lion. There's an edge to his voice. The Ranger's hit a chord.

"I am specific because it matters."

"You say 'isothermic' instead of 'mush'—"

"There's a difference in how you build an anchor in snow."

"——discharge a weapon, instead of fire a gun. Suspected male perpetrator instead of dude—"

"That's for legal purposes. I—"

"—talk like a cop. Are you going to grow a moustache to cover your glaring insecurity?"

The Ranger is on his feet, but calm. "Maybe you hate the fact that you wasted four or five years in university and are now a working grunt on the trail crew, but that's your problem. Technology could even save you, if you knew how to use the rope and anchor it. Philosophy comes from people sitting around and watching, not acting."

The Lion shrugs. "Without imagination, we have no rudder. Leaving just competition." He gets up slowly, his back to the Ranger, says goodnight to the Interpreter. Is he living up to the script he claimed for himself? The Lion disappears in the dark.

The Interpreter is looking at the flames. She says, "You did not need to say that to him."

"Someone must," says the Ranger, still standing.

"Why?"

"I need to tell you," says the Ranger. "So it isn't forgotten. I've seen too many accidents to want to see another when I can stop something from beginning."

"We can handle ourselves," I say.

"But he couldn't. Do you know what happened?"

"Enough. His partner fell into a crevasse, and he couldn't get him out. Almost died trying."

"Not exactly," says the Ranger, stepping close to the fire. I lean in, suddenly chilled. "He was traversing the Saskatchewan glacier in early spring. They had just passed the firn line, which should have given them enough warning."

"Which is why they were roped up."

"Yes. But the snow bridges were weak last year, and they should have known that."

"They did."

"They went anyway."

"As do you." I say this without being sure, but it sticks. The Ranger restarts.

"His partner fell through."

I'm silent. This is where my knowledge ends.

"He dropped about ten metres. You know what that means?"

I do, but I don't speak.

"It means that the rope was so slack between them as to be almost useless."

I shuffle in the hot gravel at the side of the fire. The bridge could have collapsed at the far edge; the rope could have dug into the snow and dragged the Lion until he could stop the fall. The Ranger ignores my movement and continues.

"His partner was ten metres down when he was caught. Ten metres! That's thirty feet, or three storeys of a building. It was a big crevasse. They should have seen it in the snow. Obviously he didn't. And what happened was that he braked the fall with the rope and his legs. He did that. He held his partner's fall. He dropped his pack and got his rescue gear sorted."

"How do you know all this?"

The Ranger tells us he read the reports of the investigation. The Lion's partner had fallen but landed on something that then gave way. When the Lion had dropped his pack and started to dig in, his partner fell again. It dragged the Lion off his feet for a few metres.

"So his partner froze slowly, hanging between walls of ice, calling up, the endless black around him."

"How long?" the Interpreter asks.

"Three days. Until the call was received and the chopper found them."

"Three days he sat pinioned in the snow, not being able to move until they were found?"

"Yes."

"He could have cut the rope," said the Interpreter.

"No," the Ranger and I both say automatically.

"He could have made an anchor," says the Ranger. "When they picked him up, there was still a sling on the back of his harness."

"Proving nothing."

"Just that he didn't act when he could have. Maybe he wanted the perfect anchor, the ideal rescue. Philosophy has no place out there. He needed to fight as hard as he could or die trying."

■ I catch a lift into Canmore to meet the professor who's urging me to continue my studies.

"You need to decide what you want to do," he said on the phone.

On the drive down from the park, traffic becomes heavier and billboards litter the swales. Names on posts sprout on the bends. One announces the distance to Field. I've never questioned it before, but now it looks foreign, deposited by some Midwest tornado. Field is a town inside a steep mountain valley. There are no fields there. It's named for a man whose ancestors may have been named for a field, somewhere, an ocean away. I pass, noticing communities. Eagle Terrace, Cougar Creek. Looking at the rows of duplexes, the names seem to describe what people wanted to be there and not what was. The map creates the territory. Canmore sprawls a jumble of wood and steel up the narrow valleys of the surrounding mountains, like a logjam left when a river descends. It didn't use to look like that. Now it reminds me of the Calgary of my youth, where new communities had no sense of identity. I'm surprised at how critical I am. I've changed after two months in the forest, making maps necessary for me.

I meet the Professor at a café the Lion claims has abundant portions. I enjoy his familiar face out of place from my memories of classrooms: trim beard, balding head, his eyes curious and engaged. My tanned forearm is muscular on the table. I'm out of context too.

He tells of his fieldwork in Mexico, on the volcanoes high above plains and crowds, close to the firn line, where the snow doesn't melt. He wants me to join him as a graduate student, which means another winter in the classroom. I tell him if Canmore seems a bit too busy, I don't know how I'll handle Calgary.

"It's your choice, I know you know that. This is a big cross-roads. Decisions you make now set your direction, maybe for life. No matter. I think you've always seen your path clearly," he says.

Outside on Canmore's busy Main Street, tourists wear fashions from Japan, England, Germany. In the journals I've been reading it seems like such a commitment to get from those places to the mountains—a year or two for Douglas, a season for Collie. Now people travel for a day, stay for a few weeks. My generation is the most urbanized but also the most nomadic. All of us following charts.

He talks to ease me. He talks about how towns and cities grew because of markets, not just in goods and services, but in ideas. Efficient places to trade. Throughout history we have mythical cities, cities of gold, cities in the clouds, cities of gods.

"Because we don't need to imagine a perfect forest," I say.

"Because the dream of humanity is to come together in its own environment. The Greeks had the open squares for debates, and then they created academies. Now we have universities."

"Plato's Academy sounded good. They taught gymnastics, mathematics, and philosophy."

"Body, mind, and soul."

"The Greeks affected everything," I say. Does he pick up my aggressive tone? Or is it resentful? And where is it coming from so suddenly?

"*Peri Lithon*," he says, nodding. "The authoritative treatise: *On Stones*. Written by a student of Aristotle. Unsurpassed for millennia."

Were the Greeks that good or were they just the first to reach the easy summits?

"Fill out this application," he says. "If you make up your mind, I've only to put it through."

I leave blanks. I can't recall my Social Insurance Number. It's an odd relief not to offer up such an impersonal map of myself.

He insists I call with it. They won't accept it without, he tells me, students' names are too ambiguous. I tell him about the community names.

The Professor shakes his head. "Even the old names, those of the native Indian that we have adopted for street names, have lost their meaning. It's what happens when you speak a word over and over. Take the word *desayuno*. What does this mean to you? Nothing? Try saying it aloud, under your breath, ten times."

I do. The word falls apart into sounds until I don't notice if it's starting or ending.

"Now, does it mean anything more to you? No. It's mere sounds. Try a second word. Try *breakfast*. As soon as you hear this you think of bacon and eggs, maybe coffee, the sound of milk on cereal, feel sunshine through a lace-covered window, good smells and well-being. But try saying it ten times under your breath."

I watch him for the punchline as I do. It takes a little longer, but the same thing happens. At the end it could have been a foreign word for all it means.

"And now?" he asks. "Is it the same, or has it been dislocated? *Breakfast* is a word we know. It means to break the fast, or to end the period of not eating during the night, the first meal of the day. But *desayuno* means first meal in Spanish. It's equivalent to *breakfast*, a meaning, mind you, only we give it. To you, a few moments ago, *desayuno* meant nothing. Now it smells like eggs and bacon."

He wipes his mouth and leans closer. "I trust you. And I think you'll find what you're looking for in further study. You'll get offers. Beware the corporate door, you know where it leads."

"Spoken like a true academic."

"Which reminds me," he says and mentions a classmate who's planning a wedding for the next month, at the end of summer. "It's out on the prairie, and all your friends from your graduating class will be there. He wanted me to invite you."

"We're already coming to the end of the season?"

"Depends. Is the summer half over or half started? Either way I'll need your decision soon."

"Next time you're through I'll give you an answer. We can have *desayuno*."

He smiles. "Works for every word I know, except *love*."

I grab a ride back to the park that evening. It looks like a wild place to me now, the signs dropping behind. I return to the land feeling like a stranger.

"You were in my dream last night," says the Interpreter.

The white frame of light from the kitchen casts her in shadow. I force a smile.

"Something wrong?" she asks.

"Just tired." Actually I feel shattered. My mind is still rushing along the road with the reflective squares of signs glaring out of the darkness. I slump on a couch. It feels awkward, too soft. The dark in the living area is soothing. I open my eyes and she's sitting on the edge of the chair with a glass of water, ice cold.

"You were in Canmore?"

"Yeah," I say, intending more, shaking my head.

"I do not feel at home anymore when I return to Québec," she says. "The Lion was just telling the Ranger about Alexander the Great and his Greek army marching for twenty years through Asia. The Ranger figured the troops must have preferred it to home. My home is here now."

Now my smile is real. "What did you do today?"

"I was wandering up a valley, very high. Almost nothing growing there but boulders and dust devils. I could only see the sky above. At the end there was water and a tent."

Where is she? Then I realize she's ignored my question and is instead describing her dream.

"What was in the tent?" I ask.

"I was thinking," she says, looking to the ceiling. "How much would those little gas-station guides have been worth to David Thompson? The ones that cost five dollars."

"Useless. There were no roads then."

"Yes! But it would show the best route."

Imagine Thompson unfolding a driving atlas in his heavy hands, feeling the fragility, the mass-produced quality, the perfect width of every line, trying to orient himself to it, and seeing the proliferation of humanity over that great, lone land. Would he recognize his rivers?

"Now we all have them," says the Interpreter. "But how *much* would you pay if someone offered you a map of something dear, Rumi?"

"Deer?" I ask, wondering if she is teasing me about my nickname.

"No, d-e-a-r. I am told by a British tourist that it means *expensive*. It is a word not used in Canada, but I *love* words like that. The ones that have many meanings. It is also someone you love, and also the animal in the forest. See? I only have to know one word to be able to say all that in English. French is far more precise. I looked up *Rumi,* by the way. Did you know, that is the name of a famous Persian poet, the Sufi poet of love. Listen, I wrote this down."

She pulls a folder corner of paper from her jeans.

> *Why should I seek? I am the same as He.*
> *His essence speaks through me.*
> *I have been looking for myself.*

And she looks up, smiling. I want to know what her map is.

"What would this valuable . . . *diagram* look like?" I ask, trying a new word.

"First describe it to me," she says, laying back.

That catches me off guard. "It was *your* dream."

"Describe to me what it would look like: a map to something you really want."

Imagine spreading out a heavy map of old vellum. It shows my life: there are many valleys cutting up to peaks. In one is the path of the person I'll love forever. In several places are grottos where secrets lie. I describe how at the centre of my map are two small mountains.

I roll my head over. She's smiling. Then she speaks. "You are shy, so you might not ask again. In the tent it is still. The constant wind is softened by the canvas. I am telling *you* a story."

"Your dream?"

"Yes. There is a ring of stones and a very small fire for tea. Wood is dear at this altitude. You sit close to the flames for warmth. Other nomads come and go, but rarely. The valley walls block the future from view. You carry only memories and intentions. There is no paper, no written words, because the great explorations are those of the mind, of medicine, of love."

She talks about nomadic life, how small things are traded for immediate need, not hoarded as souvenirs. How travellers' tales are loaded with advice and rumours and clues to the teller and the told. The food good, each bite appreciated, as anything is when the future is so open and unpredictable. All nomads are ambassadors representing sovereign individuals, building alliances of trust through experience with others who have the ocean, or the desert, in their eyes.

"Choose your words carefully," she tells me. "For all things given to a nomad must be carried, including words—they must be light, brief, and sincere."

She describes a nomad who enters the tent with a living document. A chart spread before her that is constantly changing and interacting, affected by anything that touches it. She and the nomad hunch over the map, watching the intersections, the passes.

"As we trace a passage, we change it," she says, drawing in the air. "As the paths shift, they smudge with moisture and crease with time. We follow a direction, but as we reach the end it splits and weaves and fades. Generations of movement have left the parchment well worn. I held my breath because these were the Maps of Love."

"Can you draw it?"

"No. To transcribe the maps would be to understand love, which is not the purpose. In France, long ago, a duchess made a map of love, *la Carte de Tendre*. But it is useless for navigation. It is decoration. I will not follow maps that you can draw!"

I've never imagined such a map. The only scale so far has been life-sized, one to one. When I'm in love I'm there, with no map, helpless.

She's quiet in the dark, then asks, "Promise me you will destroy them." She looks at her hands. "People want maps for answers, but as soon as they have the answers, they are taken for granted. Then people start looking for the next map. If you did not create it, but were led to it, you would not appreciate it. I have learnt that here at the park. Promise me. If you are ever given the map to love, destroy it. So that you never take for granted this most wonderful thing."

I promise, then wonder, "Where was I in that dream?"

She starts to rise. I catch her arm, smooth and slender in the night, firm with muscles and rough at her knuckles. She relaxes, then laughs and slips away.

That's the problem with aluminum, I think. It bonds with so many elements, takes so much electricity to produce. It's not a natural occurrence. I always see her braid, her cheekbones, her open face—non-sparkling, non-magnetic, soft. I want to be honest with myself. Why pursue if not to gain? I'm afraid that when I reach the Pass in my stories, her interest in me will end. Then she'll get the Ranger to take her to the real Pass. I'm tired. My eyes hurt. I wonder if the Lion is right, that I'm only after her because the Ranger is. I try to imagine her without his attentions, but I can't separate her from them.

I make a detour off my trails and hike to the fire tower. From the dual track to the main building I see no movement. Everything stands quivering with the same vibrancy as the radio antenna. The aluminum fuel tanks shine bright; the grass hums with invisible insects, the trees brood. The tower draws attention by the very absence of movement where it's most expected. The only difference now is that I'm hoping for an encounter.

There's a simple sign: PRIVATE RESIDENCE. NO VISITORS. The road flattens before the crest of the hill and skirts the edge of the clearing. On this path I will pass to the other side and continue the trail. I don't want to look as if I've come purely as an intruder. I reach the far side, see no change in the setting. I remember the Ranger claiming deer can't make a decision. I turn and walk back directly toward the squat tower. I wonder whether she is here, but midsummer is prime season for the lookouts. My own experience of her is exactly thirty minutes long and one month old. I imagine her, mud-splattered and leering, possibly insane, lurking nearby. I still don't know her name. Without her name I have no idea how to approach her.

The lower door is open to the mesh. The grid balcony above mottles the sun like a snakeskin. Through the haze of the screen the room seems empty. There's no manufactured scent—just the sun-heated dust from the concrete pad and the tang of dandelions. I knock. The echo makes me wince. I try again, feeling the same relief I did as a teenager when the girl wasn't home and I could hang up, having faced my fear despite not achieving my goal. Silence.

I look up the steel stairs to the observation deck where we had tea. Her yell is harsh. "It says private! Can't you read?"

Just for a moment I consider running.

"It says no visitors," she says. "The rangers can be here in ten minutes."

Surely she remembers. "Wait. I'm with the Parks. We talked before," I say.

"When? What's your name?"

"We . . . never introduced ourselves."

"Well, what do you want?" Her eyes are keen.

"We talked earlier in the season. About the names of the mountains."

She squints over the railing. This look is comical coming from a professional spotter. I let slip a smile and that breaks her act.

"Well, come up," she says. "I've had the tea on for three minutes now."

She stands at the huge windows looking out over the intersecting valleys.

"The Garden of Eden. The original sin was naming things. However," she says, handing me the same battered metal cup as last time and settling back into the high chair by the spotting scope, "I've been thinking about our earlier conversation. Perhaps we're offended by mountain names because we think somehow a name will change the mountain. Or that the names can't be changed, as if they're as permanent as the mountains they name. Both are conceits."

The tea is still too hot to taste, the air stagnant inside the glass room. She says, "Names are simply labels we give things—like price tags. The perceived value of the object, not the object's value. The object already has that, with or without the price tag."

"You think we judge mountains by the perceived value of their names?" I laugh.

She stands suddenly in the hot stillness and waves me to the window. "Come here. Look out and imagine you've never known the names given these mountains. How does it change?"

Imagine the park, this conflux of valleys formed by colliding ranges, without names, as if seeing it for the first time. My mind quiets—the constant narrative that analyzes the exposed layers and ages and gives a sense of orientation slows until it stops. I'm looking at the summer beauty without a plan or reflection.

"The valley hasn't changed," I report. "It's a little more intriguing. Maybe a little bigger."

"Exactly," she says with a triumphant wave. "Names are just clouds that float in front for a while. Without them, everything looks more open and unknown. Like an Asian market place—all the possibilities and no posted prices."

"Okay, your turn. Look out there and forget all the names that you know." I wait while she relaxes. "Good? Okay. Now imagine that each mountain out there has a price tag."

She looks at me sharply, then slowly gazes out the window and resumes imagining.

"Now," I ask. "What's the first thing you find yourself doing?"

She glares, but it's softer now. "Touché," she mutters. I tell her about Hooker and Brown.

I fumble with the reason the two lost peaks have been obsessing me. "If you were to look for two ideals, the most meaningful aspects of life that you could imagine, what would they be?"

"Why the duality?" she asks. "Why not one individual ideal? Why not three? Why two?"

I'm not sure how to answer her.

"Come back when you know, and I will give you tea and my answer as well," she says.

Why would she need the time? In the square room of windows there is no hiding. As I get to the ground and shoulder my pack, she leans on the railing. "We only check the price tag or label when we're interested. Don't forget that."

At the trailhead I come out into the empty amphitheatre. It seems so simple: a sliced culvert for a fire ring, stamped earth stage, log benches. It looks exactly as drawn on the map, but I remember the first night I saw the Interpreter tell the story of the Borges empire.

■ The Ranger's words sound in my ears like a squeaky boot heel. It's not my regular irritant, those strange aches that appear and are featured for the week. Yesterday I pulled the neck of my shirt aside to see a series of blisters. They were not from my pack strap, and I hadn't been carrying heavy logs.

"Dues," said the Ant. "Think of it as dues. Lots of weird things out here from the animals." Rumour had it that trail crew workers had been lost due to the mononucleosis carried by deer.

"You can heal that during the shoulder season." The Lion laughed.

"Heard you had a chip there," said the Ranger.

His performance last night nags:

> *When the clouds catch you on a crest, and the sun drops behind, sometimes you'll see the Brocken Spectre—an image of yourself huge against the surface of the mists, surrounded by a glory halo of rainbow colour. The mountaineers of Europe claim it is a portent to disaster.*

The gathered interpreters and custodians all moaned and giggled like children at a ghost story. The Ranger walked among the couches of the living area, behind the heads of the sprawled and twisted staffers, telling of various mountain phenomena.

> *And when you are on a big wall and can't see the storms dropping down on you until the day goes dark, your axes and carabiners can start humming loudly with the electricity racing through the rocks from the lightning strikes on the ridge above.*

I hike up the Buller Pass Trail through heavy-scented pines. With each step I think about the attention he generated. The group of interpreters seemed to coalesce watching him. It was the last night before a long weekend, the last break before the peak of the season. There would be no break for those workers—they dread long weekends.

When the sky looks like it starts to clear, the worst is to come. Those openings are called sucker holes, because only suckers think the storm is over. I've had my axes glowing brightly with a soft blue St. Elmo's fire that you can't shake free, like glowing molasses, when the air is so charged that ball lightning rips out of the clouds.

It wasn't that the Ranger had held the room. It was that he claimed the experiences all for himself. The Ranger implied a monopoly on the skills and big peaks, making me feel like an amateur. The Lion had excused himself then. Today, as I step over the fat, exposed roots of the trail, I speculate about them both: what makes one seek attention and the other avoid the spotlight? I thought the Ranger was guided by stoicism, but I've noticed the gothic romanticism in his stories, and the fact that he likes telling them. Since he knows the story of Hooker and Brown, is he interested in getting there too?

When a summit is windblown and polished, forming a delicate ice layer over melting snow, and the sun is just right, you can see firn spiegel, *or snow mirror. I came over a cornice once and the whole surface was dancing, a slow, oily flicker, like it was on fire underneath.*

My mind wanders, as do I on the path, and I think of meeting the Lion in that philosophy class and what little I know of Plato, who was a student of Socrates, the wisest of the Greeks. Socrates made fun of the elders in order to establish the futility of true knowledge, made too many enemies with his arrogance, and was ultimately forced to commit suicide by drinking hemlock. He drank it voluntarily, believing philosophers should not fear death.

I stumble on a loose, grey rock as the trail rises up out of the montaine. Plato was one of thirty who sat in the stone prison attending his teacher. How Socrates' death must have shaped Plato's outlook! The thick brew of hemlock was drunk, and

Socrates paced the cell until the numbness started in his feet. As it moved up his legs, he lay down, covered his face, and told the quiet gathering about the cold in his thighs and then his groin. Soon the paralysis had reached his heart. The great light of Athens was blown out, and Plato sat at the end of the pallet, helpless.

A piercing whistle by an annoyed marmot hidden in the rocks warns of my trespass. I'm surprised to stand in the barren alpine bowl below old streaks of snow and the high pass. I'm so fit and distracted that I barely felt the elevation. Behind me, far away, soars Assiniboine. The grey-blue bands striping her east walls flare like a pharaoh's headdress. The sun catches the rock and a vague face of a sphinx appears on the stone. At the top of the pass, in the wind, I look out. I want more than anything to go north and see what Collie saw from Forbes—a vision to keep the dream alive.

"L71. L69. What's your twenty?" I radio the Lion.

"Descending from Three-Isle. Trailhead in two hours, over."

"We should be on Forbes, over." We firm up plans to leave for Banff National Park and Mount Forbes right after work. I imagine our voices, backed by the breeze, sounding wild and urgent on the listening sets in the ranger station and visitor centres.

I swing the short antenna toward the repeater in the Lion's direction to strengthen his signal. As I sign off, I hear the Ranger open the frequency to one of the visitor centres.

"Victor-one-one. Go ahead, R-two-five."

"Switch to channel six, relay." He calls for the secure channel, one that my radio can't pick up. In the same way we can name a song after hearing only the opening bar, I know it's the Interpreter's voice answering his call.

▪ I stare at the beeping map, trying to understand what it's telling me. The symbols are all in another language. There's a rope around my chest, pinning my arms.

I thrash until my head clears, then I wake from the twisted sleeping bag to stop the alarm.

As the Lion shifts, I fall back. I've checked the glowing numbers many times during the night, sleeping fitfully, muscles aching from the huge packs and the long approach, but now I feel released.

I suffered a dream in which the Lion kept asking, "Why don't you just go directly to Athabasca Pass and climb Hooker and Brown? Why all the foreplay?" Now, lying awake in the dark, I know I need to see what Collie saw and find out why he stopped searching. If I just go to the Pass and follow the maps, I'll find what they say: that nothing is there. I want to pick up where Norman Collie left off.

The Lion rises beside me. The tent's too small not to feel each movement. There's the long, loud zipper of his sleeping bag and sounds of hurried dressing. It's inevitable. I duck his elbows and pull my bag open and dress in the frigid air.

I'm pulling on climbing boots when the Lion turns on his knees and opens the double-walled door. The metal zipper mows off a shower of frost. The cold doesn't come in so much as the warmth drains out. It's the cold of emptiness. I turn off my headlamp and watch the blackness outside, adjusting my eyes like a slowly focusing camera.

It isn't raining or gusting. Tents are drums that amplify weather and ours barely flutters. If it's overcast we might not go. We might sleep.

"Stars," he says. "All around the peak." And I know he's smiling.

I snap buckles and pull laces, stuff small bags of gear into my pack. I try to imagine how I'll dress during all parts of the day, including the gear I'll need in an emergency, or when we're taking a break. Planning for the unpredictable. I clomp around the tent on the barren stone of the moraine field, a moonscape under bright stars. The clouds of our exhalation and the echo of our big boots make me feel like a casual astronaut. The taste of snow, a dry ozone in my guts, permeates my senses. There's no scent, no touch; my fingers are numb.

What I don't pack, I throw in the tent. I store food on top of a boulder so packrats won't chew holes in the tent. Then we both set off, talking in whispers without meaning to.

Across the scraped stone we walk, headlamps floating through suspended mists like other breaths, the breaths of everyone who has come this way before, walking in the predawn darkness toward a ghostly cone. Our lights reveal only ten metres, the rise and turn of the rock, and we follow it toward the glacier. The ice nears, like the wide door of an open freezer. The glacier becomes a pale lustre in the middle distance. A faint radiance seems to rise off the snow, as if the ice is transmitting the light that has fallen on it for years, melting the glow off at night in a beckoning incandescence. The dark peaks crouch. The snow spire of Mount Forbes, the highest in Banff National Park, front and centre, gradually rises, imposing.

At the glacier toe, I fasten the spike bed of my steel crampons to the bottom of my boots and tie the rope to my harness. The frozen snow crust crunches loudly. Our headlamps form blurry halos. On the horizon, the brightness grows, then stalls as we climb onto the glacier.

We wind around crevasses as empty as my stomach, doubling back often, finding our way, watching each other and not much else. I'm lulled by the rhythm of the rope tug on my hips.

The soft-shadowed snow turns dull and then bland in the morning light. As the air lightens, I become aware of my sore eyes. The Lion calls, and Forbes turns bright pink with alpen-glow, spreading around its perfect snow pyramid. A wash of cold air precedes dawn, shortening our pause.

Above the broken terminus, as we reach the long lower-grade tongue of the glacier, we stop to eat dry food, drink sparingly. Like sailors dying of thirst in an ocean, we're surrounded by inaccessible water. We sit on our packs, feet heavy and legs sleepy. My eyes feel baggy as the light moves down the high face and the sun rises, warm and yellow.

Behind is the valley we came up yesterday, a long, hot day hauling huge packs around the lake and up the river that bends down from the ice above. We were forced to cross that flood several times in consuming and painful mini-dramas. All is hidden now by the long headwall we climbed to get to the hanging glacial shelf.

I smear cold sun lotion and change my toque and find sunglasses.

"Looks straightforward," I say, looking up at the north ridge, our ascent route.

"Yeah. I wonder though."

"I don't. It steps all the way up. Looks beautiful."

"We might be post-holing if the snow is deep. Like to get on some rock."

I hear his voice choke and I turn back to see him doubled over, his hands in his armpits. The screaming-barfies. His hands have chilled in the open air; as they warm, the blood pushes back into constricted capillaries. I never know whether to scream with the pain or throw up. There's nothing to do but try not to laugh as he dances. My hands are numb; the pain is close.

The freezing happened to my feet many times yesterday fording the streams. A numbness as if I were walking on wooden pegs, turning and slipping on the submerged rocks without response or control. The tight bands of water clasping up my thighs, into my groin, lurching my heart, then the stumble onto the far bank, the burning agony as the warmth squeezed back into my feet.

As he recovers, my hands go, curled like claws. I know that the pain will pass, that it'll make my hands warmer and harder to freeze, but all I think about is standing outside his car on the campus grounds with frozen fists, watching the blurred movement of bodies.

He said nothing happened, as if he'd plunged into the River Lethe's forgetfulness.

He said she came across him after the cabaret, begged him to talk. She was in distress and tricked him into the car.

He said he held to his side of the bargain.

I remember his firm handshake, genuine. The kind men give when surrounded by people and beer. We were close then, alive with the challenge of climbing and improving together, absorbed by the depth of our trust.

But she was all green eyes and dark hair, a light laugh and a twisting, lingering look. A pop of breath on my cheek. She had a thing for climbers, for ropes and gear, and for guys looking up and leaving, and she liked being pursued, valued.

Under red and yellow spotlights, she was a primal force. The floor was sticky with beer; I danced until I was soaked. She was playing us off each other.

Outside the toilets, the Lion made me a deal: we'd both walk away and mystify the girl. We shook hands earnestly to seal our friendship.

But she turned from flight to pursuit. I agreed to get our books from the coat check while the Lion got the car. We'd meet outside the main student union building. I stood in wet clothes, freezing, outside locked doors, for an eternity of twenty drunk minutes. I knew I was going hypothermic and could barely move my arms to wave the car over.

She hopped out as I got in. The Lion didn't look over. I shivered violently in the heat of the car, my seat already warm.

The windows were fogged: I couldn't see. I could barely hear their voices. But I'd imagined the most dramatic offence I could.

He says it could just as easily have been me she ran into. But I was bruised; he was chosen.

"Let's move," he says as he heaves up his pack. Now on the glacier he seems solid and real, disconnected from those wisps of memory and disappointment. I admire his strength, want to learn from it. I flex my fingers, the pain passing. As if I've dipped them in the River Lethe.

■ I can tell by the angle and pauses of his helmet that he's reassessing, looking up at the rock bands that make up the west face and searching for a more challenging route.

"Like to try a harder line," he says. "Before we get committed."

I stop. I've no words. "Our plan was the north ridge."

It sounds weak when I say it. Too simple. As if the old plan belonged to a world below, left behind like the trees and soil.

"If that snow warms, it'll be dangerous, and we'll be trapped on an avalanche slope," he reasons.

"We didn't come for a rock route."

"That face has less snow than the ridge. We'll move faster."

He's determined. I move ahead to look. He's already passing me, starting off. Somewhere on the glacier below we've crossed a line, near the firn line, where the first permanent snows start overlaying the exposed ice. That's where we entered his realm, where his desire encompasses him and there's no stopping for discussion, just a battle of wills that resolves in seconds.

The alarm I feel is not about the mountain but about not seeing what Collie saw. The Lion's here to ascend, not to look north. I'm climbing to see another mountain while he's solidly on this one. My purpose feels small and unconvincing. I resolve to push ahead with his plan and to work efficiently to gain the view I want.

When I take over the lead, he slaps my shoulder. "We improvise and get a better route."

The stinging, open sky is too bright. It's all scraped ice below the rock bands. I kick my crampon points in easily as we climb together, running the rope through a single ice screw between us. Against the starkness of the slope and the black rock above, my mind flails without comparisons or abstractions:

Is there rockfall here? There's no scarring on the ice. What about snow? The upper slopes could warm and avalanche. What's under this ice? The rock is black, like granite, but it must be limestone. What if I slip a crampon? What if he loses his stance? What's my first reaction? How do I make the rope as tight as possible? Mathematics could never be invented on a mountainside, only in a valley. The wind is picking up, or is that just a gust?

Mathematics? Wait. Where did that come from?

I've daydreamed. We finish below the first rock band faster than planned.

The first section isn't bad. He leads. It's easier off of the snow, but the rock's smooth; with gloves and big boots, crampons and axes, it feels awkward.

I lead the second pitch. I'm forced to traverse left with blank slabs above. The rope drag compounds with each piece I place. I get into trouble on a flake of stone, unable to pull around it. My crampons twist my foot out of a crack. My axes dangle, sound like wind chimes. I stop for a while, ignore the Lion's shouted questions, and force myself to switch modes. Slow down. When I resume, I find the way. I've no idea how long it took.

We eat lunch on a snow band, the rock rising above, as if we're shrinking and it's growing. We can't see the summit, I don't recognize the fall line.

Four more traverse pitches and then cirrus starts to streak the open blue above. There's a cold tinge when I pull the Lion up. With each lead I'm so focused I don't notice the weather or time; on each belay the hour hand is lower and the sky heavier.

"It's getting on," I say, tying him in to my stance.

"Yeah."

"It's starting to turn as well. Some front moving in. We need to exit soon," I say.

He looks up as he restacks the rope. "This should be it. We aren't far."

I'm looking for a traverse back to the snow, but we're committed to the rock band, which is steep and difficult to brace our crampons on. I'm tired.

"Give me all the gear," says the Lion. "I'll try that corner. Lace it up. Remember, keep the force off the anchor. If this doesn't go . . . " He looks as if to measure the alternative, but I'm consciously not imagining that.

I pass him piece after piece as he strips the anchor to a minimum.

"Okay, this is it. Through this and onto the ridge. This will be a full rope length. Make sure your knots are efficient so you can give me every last metre of rope."

My hands are so cold I'm fumbling the carabiner gates, and I don't want to be trapped without something to work with. I keep a sling and cam clipped on the back of my harness.

"If I get to the top and I'm solid, you might need to pull the anchor and start climbing." He's grim, even happy. He starts, moving slowly. Progress is tiny pulls on the rope. The cold creeps into my layers faster than he moves.

He pulls above a crest; my neck aches. The clouds are thicker and dark, moving out from behind the peak. Spiked into the snow, my big boots look impervious, but I feel the ache in my toes and the numbness of my heel and the sharpness in the sides of my feet where the crampons press. The heat coalesces to my core and I stare at my extremities. My thoughts hunker back from the cold. Mathematics? Indeed. All those abstract ideas that dominate society seem useless here, thin and fragile, like a map in the wind. What are ideals when plastered against the freezing bands of a mountain? Within an hour the air grows so cold I'm shivering; my hands are pinched around the rope. I've daydreamed again. Time has speeded up as it does after midnight at a party. The verglassed stone grows mossy flakes of ice like windows splayed with blooming frost. I look up as the rope jerks and the first flakes start to swirl down and the Lion starts to scream.

The Word for Word Is Word

The Lion once told me that enlightenment is associated with good weather.

"The sun breaks through, the sky clears. It's not possible without first knowing storms, a period without sun. Clarity comes after struggle."

This is the struggle. When the Lion starts screaming, I'm looking at the shattered limestone, a calcium carbonate of shale. The snow is white, the rock black. A charcoal fog wraps around me, cold fingers tapping my neck. I'm close to three thousand metres above sea level, but all I remember is that limestone is formed from crushed shells at great depths and pressure under an ocean. There are faint tinges of blue in the rock. I wonder if it's a phosphate. I always got that identification wrong. It's probably apatite, it looks like other rocks. It gets its name from the Greek: that which deceives.

I can't understand what the Lion is yelling. Does he want me to come up or is he warning me he's about to fall? I brake the rope. Wait. Wish my gloves were two sizes bigger. I hear the Lion in fits above the wind, his rope tugs are indecipherable. I let some slack.

I let more. The rope whips tight, as if he has fallen.

This is serious, I'm yelling at myself. I need to wake up. Everything seems to get sucked away into the cold, empty air behind me, my focus, my determination.

The rope jumps like a string in a bass chord. The Lion yells for me to take in the slack.

The rope's pooled somewhere above, too stiff to drop. I pull it in like a cable. The Lion must be down-climbing.

Tension again, the rope solid. The wait. A tightening. Slack. Pull it in fast. Wait. Again.

And again. Finally, the Lion yells, "Lower," and I let out the rope, under tension, frost spewing from my braking device. What will I lower out of the gloom?

He comes down, legs swimming, then he's beside me with a lurch, a wet and warm jacket, the smell of sweat and fear, a glare of intensity. He swears, pushes his helmet against the rock.

He punches the rock with a bunched glove.

I restack the rope, place my spare cam into a crack, reinforce our anchor. He's in turmoil.

"Damn! I was so close! I needed three more metres. One more piece to protect the flake, something, anything, and one more for the block, maybe four metres, and we'd have had it."

I hold my breath, hoping the cam I held back wouldn't have fit the flake.

"There were stones I could use as a chock, to wedge in a crack, but I had no more slings."

He yells at the mountain. I yell to keep warm. We look at each other. Decision time.

I'm a swirl of emotions in a place where I can't dwell on them. The frustration of being stuck, of not summitting, of no good options. I tell myself he needed more gear than what I had to complete the line and build an anchor, but there's a nausea behind my words that makes me shout a bit louder than I need. I don't want to think about the original plan, about recriminations.

"I don't want to come all the way back up here."

"If we make that snow band, can we traverse to the ridge?" I ask.

"Snow's too weak now. Damn it, what gear do we have left?"

"What did you leave up there?"

"What I had to."

It's ludicrous: I'm hoping to see an avalanche, a lightning strike, something to make the decision external and obvious. I'd rather be forced off the mountain than carry the responsibility for choosing defeat. The tendency is to stall until the conditions are truly horrible and the turn-around obvious and the descent a guaranteed epic.

Then, in a rent in the clouds, a sucker hole forms. It shows a window to the north, just long enough. We must be close to the summit as there's nothing blocking our view. Another fifty kilometres across a jumble of snowfields stands the chisel-headed summit of Mount Columbia. It's bathed in light like a bride waiting at the altar, its eastern slope a long train of snow. The half-kilometre-deep glaciers of the icefields, across such an expanse, create their own weather, leaving the mountain clear of the storm. I relax a bit, having captured my goal.

"Columbia would have been the better choice," says the Lion, subdued.

As the hole closes, we both know our attempt on Forbes is finished.

■ "Ever heard of Plato's cave?"

The flaps are tied down; a storm descends out of the west. Our bags slump in the vestibule, ready to go. It's comfortable in the tent; the Lion and I have sat out storms many times. There's nothing to do after our gear is checked and packed but to sit and ponder. Dark comes and the guy wires start to whistle and weight the rocks that hold the tent down on the terminus plain. Long striations in the rock—grooves straight and smooth as ball bearing paths—lead to the headwall edge where thick ice sheets once ground on small stones over our position. The Lion is deep in thought, mulling over the climb. I try to distract him with the thoughts I had on the mountain.

Who tried to force order on their surroundings by scratching the first straight lines? What was the inspiration? The imperfect crescent of the moon, the blinding circle of the sun, the rippled surface of a lake, the smooth curving drifts of snow? Where is there a simple geometry, a natural sidewalk? Most pedestrians ignore the humble sidewalk, but I wonder whether it's a larger achievement than a skyscraper.

Even up here are the ingredients of concrete, but only humans have combined them: limestone ground by ice, baked into ash, mixed with clay for cement, then water, sand, and gravel.

"The trail crew is affecting you," says the Lion. "You're starting to see the path for itself now."

I'm taking the measure of how much humanity has changed its surroundings.

"That's because Nature is not *simply* impressive," he says. "Nature lacks the control of power. That's why churches aren't just in pretty glades. How do you feel when you're in a cathedral?"

"The same when I stand in the mountains: awed."

"But not necessarily cowed. Mountains are too complex to comprehend. Perfection is defined as simplicity. Think of the pyramids, the Parthenon, the walls of Notre Dame, with long halls of gothic arches and columns, like perfect trees on a smooth lawn. You're attracted to them because they're clean and simple. Like geometry, like math."

"I am *not* attracted to math. But the outdoors is perfect in its imperfection."

"Yes, but what impresses us is unnatural perfection. That's why I ask if you've heard of Plato's cave. Plato likened people's knowledge of the world to people sitting in a cave with their backs to a fire. On the wall of the cave they see their shadows and think it's reality," he explains. "Then one gets up, goes past the fire, and sees the sharp, dazzling beauty of the real world, the truth."

We watch the shapes made by our headlamps on the tent.

"We're impressed by the perfect because we can conceive it, but it doesn't exist naturally. Plato called that his Ideals. They didn't exist either," he says.

"If perception is reality, then right now, in this storm, Forbes doesn't exist. C'mon, this is a racket. These questions have been around forever and never get answered; they're just job security for philosophers."

He nods. "Yeah, it's the oldest question: the *Magnum Opus*. The great work. The search for the Philosopher's Stone."

"Perfect example. Turning lead into gold? Fool's errand."

But he resists. "That's the Disney version. It's the Philosopher's Stone, not the Geologist's Stone. The *Magnum Opus* was the search for the underlying idea behind everything, the pure essence, hidden in all forms. It's called a stone because it would be the reliable truth. But I never understood why gold is so valuable. You can't eat it. You can't do much with it."

"Maybe you're not such an idealist after all," I tease. "Gold is incorruptible. It represents purity. No rust or corrosion. A superior metal."

He gets up. A last stretch before sleep. I join him outside the tent, looking around at the ponderous cloud, my hands deep inside my jacket pockets.

"Nobody believes in the *Magnum Opus* anymore," he says. "Except physicists, looking for the Theory of Everything, but they'll never tell you what love is. We're still looking for the eternal truth amid the flowing change of all things. Like a stone in the river. I envy you," he says, solemn. "All the doors are open for you in your career. Geology is something solid, practical."

I shift on sore feet. There is nothing in the dark moraine to distract me from his bare emotion.

"I can't see Forbes, but it must exist. That outflow starts somewhere," I reason. "Forbes draws us up just as rivers fall away. If you keep following water, you'll eventually find the highest point."

"Like a reverse gravity? Plato believed in two countering forces: Love and Strife, attraction and repulsion. Love, Eros, was the soul's longing to return to the ideal. I always thought Gravity was like Love. I wonder which one draws us here?"

"Maybe we're drawn to summits because they are singular. High places need big foundations. That bulk has a draw, like gravity. Anything big has that pull. Mountains, celebrities, big events."

"So, the bigger the mountain, the bigger the pull? And because it pulls us we know it exists?"

"I figure. Why that look?"

"Try telling that theory to Hooker and Brown," he says.

I feel the pull of the big northern mountains. The next is Mount Columbia, highest in Alberta.

"You're looking for two mountains, but it's one ideal. Two summits are a distraction," he adds.

Is that true? Or is the second summit hiding behind the first ideal? Later, in my sleeping bag, I ask, "What happened to the guy who left Plato's cave?"

"He returned to tell the others. Who didn't believe him. He wouldn't shut up, so they killed him."

■ The Interpreter says she loves the connection of water, how it flows around and through us, how it's everywhere—in our breath, our blood, in the trees. Now she tells me she has a lake of her own, one the Ranger named for her. Everyone who comes there will ask, and they will learn her name.

The first job after a long weekend is cleaning campgrounds. I'm always surprised by what I find: constructed benches, deflated ice bags from coolers, weeds pulled from around a site. Activities of people unable to stop modifying their surroundings into order.

"Who brings a hammer and nails when camping?" I ask.

The Interpreter is borrowing our tools to clean the campground amphitheatres.

"Why do they not bring garbage bags? I am finding something under every bush," she says.

"Hey, why are you working? I thought you always have a few days off after a long weekend."

"I took the weekend off," she says. "Why did you not invite me to Forbes?"

I shrug by way of apology. "It didn't go."

At lunch she and I sit by the river. It's flowing fast, released from its winter jail, in a ripple of oily skin. Underneath the surface is a solid flow of water.

"I love how rivers carry on for so long—at any point you look it is moving toward the ocean. So fleeting, so constant. How can the mountains provide so much for so long?" she wonders.

"All from the glaciers. Like a storehouse of water."

"And from the lakes." She tells me about the lake they found. She hadn't worked that weekend. Neither had the Ranger. "We followed a moose track to our camp. It was this tiny lake. It was not on the map, it did not even have a name! Just there, waiting to be discovered."

"It doesn't need a name to exist."

"No. But how would I speak of it? So he named it after me." She beams as though the Ranger has given her the greatest gift. Immortality.

I'm unsettled. That little lake now holds something of her.

If I'd followed an animal trail near Laggan a hundred years ago, pushed through to a shore, glaciers hanging off the mountain slopes, coloured bands of shale capped with seracs, would I have named it? Could I have resisted? That lake is now known as Lake Louise. The name conjures photographs. Something of the lake itself becomes secondary. Maybe the Lookout was right when she declared naming as the original sin.

"I have always dreamed of a little lake in the mountains. And now I have one."

"Where is it?" I ask, wanting to see it.

"Just off the Columbia Icefield. We were camping there. We climbed Columbia this weekend."

In the great race for the highest, I'd just been leapfrogged.

◾ Late summer and the rhythm has changed. The trails are no longer ways to explore but exist as a larger system of weather and animals. The path is not steep or open but endless; each section is momentary and the trail spans the whole week. My fitness helps, but hiking has become like breathing, just something always there, and the tread is passing underneath my feet without me wondering when it will end because it never does. The map posts at the trailheads and crossroads mark arbitrary points, not really starts and endings, as the trails continue on, winding always to another place. The signs are like stakes trying to pin down a snake.

"There was an enchanted pool," the Interpreter says, sweeping the sky.

I watch her carefully, sitting motionless.

"It was small and round, perfectly still, like a mirror. It was said to reflect your future, show you the most important thing in your life."

"Like your purpose."

"Yes. Your raison d'être!"

"Is this in your show for tonight?"

We sit together on the ground of the amphitheatre, in the middle of the empty stage. I passed by on a trail in the early afternoon and stopped to talk. She calls me her coureur de bois. I'm flattered by the translation—runner of the woods—even though it really just means woodsman. I'm more thrilled by the possessive form.

"No," she says, shaking her head, whipping her plait. "It is a story my grandmama told. To keep me safe, I think, since I loved the water. I don't know where it is from."

"So you look in and see . . . your reflection?"

"No! This pool was special, you would see *things*. But not if you touched it. Then it would show you exactly the opposite. I think my grandmama did not want me playing too close to water."

"So that kept you away from the water's edge. Smart."

"Yes, but it made me a horrible tree-climber. Especially on those old maple branches that hung out over the banks."

"And what's the catch?"

"What is *catch*?"

"It can mean many things. But, you know, a complication. I don't see this pond just sitting on a street corner in the middle of a city where people walk beside it all the time. Something as powerful as an enchanted mirror is never so easy. It is either hoarded or lost or hidden."

"Oh, I understand. No, it is not. It is just hard to look into."

I shake my head, not understanding.

She waves her hands like spreading water. "It is supposed to be a pool. But you must look down into it, as from a tower. Perhaps a bridge, as long as what you see is not the underside of an old bridge. Or a troll! That would be a *terrible* destiny. It was always my favourite story when I was a child. I tortured my grandmama into telling it over and over. I was absolutely in love with the idea of seeing my true role. I think that is my fate."

"It's your destiny to see your destiny?" I ask, teasing.

"Yes." She looks out at the trees. "But I don't know if I believe in destiny."

I imagine polished halls of pillars that take minutes to walk around. In the recesses, robed savants attend to shelves of scrolls, each of these a map to a fate, finely written before one is born. A priest pulls a heavy tome with my name on it, turns to today's date, and reads.

"I'm not sure I like it either," I say, not knowing if I hate that my decisions have already been made or that I can't conceive of a force great enough to dictate my path.

"It is the prison of a script," she says. "I always was afraid that

I would see my destiny and then not be able to move. Because, of course, as soon as you move away from the mirror you start to change. So I never want to leave the mirror. But even here, each night, we make it up. I would hate to just recite my lines like a robot. The Lion told me that *theatre* is Greek for 'to see,' He seems sad. Not like a robot, but like his script is penance."

The stage is empty. A squirrel chatters a warning; the leaves of the poplars rustle, pages of vellum. It's a wild feeling, this stage, so possible. I imagine myself as anyone, any place. I look down at the barren earth and imagine a map of everyone at the park, working alone on each day's path, sometimes intersecting.

"Perhaps the map of destiny is like the map of love," I say. "Always shifting by choices."

"Yes!" She seems delighted. "Because I have always felt that there are some forces that dictate us. The reason we are both here this summer, both on this stage together. What do we have to teach each other? But it is up to us to decide what to do with this and how it affects us."

After a moment I ask her, "Is that what caught your attention with Hooker and Brown?"

"Yes. The pool. The way you described it. Perfectly round and small. And, not just that, but bordered by two mountains, and that it was hidden away, at the very top, draining to both sides, like the start of rivers. I love this: how great rivers come from such tiny trickles. It reminds me of the parties we would have beside the fleuve on Saint-Jean-Baptiste."

"Beside the what?"

"The fleuve. The St. Lawrence River. In French, there are different names for rivers depending on their size. A fleuve is the biggest river you can imagine."

"No, about Baptiste. What is that?"

"He is our patron saint. You know him as John the Baptist. Saint-Jean-Baptiste is the day of our patron saint. Maybe that's why his name is so important in the stories of the voyageurs."

"Baptism?" I'm smiling. "That's a good saint to follow. It's a ritual of beginning. Not a reward, but a sense of becoming. Dunked in water, emerging different. Like a decision that can still be made, not just inevitable."

I get up to go, stretching stiff legs, pulling up my axe.

She draws on the ground with the wispy double prongs of a pine needle.

"I always imagined that enchanted pool as far away as I could, as a little, quiet pond surrounded by many peaks. I would wonder which peak would be best to see down into the pool, more than what I would see reflected back. Like one is a decision and the other is fate."

■ I arrive in Calgary at the end of the week, a Friday. I'm tired and anxious with the traffic and noise. I smell the exhaust like I never have before and can't believe the power we have to get used to pollution and crowding. That power allows us to dominate nature, but it could also be our death sentence. I'm at the university to meet with the Professor. The campus is quiet. On the tenth floor of the earth sciences building, he steps from a room wafting with funding battles. He asks me to wait in the graduate library.

I'm glad of the pause. Calgary is exhausting after a summer in the forest. I look at the shelves and remember studying all night, writing papers without rereading them, juggling an over-full course load, deciding what would not get done. I'm a vacationer returning to work, looking at familiar files without any comprehension of how I managed it all before or where to start. Everything in the city calls for my attention. Every sign and advertisement and warning and caution and colour and signal light. The forest allows me to give attention at my pace, but here success is speed.

The physical sciences grad library is empty. It holds the story of humanity's comprehension of the Earth, the changing legends of a civilization. So close to the mountains, the Geology Department has specialized in studying their formation. In first year I'd imagined the mountains formed in a smash of tectonics, then worn away by exposure. But evidence is growing that mountain-building is a continual motion, with even the rain, as it erodes the stone, lightening the greater mass so that the mountains keep rising.

Outside, through one narrow window, I can see the flat, dusty spread of the prairies. This was all an inland sea once. Then the mountains rose and drained it, the runoff cutting deep ravines. Then ages of ice sheets, kilometres high, ground the shale and coals flat.

On a cross-section of the Rockies, I locate the area of Hooker and Brown. It's unique for its pocket of hard dolomite that rises above an arching basalt mantle, the way a large stone emerges above sand when it has been shaken. In these archives, as in climbing clubs, great dreams began with a touch of research: a haunting journal entry, a map with an obscure name, handwriting in the margins. A match to light the imagination of restless people. I feel that again. I pull at books. The windows darken with a storm, and the glass looks greasy. A shadowy version of the archives appears in its dim reflection, some alternative library holding answers to the questions on this side.

The *Physical Atlas of Natural Phenomena* of 1856 lists Mount Brown at 15,900 feet and Hooker at 15,700, elevations that would make them the highest on the western continents yet discovered. The *Nouvelle Geographie Universale* lists Hooker at 16,980 as late as 1893.

On the microfiche, I follow the 1897 and 1898 seasonal routes of Norman Collie. I scroll over the familiar peaks of the north Yoho and the Continental Divide, over the Columbia Icefield. Then I toggle over whiteness, without landmark, without apparent speed. Finally, far to the northwest, two peaks emerge into view with question marks for altitudes: Hooker and Brown.

"Find what you're looking for?" The Professor smiles at my immersion.

"I'm trying. Looking at these old maps, pretending to see them in the 1890s." I tell him of my interest in Hooker and Brown, and of Coleman's quest.

"He was a great mountain geologist. But there's still much to discover," says the Professor.

"Really? We have maps of the entire world. Hooker and Brown have been mapped for ages."

"Have you been there?" he asks.

"No," I say slowly. "But I've seen the maps; they seem accurate." Here at the university, back on familiar ground, I can see how much my trust in maps has shifted.

"So then it's a blank spot for you," he says, as if concluding a class. "Maps are like our theories, reflecting how we want to see things. A good geologist always looks for layers and distortions."

"Do you mean incomplete? Because on some of these old charts it's obvious: the land was not known and their instruments were susceptible to error."

"No, I mean distorted. Sometimes in spite of intentions. The Earth is an orange, and no matter how you peel it, you can't lay it flat without something going off. And that's just the surface; problems are amplified in depth. We're used to looking down into the ground, but it's the same in the mountains looking up. Techniques preserve only one aspect: distance, direction, or shape. No matter what map you're looking at, only one aspect retains its truth."

"Those flaws are quite small, especially on large-scale maps," I say.

"Not if the translation is happening at a large scale, which it is on topographical maps. As you move away from a grid inter-section, everything becomes suspect. Remember that Mercator projections preserve distance, which is our priority, but we lose area and direction: you need to add declination to your compass, and that makes Greenland huge and Africa small, when actually Africa is much larger. That's political distortion. This popular projection is a subtle reinforcement to Western schools that their countries are larger and, therefore, more important. Not always deliberate, but simply to show the part that would receive the most attention. Centring the map on North America means you must split Asia in two, hiding just how big it really is and implying that it's not a contiguous political region. The farther from the baseline, the equator, the greater the distortion becomes."

I'm surprised because I should know this. I studied geography and didn't pay much attention when maps were discussed in my courses. I thought I knew maps, and no one studies what they already know.

"How much?" I ask. "On a standard topo map, how much would features be off?"

"A degree or less, but that can compound quickly."

"And altitude?"

"Actually, even worse. Older maps were based on boiling-point determinations. These days we trust aerial maps, even though they are based on the same principles. One is based on the pressure that affects boiling temperature, the other on air pressure on a mercury gauge. The maps in the Rockies were made from aerials in the 1970s. To create this map, the government survey flew little planes about yea high." He holds his open hand, palm down, about half a metre above a spread-out map. "See anything wrong? This method works great on the prairies."

"You'd have to fly high enough to see all the mountains or they would block each other? And then valleys, unless they're right underneath, would be hidden!"

"Exactly. You know a wide-angle lens? It's the same lens they use for aerial maps. Things get bent the higher they are above the horizon. They call it relief displacement."

"You're kidding!"

"No," he says victoriously. "How many perfectly cloudless

days occur in the mountains? Ever have a smooth flight in a small plane, *anywhere*? Good method, not so good in the mountains."

"So if everything I've believed is wrong about things like maps, which I've always trusted, why would I continue studying maps of the ground?"

"Geography can get distorted! But not geology. Bedrock doesn't lie." He laughs.

Back in his office, he says, "What I need from you is a commitment."

I want to say there's no other offer, but then I'd have to explain my reluctance.

His office is simple, smelling of paper and coffee, with tack boards and a heavy, laminate desk. On a shelf sit books and a globe. Rolls of seismic plots loiter in the corners. The high, narrow windows remind me of arrow slits. He has a corner view. Out one side is a jagged horizon of mountains, luminous beneath an arch of cloud, like the light at the end of a cave; out the other side rise the office buildings of downtown Calgary. He follows my gaze.

"Sure, these facilities are not what you get in the big oil companies. But here we have freedom. Don't be deceived by the look of the buildings, or compare our old concrete to their shiny towers. Glass and steel are just processed stone. Everything is built from the earth, even the trees, even us."

His view is comforting: if there's truth to be found, it's in the rocks, not the fluttering maps.

"All this is available; the best new thinking in mountain building. There's glaciology, seismology, volcanology, probably new research streams. You're the new generation, standing on the shoulders of giants like Coleman. How far you see is up to you. Think of Coleman and how much he was able to accomplish with his field studies. And he was in Toronto. The mountains are right here!"

What I need is enough time to understand what I'm looking for, and the space to search for it. The Professor promises me that.

The image of Coleman, taking five seasons and enormous stamina to finally reach the Pass, is vivid. If I reached my goal, and it was late in the summer and cloudy, and I had time for only one attempt, which peak would I choose? How would I feel if I came through the clouds and found that I'd selected the lesser one?

I think of the wolf and the old sign lying at my feet up Mist Creek. Meaningless scribbles. I think of climbing blindfolded and having the rock open up. There must be something more to find.

I agree to pursue a master's.

"I just feel like I can't trust these anymore," I say, waving obliquely at the maps on his wall.

"That's a perfect place to start," the Professor says.

▪ I'm climbing in the shade, telling the Interpreter about Norman Collie. Collie didn't go to climb Columbia once he found out that James Outram had rushed ahead and claimed it. What was lost in his mind? I've been loath to admit to myself that Columbia doesn't draw me as much now that it has the Ranger's footprints on its summit. With Outram's footprints, Collie left off his search.

Collie was a professor of chemistry at the University of Glasgow and a pioneer in mountaineering. Already by the late 1890s he had climbed in his native Scotland, travelled to the Alps, and even expeditioned in the Himalayas. He was a legend in climbing circles before he arrived in Canada. The Rockies were yet another unmapped region, and like all explorers, he was drawn toward the greatest landmarks. I tell the Interpreter how, in 1897, Norman Collie summitted Mount Gordon, by mistake.

▴ Norman Collie's tall figure breaches the pale blue horizon and walks the level snow at the summit. He looks south, turns back to the others, and starts to laugh.

"Humph. It's not Balfour," he calls to the others' startled faces. "We're not on Balfour."

The Swiss guide squints south, surprise wrinkling his eyes.

When all ten men stand on the summit, they laugh easily, turning slowly amid the peaks that lie about them in every direction, as far as they can see. Voices mingle.

"Sweet Heavens, I wore too much! That glacier was an oven," muses the reverend.

"Norman, can I untie this bloody rope?" asks Charles Thompson.

Another regards the heights of Mount Balfour. "Why, that must be four miles away if it's an inch!" More laughter.

"We could have saved ourselves some trouble by coming up from Lower Bow Lake."

"Think of all the bushwhacking to get to the Upper Bow." That sets them off again.

"Baker," calls Collie. "Can you get some bearings on all these peaks? It's a day we may not have an equal of this season, and that map of yours will be most important.

"And can you tell us where we're standing?"

Baker sets out the heavy tripod and scope for the plane-table while the others produce pipes. "Appears we're on the summit of Mount Gordon."

"Baker, any idea what these others are called?" shouts Thompson.

"Nothing, as far as I'm aware." The others feel no wind, but the parchment flutters. Baker places his hands on his hips in a mock official stance. "I fancy that one will be Mount Baker. That pointy one, at the northern end of the ice."

"Fair enough, then I'd like that one," Thompson points.

"Very good," approves Baker. "Mount Thompson it is."

Collie scowls. "Naming things eponymously may be con-strued as self-aggrandizing."

"All right then, that one there," says Thompson. "That's a beauty. How does Mount Collie suit it? Named after the emi-nent conqueror of Assiniboine, that bastion of British climbers, guideless summiteer of Mont Blanc, and Himalayan veteran."

"Mind this, Baker," says Collie, "for that's how you name a mountain. And as the recipient of this unasked honour, I only regret I have but one name to give."

One mountain to the north stands out in a sharp fin.

"That may be Murchison."

"Impressive profile. Forty . . . fifty miles north?"

"I reckon thirty. Could take a month of cutting. But you're off to tackle Assiniboine."

"Yes, maybe . . ." Collie replies.

Later that summer he was on Mount Freshfield at Howse Pass. High on the glacier, his Swiss guide's heavy beard is pointed upwards and trembling.

"Asleep?" asks Collie.

"Yes. And why not? He's hauled the camera all the way in this heat," whispers Baker.

"We'll all be glad when we see the plates," says Collie. "No substitute to seeing."

"I'm not sure how you can attempt to frame all this."

Collie stretches, looks over at the pyramid of Forbes.

"I've never seen one as big as Forbes hide for so long. Only now is he clearly seen."

Baker resumes mapping. Collie catches him eyeing the summit block of Freshfield.

"We got started a bit late this morning to push Freshfield here."

Baker looks down at the Swiss. "He won't like the sound of that."

"Well, he can't hear anything. Besides, we named the last mountain after him. Let's have a hand at Forbes tomorrow. For now, jotting down what we can may save our souls later. That map will be the finest artifact of this expedition, keep at it. It's making order out of chaos: a Periodic Table of the Mountains. I'm going to go nose around that rock over there and see what lies north. If he wakes, tell him to prepare to head down. Don't listen to his protests."

Collie constructs a rough idea of what should be north. He savours the arousal that he feels before discovery. He could almost run up the ridge to the summit. But at the rock crest he tries to accept what he's seeing. Far to the northwest, maybe another forty miles, rises a blunt, chisel-headed mountain sloping down to a long glacier to the east, sheer for thousands of feet to the west. Just behind, he can see another giant. If between them is a pass that leads to the Columbian Trench and out to the Pacific, maybe Athabasca Pass has been misplaced. Maybe Coleman found a different pass than the one Thompson and Douglas crossed. Coleman reported nothing of stature, but here are two peaks that stand above even Forbes. If Forbes hid so well, then these were never seen by Coleman. Perhaps Hooker and Brown at last!

I read the Interpreter a letter from Norman Collie in Edinburgh to Charles Thompson in Boston, written the next year:

> *My plans have suddenly changed. I was to have stayed over here as my friend Bruce (who was with Conway in the Karakorams) ought to have come home; but the wars out there have incapacitated so many officers, his leave has been cancelled and he has to stay out there. Consequently I have enlisted the help of two crack Alpine Club men—Hermann Woolley of Caucasian fame, and another friend of mine, Hugh E. M. Stutfield, and we shall descend on the Canadian Rockies at the end of July if all goes well.*
>
> *My program is an ambitious one. Murchison from the pipestone to begin with, then Forbes, and then we shall force our way north to Brown and Hooker by the north branch of the Saskatchewan. Couldn't you join us for a bit at the beginning or come the whole way if you could? We ought to have a really good time— barring the damn moskitoes—and do some really good climbing.*
>
> *I shall start if possible about the middle of July and be at Banff by the end of the month. Baker showed me a letter of yours yesterday and you say you are keeping your movements dark. You needn't trouble about mine; if anyone wants to know whether I am going to the*

Rockies you can say that probably I am—but don't tell them what my plans are, more than that I am going to try Forbes again as we didn't get up him last year.

I tell the Interpreter that Collie bypasses Forbes to explore another valley toward the two giants. He wants to order the unknown. His map is allowing him to fill in the blank areas, and he's finding peaks that have been missed, higher than any others. He thinks he's cornered the beast and means to flush it out with cold triangulation. By late August 1898, Collie finds the two he'd seen from Freshfield, but they are guarded by the massive expanse of the Columbia Icefield.

Norman Collie steps up the last crumbling rock of Mount Athabasca and onto the solid snow, keeping the rope tight to Hermann Woolley. It's Collie who can see over to the other side first. He stops dead.

"Good God!" he whispers.

Woolley moves up beside him. Thousands of feet below stretches an icefield of enormous size. The ripples, which resemble frozen waves, make them think of an ocean of ice.

"Look there! The chisel-headed one and to the northeast another, almost as high! Hermann, they must be Hooker and Brown! If we can prove them, then we've found the way at last!"

Collie and Woolley try to make their way to the highest of the two by crossing the icefield. They turn back after walking all day and making no progress. The expanse of ice is astonishing, the last redoubt of the Ice Age.

At the end of 1898, they return to Banff, finding no better maps of the area. Collie is frustrated, saying, "Humph. These folks all claim Hooker and Brown exist sure as Jesus, but they have as much proof as the resurrection."

In December 1898, Collie is back in London.

"Now hold your horses," mutters Norman Collie. Oil wicks burn in the gloom of velvet chairs and mahogany tables. "Thompson quotes Simpson for a height of eleven thousand feet. But where did that come from? Sir George wasn't trained in the physical sciences. And here Douglas notes that the heights were sixteen thousand feet for Mount Brown. But he also reports that he didn't start until 1 PM on the first of May. Yet he claims to have climbed it all in five hours! That's five thousand vertical feet without an axe and through warm snow! He states vegetation stops halfway up; that'd be thirteen thousand five hundred feet. No mention of Columbia to the south or Robson to the northwest. This is absurd. Those mountains cannot exist!"

The Interpreter stands in a trapezoid of sun; a haze of chalk dust settles about our feet.

"What is it?"

She shrugs her bare shoulders, jangling the aluminum carabiners on her harness. They flash in the light, impervious to change.

"These maps, it is funny. They are *all* about the past. We think they are the present, but they are old the moment they are made. We stand in the present, planning our future with the past."

She's not done. She chews her lower lip. I imagine ticking, an impending explosion of hands. There are nitrates in these rocks. Mix that with aluminum and we'll have explosives. I don't have to wait long.

"Collie was such a scientist! He comes, and because he does not prove what he expects, he goes home, opens his books, and we are taught to believe the conclusion: Hooker and Brown do not exist—all wrapped up in logic, and without him ever having actually stood in the spot!"

■ I work at checking the NO HUNTING signs on the British Columbia border. These big red signs run right up mountains, like seismic lines, the manifestation of a map boundary. I sweep the border, looking for hunters' boot prints, telltale signs of poaching, all the while considering the wedding of my classmates out on the prairie.

That evening I borrow a car in Canmore and head to Saskatchewan. I find myself almost on the border of Manitoba at noon the next day, and before I arrive, I have crossed two full provinces. An hour after Yorkton, there's no indication of a boundary, or towns, just a grid of dusty roads and fields, shimmering heat and bleached blue skies. At the farm I feel stunned from driving, and so lost that I don't stray far from the group. Amid a break in the reunion, I stand up to my waist in a field of rye. I can look west and pretend that mountains don't even exist.

The groom finds me. He's like a favourite jacket pulled out again with the change of seasons. He points to the clouds building on the horizon. With no land feature to compare them to, their scale appears gargantuan. In the mountains, clouds like that are on top of us within an hour, but the groom kicks the soil with his boot and promises rain the following evening.

"You can see weather coming a day away?" The sky towers, sun hot on my cheekbones.

"Yeah. Guess no rain's good for the wedding, but we sure could use the moisture."

"You talk like a farmer, never satisfied."

He smiles. He's also a geologist, working in gas exploration. We talk about the choices our graduating class is making. I ask him how he likes working for a big corporation out on the prairie, and if it's enough.

"You're a hick," he says, laughing. "I love it here. You're happy in the mountains, you got into climbing and all. But look around. More importantly, look down. Feel what you're standing on. These prairies are unformed mountains—horizontal strata that haven't been folded up and whittled down into peaks yet. They're potentially far taller than anything raised so far. Just waiting. Underneath all this lie pools of gas, like treasures."

"Is that interesting—searching for little pools?" I ask. The Punch

Bowl gleams in my mind and then turns into the Interpreter's brown eyes. I've driven all day and I'm barely a quarter of the way to Québec.

"The pools are hardly little," he says. "Last week my team solved a problem: every four weeks our pumps work three times as hard, sucking up power and producing little gas. We thought it was an issue with the power grid or with the suction heads or sand in the collectors, but it was none of that."

He pauses in case I choose to guess.

"It was the *moon*." He lets that sink in. "These pools are so big, they're subject to tides. Each month our pool levels drop like the Bay of Fundy."

Across the fields, with the rock layers and the ocean below, I'm not sure whether I'm standing on the side of a sleeping mountain or on a mantle above a subterranean sea. I gauge the clouds' progress in the languid afternoon. They move slowly, like sheep without mountain lions to shred them.

As the sun leaves, the night pops with stars and crickets. The horizon is uniform and dark. The compass was invented for the ocean, but it could have been for the prairie.

The ceremony commences with nightfall, under awnings stretched between old farmhouses. The couple is jubilant. The groom begins his vows:

> *I fully commit myself to join you in perfect love and perfect trust. Let us be as one. I will walk beside you wherever this life leads us.*

The bride reaches across and pushes his nose. "Beep! I am recording this." This is a celebration of two people finding their ideal.

> *I will guard our unity and cherish the respect that lies at the heart of our union. I will accept and honour you for who you are. Let us grow together.*

The bride and groom face each other. They remind me of two mountains, and only with at least two can something new be born. Why always the need for the superlative in our society, where we are consumed by comparisons and competitions? Must one peak be higher?

I give great thanks that the pattern of our lives together shall be a perfect and loving expression of the Creator's will. Let this be my prayer and my vow.

I wonder about the vows we all make to ourselves—the promises to pursue what's meaningful. The early climbers hacked hundreds of kilometres to reach Hooker and Brown. But their motivations diverged: Coleman loved rocks; Collie loved mapping; Outram loved God. In essence, they all searched for different things.

In the shadows and expanse beyond the lanterns, I conjure two grand peaks, starlight illuminating the high glaciers. If they were the ideals that I strive for, the Hooker and Brown of my life's map, what would they represent? Which would be higher?

Among the guests, the first question is always "What's your name?" The second is "What do you do?" Instead, I ask them about the two highest ideals in their lives, during quiet moments, between laughter.

I found a classmate swaying to the Western music. "Happiness and Love," she answers immediately, her gaze going to the stars.

Another who loves to work out in the gym stands tall under the reception tent, quietly approving, nursing a large beer, and eventually replies, "Fulfillment and Purpose. And of those, Fulfillment is the higher peak."

His girlfriend, who ran on the university track team, looks down at her feet, perhaps because she trusts them more than her feelings. "Friendship and Self-awareness, I guess. I don't know which is higher," she says, relieved.

I catch up with a graduate from my class who has been backpacking around the world. Having had many long nights of solo travelling, he's eager for his turn. His succinctness is testament to thought invested. "Direction and Acceptance," he says.

Another schoolmate surprises me by choosing Comfort and Self-sufficiency, with Comfort the most important. Her date is polite, asking for Destiny and Strength, recognizing Destiny as unavoidable, but believing Strength is the key to realizing it.

The next afternoon, as I pack for the long drive back to the mountains, the sky looks as if it might rain hard.

The woman on the track team walks over as the crowd disperses.

"I read the other day that the mark of a good athlete is not one's ability to perform but instead to recover," she says. "About what you were asking last night: I think most of us are looking for answers in our lives. Perhaps once we find them, we think it's just happily ever after. Does anyone consider what comes next? A relationship doesn't end with marriage. More important is what we do with the answer when we solve the mystery. That's the mark of the good seeker."

■ When I arrive back in Canmore and return the car, I call dispatch at the park office to see if any staff happens to be in town. Eventually, the Ranger arrives in his truck, pulling aside heavy folders of paperwork from the passenger seat and sending his dog into the back of the pickup. I feel more tired than I expect as he turns down to Kananaskis.

"Is it me? Or is Canmore growing too fast? It feels like the pace has picked up."

"Yeah, it's becoming the hub for everything between Banff and Calgary," says the Ranger.

"It's growing faster than the planning." I'm thinking of the litter of signs everywhere.

"It's efficient. Hopefully so much so that people stay there."

I've heard it before, this idea that only trained people should be allowed into the backcountry, but never so blunt. "Only the worthy should walk the woods, eh?"

He looks over as if my job is to blame. "When you spoon-feed tourists, you don't teach them respect. If there's no trails, there's no amateurs. I say let them grow over."

"I heard you studied town planning."

"Not for long. Trouble with school is everything loses its attraction when you study it. The only learning is figuring the underlying game, which is usually saying just what the prof wants to hear."

The drive continues in silence; I look out my window, biting my lip.

"Summer's over," he says. There's snow caught in the ditches and on the peaks. The nights are closing sooner, aided by dark clouds.

"It's not over yet," I say. "Just changing."

"What are you going to do?"

"Finish the season. Then I'm back to school."

"Leaving the mountains?"

"*Studying* the mountains. I have to leave to stay. Some things are necessary."

"Just don't get trapped in a dead-end job down here, like some of the others."

I guess he's referring to the Lion, who's accepted a position at a visitor centre through the fall. No one visits the park between Labour Day and Christmas. His job will be a lonely vigil.

"Where are you off to?" I ask.

"North Boundary. Jasper National Park. To the real wilderness. Interview on Monday."

"Not for sure yet, eh?"

"It is. I've paid my dues. Time for those mountains you've been telling stories about."

I'm shocked by the possibility that he will scoop me on Hooker and Brown. "She told you?"

"She does a show, you know. She tells everyone. She told one of mine: the Mad Trapper."

"That old Shuswap myth. Every big lake has a recluse like that."

"Not a myth. He's real. They've just never searched hard enough."

"Like a sasquatch?" I'm surprised that he believes in these romantic beasts.

"Now there's a mystery that keeps on giving." His face washes with the faint purple of dusk.

"How could creatures like that survive? There are roads everywhere now," I argue.

He shrugs. "Just because you've never seen one doesn't mean they don't exist. Everything in nature is either essential or impossible. Sometimes I think you and your partner are trying to rationalize something else into the mix."

Again the attitude, that I haven't seen what he has. He figured the Lion was too wrapped up in his ideals to be reliable in the mountains. I thought the Ranger was just too practical. Now I'm not sure. I've heard that zinc emits a surprising sound when bent: the Cry of Zinc. The problem with minerals is they react and form everything. Sometimes it's hard to identify what they really are. The Ranger sighs in the dark and slaps the steering wheel.

"No peak is the ultimate," he says. "There's always another one. They're like magic tricks; they're only tricks while you don't know the secret."

Is he talking about the Interpreter? Or the northern mountains?

"What if there was, though," he continues. "What then? You climb it, you're done? It's not the arrival that matters but the process of arriving. We need milestones: it's natural to compare and compete with others. A healthy rivalry. Call it our *arrivalry*."

He smiles at me.

▪ "Ah, regarde! Le petit croissant de la lune!"

I follow the Interpreter's arm to the sliver of moon, a clipping on the faint porcelain of the sky. Not a single star appears; the western ranges are dark. I'm in a group above the compound. We're clustered in blankets, cradling small mugs of whisky. In the distance, Assiniboine rises above the others, her blue-grey bands and southeast ridge cold, steep, and solid.

"Is that where you went up?" someone asks the Interpreter.

"No, from the right," she says.

"Oh. The northeast."

The others are visitor centre interpreters and custodians, versed in mountain history and feeling like experts at the end of their semesters, vying to show off their knowledge. At turns acting noble and announcing facts like they are heralding guests entering a ball, they're putting on an impromptu show of melo-dramatic history. One pipes up, "The southeast was the original route."

"Nineteen hundred and one," says another. "James Outram and his Swiss guides."

The others pick up, laughing.

"Nineteen hundred and one is a grand year to the Victorians of the British Empire."

"Weren't they Edwardians by the summer of 1901?"

"Yes, and exploration fever is high. Scott has just sailed south with the HMS *Discovery*, intent upon reaching the South Pole. The Commonwealth of Australia has just been established."

"The Boxer Revolt is being put down in China, and the war with the Dutch Boers on the Transvaal of South Africa is raging at its height."

They sweep their arms grandly, bowing and presenting, mock-ing royal accents, playing off one another. Their tanned arms are shadowed with muscle, scratched from branches and rocks and adventures. They beam with the confidence of animals in their pack.

"And here, at the far end of the New World, in a wilderness cut open by a railway, the spirit of mountaineering is establishing British dominance on the peaks."

"Even as the paint on the provincial boundaries is barely dry."

"God, think of that! This wasn't even a province yet."

The interpreters and custodians are from all over; none can claim locality, as there are no permanent residences in the park. Everyone knows it'll end, that soon contracts will finish, and then they'll be back east, or off to the west coast, or to school. The conversation is liquid, without the hesitancy of strangers or the speculation of seeing one another again. Instead, the group enjoys a game-like exchange, a verbal egg-toss among the waving fireweed and bright red Indian paintbrush.

"It's all so new out here."

"Anything over fifty years is considered a heritage site!"

"Back east feels like a different country."

"And it was only a hundred years ago that they climbed that?"

"A hundred years ago this was pure wilderness."

James Outram met the climbing party of the legendary Edward Whymper, the first to summit the Matterhorn forty years earlier, which subsequently started the whole mountaineering craze. Whymper seemed finished: old and alcoholic, haunted by the deaths of his partners on his famous climb. Assiniboine had been dubbed the Matterhorn of the Rockies and was still open to be won, her summit heavily contested. Attempts back then occurred at glacial intervals: a little movement each year. Rumours whispered by the defeated parties reached the railway sidings a couple of times a season and hardened into legends over the years, like sediment, turning the mountain into a myth with a tough reputation.

"Outram was a reverend?"

"On leave with a nervous breakdown."

"Boy, he sure took it easy."

"Aren't you religious?"

The sun red-rims the whisky mug. The smell of crushed juniper rises from underneath the worn leather of our sandals. A glance, a fast and sincere smile, heads following the conversation like a school of fish. And always laughter, jousting.

"I've heard you pray."

"Only on a steep pitch."

"That's more like begging. And on the tourist hikes?"

"Throwing curses under my breath."

"Be good to the tourists, little interpreters, or James Outram will get you!"

"That guy must have been in awesome shape. He hiked to the mountain, climbed it, then hiked back to the siding in a day."

"Through a storm."

"Without boots."

"One of the 'conquered it in the name of God' types, eh?"

"He hardly mentions God in his book."

"He was English. Not a Puritan."

"He traversed it on the first ascent. I'd say that pretty much conquers it."

"He said that with skill and ropes there is no danger."

"Sounds arrogant."

"It doesn't look conquered."

"Maybe he made it all up."

"There's no way to know what actually happened up there."

▪ "Sir James Outram was a vicar from Ipswich. That's near London, I guess. He came to Canada in 1900 to reside with his brother while resting from overwork. Back then it was called a nervous breakdown," I tell the Interpreter as we walk along the lakeside in jackets and jeans. "He'd climbed recreationally in the Alps, but when he climbed Cascade Mountain and looked south to see the pyramid of Assiniboine, he was as enraptured as I was when I saw her at the start of the season. He actually went on to make its first ascent. He seemed to have coaxed an obsession for that, and became the first to summit twenty-seven other mountains, travelling with only a guide and following maps prepared by others. At least, he was the first to record an ascent. The natives climbed, but never on glaciers."

She's asking about Outram because his name came up in the stories and she wonders why the Ranger thinks so highly of him. The lake is a skin beside us, punctuated by the startling jumps of trout. We walk in long periods of silence, with the whine of mosquitoes and the shapes of the mountains against the lavender dusk. She wants to know.

I announce, "It's August 1901, somewhere in the Yoho Valley," and begin the tale.

The fire burns low and sparks as the green wood splits open in the heat of the coals. Sir Edward Whymper's snoring passes through the white canvas of his tent, the far-off roaring of Takkakaw Falls through the trees.

The Cook and Axeman have made off with the whisky. Whymper had gone to fetch a photograph to support a story he was slurring and had fetched his bed instead.

"You'll strip his boots at least?" Outram asks.

"I'm not a chambermaid," replies the Outfitter, staring at the low flames.

"As long as he doesn't choke to death in his collar. Where are the others?"

"Taking a break."

Outram tried to dissuade the hirelings from taking the half-empty whisky bottles by stating how late they were rising, how bad Whymper would be in the morning.

"He's haunted by his companions' deaths on the Matterhorn, and I'm haunted by him tellin' us every night," whispered the Axeman as he slipped free the bottle. "Think of it this way, sir. I'm keeping 'im from indulging more. I'm doing 'im a favour."

Bloody Scot, thought Outram as they slipped off to the

creek in the moonlight, leaving him alone with the Outfitter, a rugged, uncivilized man.

"I heard Wilcox tried Assiniboine again. Made a good show of it."

"Northeast ridge again?" asks Outram. The fire lights his round face and smooth cheeks.

"Aye. And with the Swiss. Again. Big news back at Banff."

"I'm surprised his Highness didn't try. Isn't that what he's here for?"

"Him?" The Outfitter nods toward the snores. "He's done. He was first up the Matterhorn. Assiniboine is a prize for someone else."

"Pity. I should think that anyone that is ambitious should gain her."

"What about you? You're fit, an' I've seen your fever near a summit."

"Only the brave deserve the fair," sighs Outram.

"Who said that?"

"I forget. Tennyson, Dryden, Our Lord. I have quoted too many in my work."

"You want her?"

"Aye, but only the well-funded can attain that prize." The moon is almost full.

"You sound melancholy, but do you want her? Oh Christ, sorry, I'm asking a vicar about a mountain like she's a woman!"

"You're forgiven. And yes, I want her. But I cannot afford you. I'm on this expedition only because Whymper invited me up from Field by Providence alone."

"I understand. But what I hear is that you can't afford a long expedition."

A sudden wind comes up in the treetops, flares the sparks into a red avalanche.

"But you could afford a short expedition."

"Short? Wilcox took two weeks," says Outram.

"I could get you there in two days. With good weather you'd summit the next day."

"What if we are bogged by early snows?"

"Two days, I guarantee it."

"Okay. I'll want the Swiss with me. I'll see if I can get another in Field."

"Two guides?"

"Are better than one. They have been there, as have you. And I've climbed with them. That gives the best chance of success. You think the southeast ridge is the route?" Outram asks, with full interest now.

"I'll let you decide, but with good weather there should be no difficulties."

"One other thing. Pull it together with utmost secrecy."

"In his prayers that night Outram mentions weather and Assiniboine in the same sentence," I claim. "And, later, he did slip away with his outfitter and guides without telling anyone, just a day ahead of another expedition. Outram got to Assiniboine in two days, climbed it the next, came down the other side, then walked through the camp of the other expedition on his way back to Banff. Outram himself, ahead of his party, walked all night in order to beat the news back to the railway siding so that he could prepare for the publicity.

"I guess you have to push to climb a mountain like that. When we did it, it was go-go-go all day. I'm not sure why the urgency," says the Interpreter.

"Some people have to climb that way," I say. "To avoid allowing themselves to fear or doubt. The Ranger's a lot like James Outram. Outram became famous in the mountains and was able to draw on patrons' funds to tackle the biggest unclimbed peaks the next year. That was 1902, perhaps the greatest year of climbing ever in the Rockies. Outram was determined to find the two peaks on the far side of the Columbia Icefield that Collie had spoken about at the alpine clubs, and so he got started ahead of Collie's group."

⸺ The Packer's been acting too casual ever since he and Outram and the Swiss had come down from the new peak, tired but exhilarated. The first climb above the alpine onto glaciated ridges after over a week of pushing through the brush of the valley. Now the forest is growing dark, the air cooling. Their drying clothes hang and throw blockish shadows onto the spruce boughs.

"We were blessed, I tell you. When those clouds withdrew to reveal Mount Columbia, I felt it was ordained." Outram is laughing over plates of bannock bread, potatoes, salt, and jerky.

"Ja. It was a good, clear sight. Did not look hard," the Swiss agrees.

"Possible in a day, I think. I'd want to be on the névé by daybreak."

"Ja. We could cut a trail to the icefall from here, make moving in the dark easier."

"It will never cease to amaze me how fearless you are on a steep pitch of ice but how you have an absolute hatred of bushwhacking."

The Swiss laughs. "We do not have this busch in Switzerland. It is uncivilized."

The Packer steps forward. "Whatcha gonna call it, sir? The mountain we just came offa?"

"Alexandra. Alexandra Mountain. No. Alexandra Peak, I figure. On account of our gracious Queen of England, as her and King Edward's coronation approaches."

The Swiss grunts. "It does not matter what you call it," he says. "I still climb her."

"A rose by any other name, eh?" Outram jibes.

The Packer presses on. "It must be exciting to name a mountain, knowing that forever after it will bear your stamp and interpretation."

Outram considers this. "One does find a knack for it. Gets to be more of an intuition once one has managed a few summits."

"Let's hope it's like last summer for you. Which brings me to mention how we spotted Columbia from the ridgeline. I reckon she can't be as far from here as when Collie tried."

"Indeed not."

"Well, I would like to come along then when you attempt her. Now you know I'm strong and able, and good with a rope. I can balance across a river better than anyone. And I can handle an axe, now, sir, please . . . one of those little alpine axes would be a trick for me. I can haul better than my load, and it might be best to have a third on the line with you. With crevasses and all it would be a sight better to have two on the line pulling than just one."

"Perhaps you forget yourself. You're an outfitter, not a mountaineer."

"You said the way seems easy though, sir. I won't be a burden. I can handle myself, and I'm not afraid of heights. We have time. Collie's party is a week from leaving."

"I won't hear of it." Outram becomes stern and rises from the log, hands by his side. "What we face up there only God can tell us, but I can't allow just anyone to step onto the greatest icefield yet discovered. It is no place for amateurs. Now no buts, I will simply not be responsible for the death of any man in this party. I will hear no more on the matter. Tomorrow you will cut a trail toward the icefall. That is your duty."

I tell the Interpreter that Outram and his guide mounted the glacier and walked to Columbia.

James Outram pauses to catch his breath and looks slowly up the ridge to the summit. The Swiss is above him at the other end of the half-inch manila rope, mechanically chopping steps in the firm névé. As the rope slack is taken up and begins to tighten, the guide looks back.

"Herr?"

"A moment, if you please," says Outram. He is having trouble catching his breath but looks away, down the steep slope of the eastern face and out along the brilliant white of the icefields. He can see the open wounds of the crevasses, the thread of their trail, and the shadow of the bergschrund below. He adjusts the smoked goggles on his broad face, careful not to let them fog, and follows the tiny path all the way back across the miles of glacier. Their track is the only flaw on the surface of the ice sheet, and he is again surprised that he can still see it, between Alexandra and Castleguard, at the point where they mounted the ice. *That must be six or seven miles,"* he thinks. *"Distances are deceiving.* He turns north and sees nothing in the riot of stone to challenge the peak they're on. There are some mountains that are big, several that are impressive, but nothing that clears the skyline in the manner of Forbes or Columbia. This is the end of the line.

"Find what you look for?" calls down the Swiss.

"That'll do, I'll take a turn at chopping for a spell," Outram says as he kicks his boots into the steps carefully and moves up to the big, bearded man, who says nothing. Outram smiles, looking around and realizing how high they are.

"We're doing well. This arête looks solid all the way to the top. Then we shall have the finest views available in the Dominion."

The Swiss nods and takes in the rope, preparing for Outram to begin.

Outram starts cutting steps with the adze of his axe and tells himself, *You're about to summit the tallest in the Rocky Mountains. Your track leads right to the virgin summit.*

From the top he looks north and sees nothing higher. He knows he has won the highest.

After a moment of silence, the Interpreter says, "I think he was very lustful, for a priest."

From deep within the nuclear furnace of the sun, perfect, simple atoms are heated to a frenzy and smashed into plasma. This is blasted out into the void, hurled out in a sizzling scattershot through the freezing emptiness. This radiation diffracts through the ozone, scatters off the long red wavelengths, tightens to a cool blue, and drops down through the air and lies gently at my feet.

I heave up my pack and leave the discordant clamour of hiking groups, slamming doors, and bursts of music and engines. The sun is still new but hot on my jaw, and I want to move. My aversion to industrious humanity comes from too many days of solitude on the summer trails.

The pines are dry and dusty green, the crags a solemn grey. A brief resurgence of summer has melted off the first autumn snows, but the feeling of borrowed time is strong. I can't bear to leave without setting foot on Assiniboine, so I plan a fast and light solo effort, bargaining an extra day on the South Boundary Trail from the Ant in exchange for a day clearing campgrounds after the last long weekend. All week I've been anxious to start, to get up high on that pyramid.

That morning I ran each piece of climbing gear through my fingers: testing for damage, measuring for weight, judging for utility. The conferred purpose of tools is a bond I share with all my ancestors: a short thin rope, a few slings and pitons, a small axe, climbing boots. I take these items in my hands and they change me. I assume their attitudes: direct, simple action.

I move quickly past the hiking loops and into a silent forest. There's plenty of signs of large herbivores. The animals seem to know it's the hunting season across the British Columbia boundary and are moving into the park for protection. Just as they know when it's the weekend and are less than shadows when the tourists arrive.

My pace is slow with the heavier pack. At an intersection where three valleys meet, I glimpse the east face of Assiniboine, like a gold-and-grey-layered Pharaoh's mask of the Great Sphinx. I'm walking in between her thrusting paws.

With the long trails I've been assigned all summer, I'm in the habit of rarely stopping, but I keep turning and listening to the silence, as if someone walks beside me. The trail follows a shaded valley between bunched ridges. There's no distant view. I sense this is my last foray for the season and I daydream through scenes of this summer in the park: the Interpreter on her stage, spreading her arms; the Lion clearing trees, smiling; the Ranger shaking his head.

At Wonder Pass the trees hold old burn marks, clawed and tattered bark. I feel an absence there, something uncertain, a mood that indicates I am leaving my domain and am now under the power of a new sovereign. I pause to see the pyramid of Assiniboine. I stash the trail tools under a drooping spruce. It's late afternoon now, and I walk across the meadows and around the lake, planning on resting in the alpine hut atop the glacier bowl below the north face.

A headwall rises between the lake and the hut, and old snow leads up in a ramp. I follow a faint trail of steps. Sweat drips off my brim. I'm an hour up the slope, maybe two hundred metres high, when the snow starts to slide.

The thump of a collapsing layer seizes my heart, catching my legs off guard, unbalanced. The slope shifts down a metre and settles in a soft ripple, like sand on a dune. The snow is too warm to hold itself at this angle. I'm high above the lake, yet still far below the glacial carved bench.

I've daydreamed, wandering somewhere back in the amphitheatre, back among the conversations in the park. That was a mistake, this is the consequence.

Get serious, I tell myself. *Get present*.

I'm too heavy to move on the snow. It has gathered warmth from the sun, and in a few minutes has changed phases from stable to isothermic. I'm standing in the middle of a potential slide, and I'm the trigger. My head clamours with thoughts and analysis and plans and options. They're deafening.

I carefully compact a small square of snow. The faint tracks of an earlier party lead up, impossible to follow. The sun disappears and the air sweeps down in a cold draught. The snow needs time to lose its heat and regain strength, but it's surprising how fast I get cold.

My shirt is soaked from hauling the pack, and I wonder whether I'm already hypothermic, and whether I'd know. I tell myself to calm down, and people the dusk with my colleagues. It's easy to conjure them in the twilight: the Lion, encouraging me to become what I dream; the Ranger looking back, warning about the snow; the Interpreter laughing, begging a story; the Lookout off in the dark, muttering inscrutable wisdom; the Ant stretching his back, deeply tanned and dirty; and the Professor, waiting for me to decide my next move. Their movements and words surround me like an orchestra, warming up, tuning discordantly.

I shiver. The darkening lake becomes a litmus to the night. Along its rim, campers are setting up camera tripods in case they forget their experience. I imagine conversations with the Lion, the Ranger, until stars wheel above the north face. Between the stars, the night tunnels into infinity. I look there to places that never end, more plentiful than stars. I stand amid an infinity of infinities. Is it my choice to be bold, or is it just inevitable that I reach for the highest point?

The night is alive with simple distractions—the gurgle of water under the snow, the clump of snow consolidating, the lurching boom of rockfall from far above—each an event on which to focus, until my senses ache for more meaning, more cause from each effect. And through that ache comes impatience and banality of thought, flitting from tune to tune like you're dialing a shortwave radio across the spectrum, until the only thoughts left are whispers of my fear and urgings of my determination, and the choice between the two at each step.

I start up again with the moon when the snow is cold and firm, spending careful hours negotiating the headwall, surprised that when I pass the dark hut it's almost morning. I decide to continue, not wanting to risk falling asleep in the hut and missing the day. I move up an easy rock slope before the dawn. Above me thunders a rockslide. I imagine the Ranger glancing back, furrowing his brow, and the resentment of his judgment is like crashing cymbals. The Lion I remember as a steady drum. The Interpreter hums. I pick through the rocks, my axe handle rattling on the edges. It all keeps me moving and warm. The sun slowly rises, red like sore eyes, washing to a pale haze.

I pass over yellow stone, shattered and unstable, forcing my focus on the broken pieces underfoot. I'm moving fast into altitude. The Ranger crowds my mind, debating my decisions even as the slivers of rock shift in my hands. The rock band becomes steep and loose. I gasp, pull through, as if surfacing, and throw him off, leaving him below.

The summit is lost by the angle of the face. It looks huge up close, an endless stretch of rock above. That summer, while working with the Ant on a bridge, he told me how the end is closest when we first plan a project, and how it moves away as we realize the problems of the project. I climb up to a steep ochre band. It's twenty-five metres high, and broken only in a few places, delicate and slippery. I visualize the Interpreter holding back, waiting for a lead. The Lion shakes his head at the fact that a twenty-five-metre cliff doesn't show up on a fifty-metre topo map.

I swallow water. Clear my head. I wait for the light and the mountain to show the way. I pick a spot and test it, then another, then move back, thinking my intuition is reading some invisible signposts. I commit and work through the weakness. My mind sees the Ant and the Lion kicking stones below, left behind. I'm feeling lighter, clearer.

I climb through pink slopes of loose apricot talus with the Interpreter. The face is not steep but crumbly. Around me, thin clouds are forming as the mountain heats.

I dig my way through pink dolomite, imagining in each a sky-clear rock. Each stone that pulls free under my grasp shows more broken layers. What if I were to scrape them all away? Would I get to the heart of the mountain, where there is no weathering and no cracks, where the water and air do not penetrate? Would I reveal the crystal core? Would Assiniboine rise like a tremendous jewel, cut on clean edges?

There is a grain of truth in every myth.

I check my progress. The mists have grown. The sky is hazy. I sense the massive drop through the moisture. I'm beside the huge east face with its bands of gold and pink and grey. I hear a metallic tapping, clear and distinct, beating time to my heart. I see nothing, but sense someone above. It's the same feeling I had on the long trail from the park.

I come to a golden band, loose, almost vertical, but short. The rocks are so similar to the one I split for the Interpreter around the campfire that it could have come from here. I pick through the holds. Eventually I concentrate on nothing but my footing. At the top of a worn groove, where I stem out my feet onto wet, vertical gravel, I see a piton, rusted and heavy, newly beaten, flakes of corrosion like moss growing from the yellowish stone. The desperate moves hold me at the top of the band. A person caught up in a transcendent piece of music becomes aware of the conductor only when the instruments fall silent. Above the rock band I'm alone.

Beside me the east face drops into clouds. Water trickles down the rock. I pass several rappel stations where rotted bunches of slings, stained with mud and sun, nestle around dubious blocks. I traverse in toward the face as the ridge becomes loose and narrow. The stone becomes a grey shale. I scramble upward, clattering, balancing on stones I barely trust with my weight. Above me the mists clear, as if I'm clawing up the muddy bank of an ethereal ocean. The clouds keep the height hidden, helping me concentrate on the next hold.

As I look for the route, a silhouette descends the skyline. A grey figure, quiet as memory, settles on a large block, pulls his ropes, then notices me.

"It seems easier here on the ridge," he says, his voice normal, pleasant, involved in his work. It carries easily across the top of the thinning cloud. Then he's gone, rappelling into whiteness.

A raven croaks far too close, startling, as it wheels on the thermal updraft near the east face, shifting the tiny bones in its shoulders to challenge me.

Into the clear and colder air, up over bigger slabs, onto a black band. The stone is solid but a dangerous sheen of verglas laminates it. I snag edges with the axe, trusting my feet only against the larger grooves. The climber wore an old style of clothing, I think, or was that the effect of dimming clouds? I've seen all types in the mountains during the summer. I'm not surprised by anything people wear.

The summit is near, blocked by a last wall. I straddle the ridge edge and see nothing higher. But the last step is intimidating: a sheer wall with an obvious cleft. I position myself under it, test the stone and figure my motions, and plan how I'll reverse the moves to get back down. After a summer of climbing, I know I can do any individual move. But it's the combination, the remoteness and exposure—the consequence of a mistake—that stalls me.

The memory of the Reverend James Outram, indefatigable, spurs me on. I restack my pack to keep emergency gear close, then move with slipping boots. Only the single, slow violin of the wind accompanies me. *Violin.* A word close to violence, but meaning peace and art and harmony. I'll tell the Interpreter. She'll appreciate the word's devolution.

There are no birds. In a scrape of the stone, I click together the pieces of a simple puzzle. It's just me, the mountain, my intention. Even my doubt is now left below.

I grasp at cold blocks near the summit, staring intently at my fingers to prevent them slipping as my boots edge up. A final compression step, my knee in my gut, and a slow rising, a precarious ramp to a cornice. There, a large stone cairn. The verglas at the top is hard and slippery and makes the rock dark. The summit register, that log of passages in this singular space, in its black pipe nestled within the cairn, is iced in and untouched. Above me a snow cornice, the final summit, arches over the east face in a dangerous wave, unlikely to hold my weight. The final metre is out of reach. Under the surface of its wind-scoured snow is pure ice. Without the weight and movement of a glacier, this ice remains unfractured, so translucent I can see it only by its far side, like thick glass in an aquarium. It's not water ice, but the pressed foundation of snow, gathered for eons. I think of what the Ant said about frost clinging to trees. What had this ice supported?

I eat by the cairn, above the clouds that float over lesser summits, so near the outstretched fingers of cirrostratus reaching from the west. Mount Gordon is hard to discern out of the northern jumble. Forbes is too far. I stand at the highest point in the southern Rockies. The edge of the world, and suddenly I have a sense that I've gone the wrong way. The answers I want are the other way. North. I need to finish the quest, but then I don't want to solve Hooker and Brown. I want their mystery to keep inspiring me. I'm caught in a paradox. Science and magic don't mix.

I wish for my ice axes. I wish for crampons. Then I might swing a tempered pick hard into the crystal blue sky above me and fracture it, splinter the frozen air with kicks of my front points, pull myself up, one small step at a time, above the mountain, and ascend the sky.

■ I find myself wrapping duct tape around my boots like the Lion does. I thought these steel-toed boots would last years, but they are so broken by use that I rely on any reasonable waterproofing.

I work with the Ant in the last hot days, repairing the trail to Three-Isle Lake, hacking slide-alder, a rubbery bush that bounces our axes back at us.

"Autumn," says the Ant. "You only see weather like this now.

When it gets hot like this for such a stretch, it means there'll be an early and heavy snow. Summer has a certain number of good days, and when they're packed in at the end, you know it's just trying to complete its quota before winter starts."

We cut a new section where swampy ground has bled and washed out a switchback.

"What's the largest organism in the park?" he asks.

I guess elk, then moose, finally bear. He shakes his head disappointed, points across the valley to a patch of aspen, golden with the cold autumn nights. "They all change colour at the same time because they all come from the same tuber." The Ant continues to educate me in his own way. He waves at the swampy ground through the trees, at a tall, slender plant with sawtooth leaves and little clouds of white blooms. "Water Hemlock. Now there's a poisonous one. Eat that and you're dead by dawn."

My turn. I tell him of Hooker and Brown, a legend he's never heard. That's surprising: he of all people should know about it. But the two mountains have been forgotten completely, like the trails that once led there.

"Too far north for my experience," he says.

He asks about my plans, and my hesitation must be apparent. He asks me to identify a tree and I do. Then he straightens. "See? You don't understand the tree by recognizing it, but by knowing its story. It starts as a seed, broaches the loam as a seedling, becomes a sapling, and finally, one day, it will lie on the forest floor." He points to a dense tangle he's cutting: a thick spruce root that's grown in a sharp right angle.

"Know why it grows like this?" he asks.

The root is bigger than my thigh, twisted strangely within a papery reddish skin.

"Have you ever seen a tree with a trunk that suddenly dips in a U-shape then grows straight?"

"Yeah." I nod. "I loved climbing on trees like that as a kid."

"Think it just grew that way?"

"No, it was pinned by another fallen tree and the sapling just grew up from under it. Years later the fallen tree rots away and the sapling is a big tree with a strange bend in it."

"Exactly. The same happened to this root when it was just a tuber. As it grows it hits a pebble in the hard soil. A tiny pebble. The tuber grows around it, changing direction. Years later, this root that breaks our axes still shows the same right angle that the itty-bitty stone caused it to take."

"The tree doesn't make a choice. It just grows around anything it can't get through," I say.

"Maybe it thinks it's making choices. The point is, after many years, that choice hardens and becomes significant. The choices we make, they're not just now. They grow with each day."

"But what if the rock that turned that root was imaginary?"

"That doesn't happen with trees. Only with humans."

He reaches out a callused and dirty hand to shake mine. "Nice working with you this year."

Just before I reach the clearing of the Lookout's fire tower, an engine revs; through the branches the splattered sides of the Ranger's truck jerk slowly down the fire road, piled with boxes, his dog in the passenger seat. He's helping the Lookout move. I don't want to be seen, I don't want him asking why I'm off my assigned trail. I hope I've not missed her. Just for a second I consider turning back.

The Lookout stops her packing to pour tea. The air above the trees is chilled. The empty room impels me to be direct.

"Why are you up here?" I ask her.

"Know what monks in the Middle Ages said? 'Go where we have gone, and you will know.'"

"So I can't know or you won't tell."

"I wonder, do you think you've finished your quest for the two mysterious mountains?"

"They represented my choice: to continue school or start a career. I made up my mind. It was a good way to look at what was important to me."

"See, that's the power of stories: warriors fight because someone convinces them with a tale. Most people are not motivated by some Valhalla or Elysian Fields anymore, now it's retirement."

"I see you've mellowed."

She laughs. "Stories have always driven us. Stories of buffalo, of wild spaces, of gold. People came because of greed and images of grandeur. The stories were about conquering. That's what made our history." She sweeps her hand across the peaks. "That inspiration rose like a tide and crested there, at Athabasca Pass, at that little pond. And mind you, it was a tide that didn't wash back but splashed up, making those two ice-covered peaks. Then it just vanished."

"But the story remains." I stand looking at her, at the valleys, at my tea.

"Yes! The heights come to us in legends, but our imagination constructs their bases."

"I thought the bases were not in question; it was the heights that we imagined."

"See? That's the problem: stories are not easily simplified. So you must go to the Pass."

I shrug. My decision has been made, my tea is finished. There's only loose ends to tie up now.

"What are your two mountains? What two ideals do you aspire to?" I ask.

She pulls herself backwards onto her lookout chair, looking inward, leaning back. "Truth and Beauty," she says. "Of that, Truth is definitely higher. But be careful, for as you near any summit, the way becomes steep and narrow, as mountains are apt to do, and increasingly difficult."

"Where are you off to?"

"Maybe up north. I'm going to see if I can get posted to a really isolated tower next year. This one is getting too popular," she says.

"Did you see many fires this year?" I ask from the stairs.

"Oh, pooh!" She waves. "There hasn't been a fire here in seventy years."

■ I probably shouldn't have told her that her dream was childish. Maybe if the Interpreter hadn't been telling me about the Ranger, I'd have been more circumspect. We're by the lakeside, skipping stones, rippling the water.

She says the Ranger grew up beside Lake Ontario, always watching the big storm clouds form. He wanted to be a pilot, so he could fly through their columns. But he also wanted more: to be able to walk on them, step up, climb to their tops. When he came west and saw the Rockies, he'd found a range of clouds settled on the prairie floor and he set off to climb them.

I say nothing, not wanting to encourage her talking about him. She asks me about the Pass, about the pool. I'm reticent now, and her insistence makes me realize that once I reach the pool in my telling of the story, she'll leave. I'd rather leave a shred of the story to intrigue her, in case I never see her again. I tell her the story is childish.

"Childish dreams should be our guides," she claims.

I'm annoyed by this thinking that dreams never evolve. I'm trying to evolve.

She pushes. "It is like what you told me Coleman said: that he wanted to sneak up and catch Nature unaware, in her act of creation. And then see what he believed could be."

I say, "The Punch Bowl is irrelevant. The lake the Ranger named after you is not yours. You've just placed a map on top of the water; you haven't changed anything."

She grows cold. I feel it right away.

"Those mountains you looked for? They were just two of many. Why did you single them out?"

She walks quietly up the trail to the cookhouse. Only then do I realize how much the dream of an enchanted pool means to her. Now that I'm preparing to return to university, I sense myself reverting to the attitudes I had in the spring.

■ "Everything that deceives may be said to enchant."

The Lion says this as if he's quoting someone. He looks out at the weather, pining for summer. The autumn is as sudden as summer was reluctant. On our last day of trails it rains a cold mist; the mountains sleep late, with their heads in white pillows. A few dirty clouds pass forlorn, hinting that this is not a rogue system but the start of winter. There is sadness in the chill, in the dying leaves of aspen and alder, even in the waning of the moon.

I try to attend to the trail, but my thoughts race ahead. I'm struggling with saying goodbye to terrain that is going nowhere, that's not bothered by fleeting passages. I return tools, write the last trail report, walk out feeling light and free and abandoned and lost.

The compound is deserted, the cookhouse empty and swept, the windows dark without curtains. Through the trees the Ranger's truck pulls out of the parking lot, pauses, then growls off, bright with duffel bags. My boots echo on the thin plywood floor of the cabin. The door swings lightly, reverberating in hollow construction. I'm thinking about the Maps of Love and how much they'd be worth right now. There's a folded paper under my door.

> *Mon Cher Coureur de Bois*
> *Thank you for making my fingers see and keeping my ears warm. Endings are just beginnings of something else, no? We do not have to know our destiny for it to happen. I do not know mine, but my fate is . . . a car outside that is leaving now! I'll look for you . . .*

■ There's always a pause before change. A deep breath before focusing. I sit in the grad lounge watching a kettle, waiting for it to boil.

"It's easy to be a holy man on top of a mountain," the Lion says on the phone, his voice calm, a world away. I sit on a worn vinyl couch under the fluorescents, the arrow-slit windows of the earth sciences building looking out at dark winter clouds, not a breath of wind or fluctuation in temperature. I feel dizzy occasionally.

"This place is an age-incubator," I say, irritated by clothes that aren't functional. I'm wearing slacks: presentation day. "I'm getting fat and comfortable."

"Least you don't have a tie." At the visitor centre, he walks through exhibits to stay awake.

"I'll do anything to stay here in the mountains," he had said, but his convictions were wavering. "I had no idea this would be so slow. I've had two visitors this week. Both were lost."

"Here it's fast-paced," I say. "But I don't know what's getting done. Everyone just shuffles things around."

"How is Cowtown? Our old haunts?"

I feel like an anthropologist. I'm amazed at how many things there are to do each day. He misunderstands.

"No, I mean *little* things," I say. "Like needing a car to get to class, and needing work to afford the car. Now I'm trapped in a job, because of payments for things I just need for the job. When did this arrangement that is a city, designed to bring together people, get so out of hand that it's no longer efficient?"

"How're the other advisers, the other students?"

"Okay, I guess. They live here, and some have never been to the park, or left the city."

"Because the city's too efficient." He laughs.

"Or too hard to get out of. Maybe they're sedated by routine. They seem vaguely surprised to find themselves here and looking at the obvious road ahead."

"Harsh."

"Not really; there's too much to do to conduct a life here. Everyone meets and talks about how much there is to do and see, but they're always talking about the future."

"That's forward-thinking."

"But it makes time go so fast."

"Time flies when you're not watching it."

"This kettle is broken," says a student, shaking it. "It's always cutting out before it boils."

I still remember chemistry lessons, like watching a storm build over a lake, over the peaks. As the water gathers energy, it increases in temperature, until, just before it starts to vaporize, it finds a plateau. The water quiets, gathering the last push before a phase change. It's called the Heat of Vaporization. The Heat of Change. Then the kettle boils.

"There's always a calm before the storm," says the Lion. "Between caterpillar and butterfly. Just be careful what you're turning into." There is absolutely no sound behind him.

"Sounds like we both need to get out on something big."

"I'm turning soft. Maybe something glaciated?"

"Columbia?" Even as I say it, it feels wrong.

"That's a savage amusement in the winter."

I think of his accident on the ice last year, of Collie turning back because the ice was too big to cross. Wrong direction. Arthur Coleman followed the old maps and found disappointment. Norman Collie followed Coleman and gave up. James Outram followed Collie and faded away. I know now I can't follow any of them.

"Okay," the Lion says. "Call me when you decide. Don't leave it until you have holidays."

I hang up and the silence crushes. I thought I could hold on to the magic of Hooker and Brown by nurturing it, but now I realize that not pursuing a mystery will kill the inspiration just as fast as solving it. I want to do something before the feeling is gone for good.

I pour my tea, walk slowly to my office. Even in the university, there seems to be no space for big ideas: always another assignment. But Hooker and Brown is not a weekend trip. Could I go and come back without losing the dream that's motivating me and that I may need to rely on to get through the long studies ahead? By going, I'd have to admit that I've headed down the wrong path with academia, and yet chasing mystery is not a career. Hooker and Brown is a story, not something that can be broken down into pieces and scrutinized in order to be understood. Collie tried that, it didn't work. The mystery is more dangerous than that. I have to make a choice: focus on my studies in the city and build a future or commit to the mountains' mystery and accept wherever that leads.

At present, I think, there isn't room for both.

▪ Can I leave the mountains behind? Without the Interpreter to talk to, I tell myself stories, trying to wrap up the tale.

▴ Arthur Coleman watches the peaks on the long ride down the valley. Especially the big one with the glacier that spreads like an angel's wings: the one marking the meeting of the waters. La Montagne de la Grande Traverse. He wonders why he passed it so carelessly. It is a goal in its own right. At night the mountains become grim judges. The last day in the valley they're gone. He awakes expecting to say goodbye, but he hears the muffled echo of horses and pots as he limps out to the fogs of autumn that confine his party in the valley's depths. He feels like a lover late to a train station expecting one last glimpse of his beloved. But the mountains turn away, like a note handed to him at a train platform: Forget us.

Moving back in time, to the French-Canadian men paddling the canoes.

The voyageurs fan out over the river huge with the spring runoff. One at a time, to a man, they turn red-rimmed eyes back to look for a long pause. Then the canoes rush away, and quickly the mountains, the ones they spent four months working upstream to win, are gone.

And the great David Thompson, how did he feel, leaving his great quest?

David Thompson has forgotten how big Lake Superior is, and how bad the cluster flies, biting bloody divots behind ears. He sets down at water's edge, near the brigade in their rotting skins, grateful for the breeze off the lake. It looks like a sea. Behind them is the Grand Portage, the last week of carrying canoes and bundles across swampy ground. Now they are back in known territory. But he's forgotten the strip along the horizon that is neither air nor water but the domain of the reflected sun. He's forgotten how long it takes to travel through Lake of the Woods, where horizons are as short as the next hill. And the Shield forests, where the rock is bare like scraped knuckles. He wonders how much else he's forgotten and checks the bundles that contain his journals. Mildew would spell disaster. Will he forget the mountains? They rise up to him then, out of the transparent lake, white towers of shining crystal. Squinting into the distance, he wants to remember each of their faces, like a line of children on a dock.

On my daily run, I pass through throngs of young students in the university malls. I have little in common with them now. I haven't seen the girl with green eyes whom the Lion and I agreed to ignore. What I see instead are women who are beautiful but who seem too quick to joy, too studied in irreverence. In the classes there are so many students who could distract me.

I find it hard to believe now that Helen of Troy could have caused such problems. Lovely, sure, but far from the only one. The Greeks couldn't have been the first to think of the concept of superlative beauty. Maybe she was more valued because she was stolen.

I run down the hill from the campus to the river, then to the tracks. This time I stop between the rails and think about all the people who have passed over them in the last century and the places from which they came.

Looking east, I remember the Interpreter thought the rails lead her home.

I imagine an old locomotive, a heavy iron horse, like the dense head of a pin sliding down the rails, surging. Picking up steam. Pushing the wind aside, screeching on the corners that lead from foothills to prairie, careening in a staccato clatter past geometric farms.

What are they thinking, all those people who watch the train pass by? They have their tangle of friends and family and hopes and deceits, invisible webs strung across the rails. Watching the train from a field, at a crossroads with a clanging bell, in a noisy café. They have crossed these tracks a hundred times as they trace their lives, back and forth like a tangled ball of yarn. Then a train thunders through, flickering with windows on other lives, stopping conversation in the cacophony of steel, forcing them to look up, perhaps to wonder at the stories rushing by. The engine is a needle that darts through those balls of yarn, intersecting different strands, touching fragments, scents, parts of a sentence.

The train speeds east into the hills of Manitoba and the forests of Ontario, its headlights splattered with life's moments. It races under a moon seen by everyone. It passes the Great Lakes bright as ice in the night, through the metropolis, where the tracks are almost hidden and buried by the thrusts of concrete, past the university grounds where late-night thoughts snag on the passing piston shafts, past the capital, sleeping.

Until it slows, sweating with energy, pulsing up to a stone platform under broad-leaved maple, beside a fleuve, a great river, in a small Québec town where churches thrust twin spires of tin, flashing in the dawn. Where I imagine stepping down, feeling the cool morning, bags hunched under my eyes, looking for her.

The tracks under my feet in Calgary dart to Québec. I don't know where she is, if she's even back east. They also stretch to the mountains. A fluid sluice of steel. I'm caught by obligations, distracted by desires. The rails vanish to a point at either end. It's a false choice, this decision between school and work. Just as it's a false choice to follow the tracks east or west. There is another way, one that is not signposted.

North.

I call the Lion. I hear him smile on the other end.

▲ ▲

The Height of Land

"People are motivated by fear, hope, and curiosity," says the Lion. "This is definitely fear," I say. The dashboard reads minus thirty-two degrees Celsius. We're up in Jasper National Park. Far from home. "All your philosophers lived in warm places, where they could sit and talk. How does temperature change our thinking?"

"Is it hope making you go without maps?" he asks. "Or curiosity? Or fear that the maps are right and you won't find anything?"

The car is finally warm. It's like the start of the summer, seeing the Lion again after an absence, feeling out of touch with the mountains. We're parked at a pullout where the Whirlpool River drains Athabasca Pass into the northbound Athabasca River. At this meeting of the waters. Thompson had turned up to follow the lesser flow, deeper into the mountains.

"I want to go see without being told. With only David Thompson's *Journal*, when the territory was unknown to all."

The Jack pines are stiff, tenacious barbs in a harsh land. I read from Thompson's journal.

> *Jan**ry* *8**th**, 1811 A fine day. Very cold and blustery. Wind NNE. Course to SW up the main defile. The men grumble about the loads. But they are the hardiest ten of a hundred men I could find. The mountain to*

the North is of Awesome aspect, snow covered in ice,
like a flowing angel.

The back window is already blurry with rime. "When Hooker and Brown got mapped," I say, "something about them was lost. That's what makes the story appealing. It's like studying something but having the magic disappear in all the details."

"They're just mountains," he says, but he's pulling on his chin.

"Our science is about defining things, limiting them. But if those mountains are possible, it makes everything else so."

"It's human compulsion to define and solve. You'll be hungry for more."

Dawn crests the eastern ridges, shines through the ice fog over the Athabasca. The forest is frozen, the river broken with sugar-cakes of ice. Holes steam where the water moves too fast.

"I'm not sure how I'll feel. I have to go to know. I do want to see what they inspire."

"Pretty thin excuse. You know there's nothing there," he says.

"There's Collie in 1898, headed north to find mountains Coleman dispelled *five* years earlier."

"Pretty thin."

"Collie went again in 1900, even though he'd decided that Hooker and Brown were frauds."

"Going for a high peak is justification."

"But he didn't make it. So he went north a *third* time in 1902, looking for Hooker and Brown."

"They stopped once they mapped the area, realized the truth."

"Exactly, remove the map, resume the motivation."

"At least the service knows where we are." He mentions the Ranger.

I feel a weight, a stab of heat. "I didn't know you were friends."

"A courtesy call. I need the contacts, I might apply next year. Seems this is the first weather-window of the winter—no one's been able to get far into the backcountry for a month or more."

The forestry road follows the river upstream, the trees impassable with deadfall. "At least we have a road. Our packs are going to be first-degree murder." He thumbs the door handle. "Only my sense of touch says it's cold. The sensory world is an illusion."

I try pinning the Lion's motivations to different explorers, giving hope to Coleman, curiosity to Collie, and fear to Outram, but none seems to fit so simply.

I open the door and the cold stings so hard I forget philosophy.

■ We've driven a two-kilometre baseline on a stretch of road perpendicular to the valley, at each end making bearings on the prominent peaks. I can take a bearing on a peak from both end points to make a triangle. With half-forgotten trigonometry, I find distance and use the converging lines as a reference for the next, farther peak. I extend the connection, like radio waves bouncing from repeater to repeater, moving our understanding up the valley on stilts. Meanwhile our own legs alternate through drifts and barren ground.

"That tells us where we are, but it won't tell you the heights," reminds the Lion.

The methods to determine altitude rely on the same principles as those for lateral distance—establish sea level, then walk the measurements to the next point of reference, fix it, move deeper or higher. It's laborious.

The car behind us is already a cold lump. The river steams, the forest is a solid barrier. Our packs freeze and start creaking. We're alone in the park, not even Rangers are patrolling. Unable to ski the river, and reluctant to thrash through forest when a broad road splits through it, we hike the road, rocks popping under our boots.

Midmorning finds me turning a circle, fixing peaks. The Lion, to keep warm, continues. I get cold so fast I can barely turn the compass dial. I hunker down in my jacket. I feel disoriented, my balance off. This time, when I look away from a peak, the hard face of a voyageur stares back from the tree depths.

I lurch, one foot slipping, and he's gone. I fan my breath away and wipe crystals from my toque, but the forest is empty. I linger on the image of a heavy beard, dangling, icy tubers, old leather around eyes that burn at me with feral distrust, a fur hood that seems to grow from his beard. Like DuNord, the beater of dogs. This is voyageur territory. We're rounding Mount Edith Cavell, La Montagne de la Grande Traverse. Their mountain, their landmark.

The voyageurs had always been in books. I'd conjured them, but they remained a fairy tale. Now I'm travelling their path, touching the same trees. My map is merging with theirs.

We turn onto an old logging road, start up the main valley of the Whirlpool River, heading southwest toward the Pass. The road has only a skiff of snow in most parts, not enough to ski. We hike and post-hole through the odd drift. My feet tire quickly in the ski boots. Fifteen kilometres later, when we finally come to a point where we can see the Whirlpool River, we hike to the bank and kick on our skis.

"'Bout time," the Lion declares, hoisting his pack. "These boots were made for skiing."

The river at this part is flat as a white painted path through the wild marsh grass and trees.

"This is so easy," says the Lion on the river. He's elated by the motion of skiing, the reduced weight of the packs, the route laid out. I laugh, remember the tangle of icy streams on our path to Forbes. Now we move straight over those obstacles. The day warms quickly, and we're down to our under layers from the heat we generate.

"We can just glide right up to the Pass on this river. It's like a sidewalk. Those voyageurs weren't as dumb as I thought, always travelling in the winter."

The winter days are short and our horizons high. The sun arches down to the stone within an hour and we start to look for camp. We ski into a small cirque formed by a cataract in the river. My legs ache climbing through the dark pines in the unconsolidated snow. From the top the river stretches away, branching off in a widening valley.

"No shelter," I say.

The Lion points. "Someone's been here. Ski tracks. Maybe a day old."

The sun doesn't set so much as fade. It's hard to discern the cut. I eye the double tracks, like a railway into the distance, and think of Coleman, always in front of the group, searching. There's no sign of a tent in the valley ahead. Around us are the same trees that Thompson had brushed past. We retrace our steps into the grotto, dig out a platform for the tent. On a break I read from Thompson's journal.

> *Jan^{ry} 9th 1811 A fine day. Course SSW crossing many small streams and cutting Pts. of alder that is impossible for the sleds. There is much talk among the men that this defile is the haunt of the Mammoth, and though they agree that such an Animal would leave great tracks and signs. Neither can they point these out to me, nor Nothing can shake them of their belief. When men walk into Strange lands, fear gathers with them.*

The snow is sugar and unpackable, like loose sand. I stomp while the Lion hacks at the river ice to draw water. In my cloud of breath I see the eyes again, steely green, steady. Eyes perfectly motionless, a mottled leather hood that doesn't flutter, the five-foot musket barrel protruding from his shoulder. Baptiste the hunter. Behind him the brown and white of curled dogs, the furs and stained leather of the brigade, huddled, sleeping, mingled among the pines and trembling aspens.

Even as I look to the Lion and back I know the figures will be gone. I search the trees for their navigator. Koo-koo-sint, the stargazer. But there is no sign of David Thompson. The green eyes linger a moment longer, fading in the pines.

"Been in the city too long," I say when the Lion questions my stare. I shiver. Can hypothermia become chronic, a living state?

I take a break, standing arms akimbo—the collapsible shovels not tall enough to lean on.

"Forgot how much daylight we need in winter just to prepare to sleep."

"Free your mind and your hands will follow," he says.

That notion troubles me. My mind is feeling a bit too free. Even now, I can hear Norman Collie arriving in 1902 for the most significant season the Rockies had yet seen.

"Those tents look fine," calls Professor Collie. "See if you can't get a draft moving through. Those squalls this morning have soaked everything."

"Say, is this near where you camped with Baker four years ago? I overheard, excuse me."

Collie laughs. "Down to the last rock."

I can hear these voices clearly. I know they're in my mind, stories unfinished. But the glimpses of men in the trees are startling. I decide it's just my mind quieting, adapting, shedding noise like a hangover from life in the city. I decide not to say anything to the Lion. He'll worry.

I dig a cooking area and rig up a support for the stove with our skis. The stove's fuel canister base is too cold to touch with bare fingers, even as its top burns. Packs become seats. The roar of the stove reminds me of present time and pushes away the stories like a candle does the dark.

The Lion stirs pasta into boiling water. Around the stove we're enveloped in vapour. The daylight remains only at the height of the empty sky. The air cools quickly.

"Being here is like childhood," he says. "We'd be outside and climbing more than sitting on chairs. I think summers lasted forever when we were kids because we didn't think of time. We just thought of what to play, not what was for dinner."

"Or where to sleep. It was taken care of. Here we have to."

"To the exclusion of distraction. We're so focused on survival, our attention stays present."

As a grad student, I've felt time speed up, to race by, maybe pass me by. I've caught myself trying to justify the studies that keep me in a room, in a chair, wondering what others are doing, whether I'm making the best use of my life.

"Everything is new to a child," I say. "But how can you retain that awe?"

He mulls that for a while. "We grant mystery to an object. It's not inherent in an object."

He stirs in powdered sauce. "Bowl," he orders. "It's feeding time." He keeps talking. He likes reflecting on these ideas. Part of me listens, the other part hunches, watching him pour pasta into my bowl the way primitive hunters might watch blood draining, the division of a heart for the hunters. I'm devouring the food even before I cup the hot bowl inside my jacket.

The Lion proposes we gravitate to mysteries because they give us purpose. Purpose gives meaning. Otherwise, all of life's activities are just reorganization. According to this idea, the farmer reorganizes seeds from bag to earth, reorganizes water from stream to field, plants into bushels, and, finally, bushels for money. Trade is the reorganization of resources. Growth is the reorganization of minerals, water, and air into roots and leaves. The real mystery is the motivation to reorganize.

Spoonfuls of heat pass from bowl to mouth. The stove light blares from chinks in the windscreen. Around us could be anyone, invisible. I tell him his philosophy appears to be circling.

"Your words are organized sounds," he counters. His words bloom from his mouth in clouds.

"Some of those sentences make sense," I say, but I'm thinking *desayuno*.

We stamp in the darkness. I remind him of the wolf attack I witnessed in the summer.

"I didn't do anything. Fell on my butt, actually. But that's my most significant memory," I say.

"The things we do that involve the least reorganizing also have the deepest meaning. You climb a mountain and come back down to the same place, but as a different person. You've accomplished nothing really relevant, but you've changed. Mystery is outside of the usual reorganization, it has a sense of the divine. Survival is motivation for movement, but curiosity is its inspiration."

"And without mystery in our lives?"

"Comfort dulls the skills you gained to achieve comfort. It kills itself."

"But a tree doesn't have that sense about its own growth. It does it because that's its nature. The seed reorganizes minerals and water and air into a solid hardwood, but why?" There's nothing else to do but philosophize when the sun is down so early and it's too cold to sit still.

"Aha!" he says, excited. "Why? Plato called it the question of Causes. What is the Prime Mover, the Formal Cause? To answer that you need to believe in either God, Fate, or Science."

"Hope, fear, and curiosity, huh?"

We boil clean water, fill our bottles, snug them deep in our down-filled sleeping bags. I huddle around the stove, face hot, back freezing. Mercury orbiting the sun. In the silences I hear the voices creeping in:

"Don't worry, boss. We'll have this truck all square in a jiffy," says the Outfitter.

The moon comes up fast, spotlighting bluish light through the trees. We cut off the stove. Silence and cold dart in. Water gurgles under the river ice. We're surrounded by water. I stand, reorganizing nothing. Meaning creeps out like roots. Water in all its forms is a medium: it conducts.

I pull off a glove and touch the snow. My heat bleeds down through the hoary lattice, becomes a message, lancing across the ice and seeping into the river. The message catches the current down to the Athabasca, sweeps out of the mountains and through the cold lakes of the northern woods. The connection hits bottom and arcs through rapids, races along torpid coils that feed the sea. It bounces, out into the gulf, the Great Bay, like a whale song, off the surface tension, off the shore rocks of a lost island, past the beaches of an eddying cove. It's pulled into clouds, passed through as rain, as early morning mist, into a stream that runs into an aquifer, through limestone pores, spurting from a spring into the stillness of a reservoir. It is untouched through slow turbines, past pumps and filtration tanks into pipes, taking this junction and that main, through valves, out a tap. Somewhere out east it gushes into sparkling daylight, into a glass, which the Interpreter might lift to her lips.

The moon sees the other side of all mountains, the valleys and people in them. It watches paths diverge, converge, and move toward the heights of land. No parent ever tells children not to stare at the moon—unlike the sun.

I crawl into the tent, trampling the Lion. He rolls without touching the tent walls.

"I wonder what Thompson would have written when it was this cold?" he says. "The men are mutinying, desperately short of food, minus forty, might have to eat the dogs. A fine day."

I fall asleep thinking of all the water draining from the passes, stories not yet finished.

"Great Caesar's Ghost! That's a sight for sore eyes!" says the Outfitter, pointing across the shingle-flats of the Freshfield drainage to horsemen in single file.

"That's not quite cricket! Why in the blazes do they need so many horses?" mutters Norman Collie as the others stand. "Do they not know how to pack properly?"

The Outfitter recognizes the horses. "It's the good Reverend."

"Already been out four weeks. He aimed to explore the Lyell area," muses Collie. "I'll be curious to see what they've gotten themselves up to."

One of Collie's climbing partners speaks. "Frankly, I'm surprised by this, Norman. Outram has not been jolly open about his intentions. Ever since his secret mission to Assiniboine, it's become his modus operandi. And a distinct lack of partners. What will he gain by joining us?

"Credibility, perhaps? Now, gentlemen, the Reverend must be an able mountaineer, and I look forward to climbing with him. Besides, what better way to keep an eye on the interloper? He's already stolen too many scalps. Let's see that it doesn't happen to us," says Collie, turning now to their own packers. "Help them bring in the horses. It will be an infernal riot if that train scatters. And a pot of tea to welcome our guests to Freshfield camp?"

The others clear baggage and order the boxes to make room for more tents. Collie stands tall, tapping his pipe. The first to ride up is Outram's packer.

"Well, well, what have we here out in nowhere?" says the Packer, "At last some new faces. Let me tell you my group isn't getting any prettier. Professor Collie, a pleasure as always. Well, this mud certainly is pleasant, eh? Did you get our note at the shack?"

"Yes. Do you mean to say that you stayed in that tiny thing all winter?"

"That's a fact, Professor. And a mighty long one it was. We built her from green poplar and our fire kept the roof bloomed in full leaf mosta the time."

They all laugh. "Well, hope you won't mind us storing our provisions there for now?"

"Oh no! We've heard about you storing things," says the Outfitter with a laugh. "Was that a joke, you buried two bottles of whisky near the cabin? What—twenty-two paces to a tree with a blaze, twenty-five to a white stone—I measured that from every tree!"

"Oh, I assure you," says Collie, "they were there. A tree had fallen over the white rock."

"Oh, for Pete's sake!" fumes the Outfitter.

"Long winter, eh?" Collie's eyes move to a well-built man, his riding trousers stained but his moustache trimmed. He seems very fit.

"Professor Collie, I presume." The stranger offers a hand, eyes sparkling.

"Indeed, Reverend. Accept my belated congratulations for Assiniboine. You're our guest at this . . . ah . . . country club." There's laughter, and postures loosen.

"An honour to meet you and your esteemed colleagues. Your reputation precedes. I'm sure we're in for a capital season. Teamed up, what can defeat us?"

"Well then, you've been out from Glacier Lake. Pray tell!"

A chorus of ayes erupts. Outram, overwhelmed, quickly warms to his congregation.

"Well, we made our way north toward the icefields the Professor discovered four years ago. I should like to see such a sight myself, I said. We never made it. Turned before all that, up what we called the Alexandra River. I managed, after an absolutely gruelling twenty-two-hour push, to reach the summit of Columbia."

Collie clears his throat. "Well," he says. "That calls for congratulations." He throws his tea aside. "Bring up the rest of the number-four Scotch, if you would, please. To your success, Reverend."

■ "We must have courage," mutters the Lion to the rip of a zipper. I burrow deeper into my bag.

Past the breath-damp bag opening, there's an immediate wall: yellow and stiff with oil spots of frost. Spindles of white rime hang from invisible hairs. A cavern of delicate construction. The tent shakes heavy like canvas with the Lion's movement. Barbed crystals rim our boot liners. My motivation crouches by my feet, back in the warm darkness. I try to stretch. It's a quiet space, muffled. Then the Lion opens the tent flap to an icy billow. We fumble on boots and layers, walk like tin men. The stove roars.

"Good god, it's cold," he mutters, feeding snow into the brew-pot.

"But clear," I chatter. "At least it's clear. We should make it today if the weather holds. Though right now, the sooner we move, the faster I'm happy."

"Amen. It must be minus forty."

I unpeg the big yellow tent fly and flip it inside out. The trapped breath moisture opens to the forest, quickly freezes, spreads a white sheen across the nylon ripples, like winter over mountains, then contracts, tearing free of the fabric, and stands in a winking hoarfrost that I brush off like dust.

I fold the fly like cardboard. The poles creak in my hands as I pull them apart. The inner tent collapses in a crinkling cape, hollow, the magician inside gone. What flimsy constructions we hide our comfort inside.

After we cut the stove the quiet comes back like a determined set of rules. I read from Thompson's journal to start the day.

Jan^ry 8th 1811, Tuesday Ther +4° A fine day, partly Cloudy & partly Clear, wind SE in the Evening, & Night a Gale. At 7¾ Am set off, Co S40E 4M then we entered a small brook, but still seemingly the main Stream of the Waters we have lately followed up, but they have dwindled away imperceptibly to a mere small Brook—cut a small Point, very bad with Willows &c. Our Co for the rest of the day S22W 5M—mid of Co up another point, but not so bad as the last. Camped at 4¼ Pm—we lost an hour in mending a Sled, other-wise kept on continually. No Animals. Much Ice left in the Mountains & they are ab^t 1M ascender—but not above 2000 ft high, & the highest not exceeding 3000 ft. 9 Pm Ther +22°.

We climb out of the grotto. Above we find the ski tracks again, like train tracks never touching. Coleman used horses. All the climbers came looking in the summer. Only the voyageurs travelled in winter. Nothing moves in the distance. When I step onto the tracks I feel connected to whoever made them. If it's the spirit of Coleman pushing ahead, searching, what would he say if we catch him?

We follow the frozen stream, and as it tumbles over boulders we diverge into the trees, tracking deep into the forest. Around me struggle the silent dog teams of the old brigades, shadowed men in furs, indistinguishable from the dogs save for their posture.

By noon we surface onto a wide gravel flat, the expanse swept free of snow except for patches of ice-covered depth hoar. We ski close to the river's edge, where the snow is caught on the bank. As soon as we're out of the trees, I stop to make compass bearings. Beside me . . .

    The skids clatter on stones, driving the dogs mad. They bite at the tough juniper and tangle themselves. The men walk in a dream, packs heavy now with no ground to distract. They think of the boardwalks of York Factory, of the sidewalks of Montréal.

. . . is the springy juniper smelling musty in the sun. Above the trees in the western distance, a haze is rising slowly behind the peaks.

"Doesn't look like we're in luck," the Lion says, resting on his pack while I draw vectors.

"How's that? These flats are perfect for mapping. We'll make great time."

"We must be a good seven or eight kilometres from the other side of this washout. If there was anything as high as Hooker was reputed to be, we'd be able to see it across such a distance."

I ski over to him, bindings squeaking with the cold. "What would you call that peak at the left, surrounded by the glacier?"

"Glacier Peak? No, there must be a thousand of those. Maybe that's Hooker?"

"How high do you think it is?" As I ask I hear an echo . . .

⬒ "Watch!" James Outram says as he tests a hold. "The only rocks on this pitch are very loose!"

"Three thousand metres?" asks the Lion. "Hard to tell our elevation; you've left us sans topo."

"Do I hear the cry of a goal-oriented climber stripped of his ability to find the biggest peak?"

"Tone down. Three thousand metres above the sea will do. I wouldn't mind that eastern ridge."

In the background of my mind the characters play their drama, unable to pause.

⬒ Collie's rope team shuffles, but there is little room on the ridge. In front of them Outram's rope inches up the almost vertical arête. The rope hangs straight between the men, one of them moving at a time as they straighten and hold, the climbers like human staples. The Swiss calls of "Roche! Roche!" become mundane, but the sounds of shattering rock smacking the ridge keep the team jumpy. They are all experienced, but Outram encourages like a spiritual guide.

"Keep up that chin. Good move. See if you can lever off that small flake outcropping. But test it first, man! One needs exceptional balance to keep from weighting a hold too much. Capital lead. We'll be out of your way in no time."

I decide to ski in silence, let the stories work themselves out.

⬒ "Anybody else wish he'd shut up?" mutters one of the men on the ridge. Collie says nothing.

Their Swiss guide turns. "Herren," he says, indicating they'll begin.

Collie looks up at the pitch and takes a deep breath.

"I believe you should continue on without me," he says. "I'll wait here." The others protest. He waves them down.

"They are three on sixty feet of rope, we are four. You've seen they need thirty feet between them to safely manage this pitch. I'll remind you, gentlemen, that we are very far from a hospital. This peak is a different kettle of fish. There looks to be another difficult step of one hundred and fifty feet yet to be mastered. Remember, we must come back down. We may have no further opportunity for a decision. I will wait here for your return."

"You can't!" his partner protests. "After stealing Assiniboine from Wilcox and Columbia from you, it just isn't right that he should take Forbes as well. I will stay here in your stead. You're right about the rope, but it's I who'll rest."

"Now, mind that your voice carries."

"Blast it! He took all our hard work and our maps just to get the summits himself."

"If we didn't want him here, we shouldn't have published our maps."

"How's everything?" Outram's chirpy voice is clear above. "The pitch is a nice piece of work. You'll need care, and it looks like a good bit more is yet to come."

The partner turns back to face Collie. "This is your prize."

"I've done nothing but earn this incredible view. Go on."

The second rope team starts up the cliff, leaving Professor Collie looking impassively across at Mount Freshfield, which they'd summitted days before. When the second team pulls itself up onto the thin, sloping ridge at the top of the second cliff band, the men gather and loop their ropes and talk about the near-disasters all have experienced with loose holds. Ahead of them one more arête with snow keeps them from the final summit ridge. They are high up on the mountain on a perfect day, with little to stop them from reaching an untrodden summit.

"Now where's Professor Collie? This won't do." Outram sounds offended. "He deserves the summit more than any of us. The lack of rope won't be a problem from here on up, and we seem to have plenty of time." He turns to the guides. "Would you mind running back to bring up the good Professor, please?"

In my mind I see them on the summit of Forbes even though I've never stood there. Maybe that's the story that needs to be told so I can complete my quest. Or maybe all these voices in my head want to tag along for Mount Brown.

▪ The gravel plains are a washout from the remains of the glaciers that filled this valley. A thin streak of an airplane contrail splits the sky. The Lion tells me small planes used to cross the mountains by following the valleys. If they took a wrong turn they would disappear and be discovered years later on the upper slopes of a mountain. He wonders if the valley is haunted.

I know he's joking, but it's an opportunity to admit that I've been seeing afterimages and hearing voices of early explorers. I tell him to watch me for hypothermia. He laughs.

"Ghosts are more prevalent in philosophy than you'd guess. I believe they're around because of some wrong done to them, or done by them. They're trying to tell you something."

"But they're done with Hooker and Brown."

"Maybe not. All these fragments you're telling as stories aren't part of the historical record. They need to be connected to be complete. All those guys were competing for the high point. Maybe they lost sight of the original inspiration. Without mystery, all you have left is competition."

We ski to the diminished skirts of the old glaciers, the afternoon stretching ahead. Within an hour, slow flakes begin to twirl down, as if angels are moulting from the hazy cirrus. We lose the peaks soon after but watch the plaster form on the steep faces.

New snow means avalanche danger. The cornices hang over the dark walls like eyebrows, sagging, weakening from the sun.

"At the mercy of gravity," I say.

The Lion laughs. "You come looking for mysteries and look what you find: gravity. Nobody knows what it is. The most common force and not a single physicist can say what it is."

"Not true, there're formulae, Newton, Einstein . . . "

" . . . That describe the effects. Newton said how it works. Einstein said gravity's just an effect of space curving. But when we dig down, there's nothing there."

"Jeez, it's a force that pulls us to the ground."

Around us, total silence.

"What makes it? No one's ever found it, be it a particle or side-effect. Gravity's emergent. You can't find it in the dirt, but when you have enough, it's there. Like consciousness in brain cells."

I think of the Interpreter. "Like dreams from a map."

"Yes. Like ideas emerging between people. All these things draw us, attract us."

"Like Love," I say.

He looks up toward the narrowing valley at the end of the flats. "Or Strife."

The day is fading. We decide to camp at the far trees, where streams drain from the Pass. The flats are good for moving side by side.

After a while, he says, "There was an order of knights that distrusted any map that purported to show the Holy Grail. They wanted to trust their faith to lead them in their quest."

"I have to get beyond asking if the mountains are real or if they're a Grail and just search for the answer to why they compel us. This isn't religious," I claim.

"Neither was the Grail, especially," he says.

"What were the knights supposed to do when they found the Grail?"

"Have everlasting life."

Is that all that's left? After finding the highest peak, is the only thing left to climb it?

"And then what?" I ask. "Wasn't dying the entrance to Heaven?"

"No one thought too much about that. Go where I have gone and you will know."

I skid to a stop. "Have you been talking to the Lookout?"

He looks startled. Eventually he nods. "Once a week. A little divergence the Ant needn't know about. She asked me what my Hooker and Brown would be, figuratively."

I laugh, surprised. "She ripped me off!"

"Wisdom and Peace," he says, turning to gauge my reaction.

"What else did you talk about?" I ask.

"The *Magnum Opus*. She said that in order to transmute lead to gold, the Philosopher's Stone must be something else entirely. What transmutes an ordinary mountain into an extraordinary one?"

It was on gravel flats like these that Collie and Outram met and, later, gave up the chase. They never made it this close to Hooker and Brown. They got caught up in their competition and lost sight of the mystery. They never found their extraordinary mountain. We're skiing on, going farther than they did. Under the rasp of the snow and squeak of the bindings, I tell myself of their parting, imagining it's August 1902, the season almost done.

   "What should we call him? Or, rather, why don't you take the honours?"

James Outram turns to Norman Collie, smiles as to a member of his congregation.

"I see you've been naming mountains after your guides, Mr. Outram," replies Collie.

"Is it not the way of things?"

"What does the Good Book say?"

Outram tilts his head, raises an eyebrow, pleased. "I believe it is nothing but clear. Genesis. The first book. Our Father does not waste time addressing the matter."

"Obviously of importance to our existence."

"Exactly. Chapter 2, verses 19 and 20. Adam recognizes animals need names. God parades them and Adam bestows their names upon them. Order comes to the Garden."

"That was, if I recall, the same day that Adam was wrought

from clay. The parade of animals shows Adam that he's alone. If I may: 'He found none to pair with himself.'"

"Quite so, and God bade him sleep and woman was created from his rib."

"Busy day, that. You've had a few as long in these hills. Imagine, naming all the beasts and the birds and everything in one afternoon. Is it true that only after the Fall from Grace did Adam name his wife?"

Outram walks on. "I don't follow your lead. But you are a man of science."

Collie smiles sardonically, calling after Outram:

> 'Tis but thy name that is my enemy;
> Thou art thyself, though not a Montague.
> What's Montague? it is nor hand, nor foot,
> Nor arm, nor face, nor any other part
> Belonging to a man. O, be some other name!
> What's in a name? that which we call a rose
> By any other name would smell as sweet.

"Always pleasant to hear the words of the bard in the wilderness," says Outram. "So you think that a name does not change the object. I fancied you scientists more circumspect. In the Holy Land, names were thought to be extremely powerful. In some ways, the name of a person was almost a separate manifestation."

"Is that the reason that in the Hebrew texts—of which I know almost nothing, this is hearsay mind you, I am not an expert as yourself—there seems a reluctance to use the proper name of God?"

"In the book of Luke, the disciples claim to see a man driving out demons in the name of Jesus. By calling a name, you may evoke or summon that entity's power."

"And yet," Collie muses, "Hebrews, as I understand it, do not have a surname which is passed from generation to generation. Instead, they are known as the child of their father. In a sense, they use their fathers' first names as their own last names."

"The sins of the fathers will be carried by their sons."

196

"And so you grant names on mountains. Perhaps you want a more lasting lineage?"

■ The Reverend James Outram smiles and shakes Norman Collie's hand. The two groups move away and wave to each other as they part; Outram goes north, Collie south.

◢ "Back to the Alexandra River," calls Outram to his Swiss guide on the horse ahead as soon as he is out of earshot of Collie's party. The Packer rides up smartly.

"All horses are in fine form and well fed, sir. We have enough provisions for four more weeks, provided that we hunt some for the larder."

"Splendid. Let's see if we can't get back to Alexandra camp in record time."

"Are you going to make for Columbia again, sir?"

"We'll try our luck on Mount Bryce this time."

"I'm wondering if a man of faith such as yourself believes in luck," the Packer says.

"A figure of speech, to be sure. I believe that we are all provided for."

"You certainly seem to be." They ford the braided glacial runoff that leads to Howse Pass. "How will you reconcile the staid life of a preacher with the fame these hills have brought you?"

Outram looks over as if deciding a punishment to quote, but then he smiles under his heavy moustache. "True, England and the rigid life of a vicar may never seem the same again. There's no question that my life is different. But you can never cross the same stream twice; you and the stream are both different at the next meeting. But what you must understand is that I have never left the church. I am attending church even as we speak."

Outram smiles and waves out at the mountains. "God is our monarch and men do as He commands. He has given us dominion over all and we worship His glory. In England that is an easy thing to notice; the clergy is a respected career and the King represents the monarchy that brings order under God. And the cathedrals! Ah, but you of so few of the outfitters have been there and seen them: they are perfect monuments, well suited to bring the awe of God's majesty. *Omni Tenebrosum Pro Magnifico.*"

The Packer rides silently, wishing now he hadn't asked.

Outram continues. "But here in the Dominion of Canada, district of Alberta, your monarch is half a world away. Your churches are shacks, serviceable, but nowhere close to grand. The clergy in this frontier is only respected by gentlemen tourists, and more so by the Stoney Indians than by the residents of Banff, who are commanded by their own savage impulses."

The Packer, who appreciates the lack of authority and societal structure, grins, remembering his own reasons for moving to Banff.

Outram barely notices in his effort to press his point. "But out here, among these mountains, we can walk amid the works of the Creator, unblemished by man's enterprise. These peaks are the monarchs of Canada, these cathedrals of dihedrals are His church. This is where we worship. And if you have ever believed that there is an expression of the artist within His masterpiece, then you will understand that these mountains reveal God, and stand in for power, grace, majesty, and dominion."

"Sounds like you have a fine sermon there, sir, for when you return to England," the Packer says and rides ahead, ostensibly to check on the horses, but vowing not to ask careless questions and to be discrete with the whisky.

Outram rides, already descending his life's map, his Map of Ambition, in which there is a cluster of peaks, surrounded by white space. Hooker and Brown are not among them, discarded.

■ Norman Collie smiles and shakes James Outram's hand. The two groups move away and wave to each other as they part; Collie goes south, Outram north.

"Where do you reckon they're to?" asks a partner when Outram is out of earshot.

"Bryce, I imagine," replies Collie, walking back to their horses.

"I still can't believe Outram stole Columbia. You sure seem to take a knock on the shoulder without flinching. But I know you better than that. You came back this year for that peak you saw from Freshfield and that you saw from Athabasca. That must smart."

"True enough. But there are other summits. We'll go now and try our luck on Howse Peak, and then," he says with a shrug, "who knows? There are always mysteries to solve."

And so Collie rides, traversing one high point on his life's map, the Map of his Ordering, where there are many fine peaks, neatly laid out, with no more blank spots to be found.

I feel Collie and Outram walking away. Only Coleman is left, ahead on the snow.

At the border of the trees we find a bright tent dug in behind the drifts. I yell ahead to prevent shocking the inhabitants with our sudden arrival, and the Ranger piles out wearing a huge down jacket and a grin. Just for one irrational second I think it's the Fire Lookout and consider turning. We ski up and shake hands. Moments later the Interpreter appears.

"I have moved here to Jasper National Park . I have just started," she says.

A glacier descends beside us, washing us with cold drafts. It grows from the Divide, touching down in an agony of split crevasses, like a giant wrinkled hand, fingers dropped into a lake of their own ice blood. I can't believe they're here, that we're clustered together so far from the summer and the park. But the Lion told the Ranger we were coming. This was the only weather window since the snows had come and had consolidated enough for travelling on.

The Ranger talks to the Lion about how bad the weather's been, how he had to take this opportunity. They've been camped a day, exploring the glacier, taking it easy. The Interpreter tells me she asked the Ranger to help her find the Pass, that she didn't know I'd be here. She's happy. She tells me that this is the last park that she'll move to; she's crossed the country and there's nothing higher than this.

The Ranger is in his element, and I imagine him like Outram, coaching and leading without being asked. I resent the possibility of him taking over the trip and slip off to do the chores. I need to be alone for a few minutes.

The stream from the Pass pours through a narrow chasm and out into a small lake. I kneel at the gravel and chip a hole in the ice. The water's so cold it feels thick. There's an aching grip on my fingers, like someone trying to hold on to me against the current. Something catches my eye above the chasm. At first I think it's the Interpreter, but then I see it's a woman, distraught, in a gown of white. She vanishes.

Before I've filled the bottles, the other three crunch over on the gravel. The Ranger is telling them about a suicide during the fur trade. A woman, Margaret Harriott, crossing with the brigade to her husband out east, driven mad thinking of never seeing her family on the west coast again, wandered off in a stormy night, her footprints leading to the edge of the ravine above.

We all shiver, but I'm doubly alarmed: seeing visions of stories I don't even know. At my feet the water flows on greased stones. By the time it crosses the plains and empties into the sea, it forgets all this.

■ I shake bags of powdered sauce. There's not much else to look at—snow falls heavily, blotting the trees, filling the spaces between us. At least the clouds hold the warmth so it's not bitter. The others are in their tent.

"Butter and herb or sour cream and chives?" I ask.

The Lion looks up from the tent poles and slowly rises, facing a test. "What's the difference?"

I throw one in the cook pile. Over dinner he tries to guess which one I used.

"Simple choices out here," I remind him.

"False choices. Like the Lookout asking which peak is higher. I assume that came from you."

"Yeah, she doesn't think they exist. Not that it should change the fact we're here."

"Well, there's two types of peaks. The ones you search for aren't possible, for instance."

"Oh. Plato again? We're looking for those mountains because we think them ideal," I say. "That is, if I'm allowed to argue with Plato and Mount Olympus, domain of gods."

He's delighted and doesn't hesitate. "There's the idea of a mountain, and then there's the actual mountains. Mountains come in all shapes and sizes, but we still recognize them because they all match the pattern, the 'form' of a mountain. Just as a cookie cutter is perfect, but none of the cookies it makes is exactly the same. Children draw this ideal mountain. Ones that come close in shape, like Assiniboine or Fujiyama, are revered. However, the ideal can't be found in the wild because it only exists in our minds."

I scrape my bowl. "But where did that ideal come from? Isn't it just what we imagine after seeing a lot of imperfect mountains and then constructing one from their perfect parts?"

The Ranger's voice comes muffled from his tent. "Amen. There's no mould. The 'idea' is in the thing. Don't confuse imagination with reality. G'night."

I hear the sound of sleeping bags, see shapes behind a headlamp. I don't want to imagine the interior, so I shove my hands deep in my pockets.

The Lion notices my face, looks back at the tent. "What's your twenty, Rumi?" he says quietly. I'm silent. He starts to speak, stops, tries again.

"So this is what you saw," he says, stunned. "At the university. That green-eyed girl. This is what you saw. Standing outside my car. Listen, man. Nothing happened."

My hands are suddenly so cold I may throw up.

"I kept my side of the bargain," he insists. "You might think I didn't after she got out of the car. But she was actually after you. She cornered me. She said you had asked her a question and she wanted me to pass on her answer. That's what she was doing. I didn't tell you because we had made that deal. She wanted me to tell you the answer was Elysium. What did you ask her?"

Relief washes down like a glacier wind. I realize she never meant anything to me; it was the Lion's friendship I sought. "I compared her to mica. It's this thing I do. I asked her where we could meet. This was before our agreement," I say. Elysium? A place only for the brave? She was so unresponsive that night. Elysium is a stone transformed by lightning. Perhaps she was telling me to be brave. It doesn't matter anymore. Now I can put this memory behind me. I'll leave this valley a lot lighter.

The Lion whispers. "Let's get up early and get going. I want to get there first."

I'd like to ski with the Interpreter. But then I imagine the Ranger, moving fast and efficient, teaching me tricks, but with the unspoken disapproval, the judgment. Like a battery, a zinc-carbon cell produces reliable power, but eventually leaks poison. I agree with the Lion.

■ I've no idea if the trail through the trees is difficult during the hiking season or if there even is one. With the undergrowth buried under the snow, we travel through a wide-open cathedral, the ground like clean marble, the trees spaced like columns.

We spread out as we pass underneath a looming mountain

that hangs cornices like buntings. They bulge with weight and compressed snow. If they break, they'll drop like bombs, exploding on the face, knocking down trees. I feel alone. In the trees I expected to imagine the traders, weaving dogs, pushing sleds. Instead, a wicked bend of antlers, muffled in reddish winter fur, catches my attention. My skis stick.

An elk stag stands in the trees, watching me with expressionless eyes. Down one massive shoulder ropy grey scars scissor. A wolf, perhaps, trying to pull the elk down even as he surged free. The elk turns, disappears among the trees, in the direction of the Pass.

We turn into snow-filled glades, oblong meadows, crossing one after the other, pushing through tree bands. We follow the steep depression of the stream that comes from the pass. A V-shaped rent in the snow. At the widest space, as the valley starts a lumbering turn to the south and the Pass seems obvious, we stop for a cold snack.

"I think all of those guys expected perfect mountains," I say.

"Maybe that's what compelled them."

"None more so than Coleman. But Outram is the one that intrigues me on this because he didn't seem to care at all about Hooker and Brown. I mean, he knew of them. But I think he didn't try because no one had a map or a quick way to them," I say.

"He wasn't stupid. He wasn't about to waste a season on fantasy."

"So you think he was motivated by a need for success?" I ask.

"He was motivated by fear. That he, the instrument of God, might not overcome. But he wasn't anything but pragmatic when he considered his attempts at the big peaks," the Lion argues.

"So the man of God went for the guaranteed accomplishment, and not the mystery. I wonder how faithful he really was. He stopped looking after their joint summit of Forbes."

"Outram had already claimed Columbia. From there he knew he had the highest."

"But he couldn't see Robson, which *is* the highest. So big peaks were still to be found."

"They obviously saw enough from Forbes." Something finally made their dream seem childish.

It's early in the afternoon; the snow is getting soft and sticks to our climbing skins, causing us to step down sideways when we need to cross the creek. A rocky crest rises to our left and runs south in an unbroken wall. To our right, open avalanche slopes with sparse trees lead to a long open col where a high summit stands. Its ridge is overhung with a large cornice whose upper crust sparkles in the bright day and runs the length of the mountain's northern aspect. It threatens any approach up the vertical face. The Lion stops beside me.

"Mount Brown?" he asks softly. "It's higher than I expected."

We look at the mountain that Coleman decided had to be Brown, even though it looked nothing like what Brown was supposed to. Could there be another? Still unfound?

"It's rounded and squat. No kind of pyramid."

"And that must be the Pass."

The Lion points through the trees at the shallow U that forms between the rock crest and the snow-piled summit. Apart from a rocky buttress that steps up to Brown's sloping ridge, the pass is a natural extension of the valley we're skiing up.

"It's not even much of a col," the Lion says. "It's probably not fifty metres higher than we are."

"When Thompson talked of the height of land, I always imagined a tiny lake slung between two steep peaks, with waterfalls pouring from either side down though the clouds."

The Lion nods. "Let's get up there before the snow starts to collapse under us. You're sleeping on the edge of the Punch Bowl tonight, my friend."

We break trail slowly toward the broad cup of the pass. The snow warms fast under the overcast. As I slide forward, I weight the lead ski, packing the upper layers to hold me. We lose our speed as the snow loses its strength, and the Pass inches toward us. Now that we're so close, I want to charge ahead, but I'm already sinking, even with wide skis.

At the final rise we spread out, breaching the crest together and looking down at a small snow bowl with a flat bottom, indicating frozen water—a tarn, perfectly round.

"God, it's tiny!" says the Lion.

"It really looks like a Punch Bowl."

"I can't believe something so small was as famous as the top of an entire continent!"

"You sound like Coleman."

"A twisted knee ain't bad if there's no decent mountain to climb, Professor," says the Outfitter.

Coleman swears. "A twisted knee, no peaks, another summer, and packing a bloody raft to boot. I feel like the peaks asked us to get dressed for the big event and, like fools misunderstanding the invitation, we show up wearing a disguise to a dinner party."

"Well, aren't you surprised?"

The bowl seems perfect in its roundness, the Pass too sublime in its simplicity. Around us the snow is too pristine, the sky high, the peaks emerging distinct and shining.

"It's unreal, like reality outshines my imagination, I can't conjure what I expected."

"You certainly don't sound like Coleman."

"No. But I knew I wouldn't see giants. Instead, this place was played down so much that I expected smaller mountains, or even holes in the ground. But these are spectacular!"

"Let's go." Coleman limps over for help onto his horse. He knows it's at least a month to get back to his brother's homestead in Morley. The bitter taste of silty glacial water that flows down into the pass and out the Whirlpool is caught in his mouth.

"Come now," says his brother. "We've learnt the truth of the masquerade. It was the mountains wearing it and not us. There's some comfort in being the revealer of truth."

"Just think, fifty years after this place was forgotten, Coleman came and stood here. Not even Collie saw this. And Coleman stood here more than a hundred years ago."

I nod. "Gives us a sense of place in time, no? I just keep imagining the annual fur brigade struggling up here with heavy sleds. Stopping to come together and perhaps plead tradition to bring forth the whisky from any gentleman accompanying them, and raise a toast to a committee of their company way back in England."

"A group of men that they had never, nor would ever, meet."

"I think any excuse for a drink after four months was worth making."

"True, or for that matter, a short trip. Break it out while the snow's soft," the Lion demands.

I pull a small silver flask from my pack and unscrew the top. The single malt tastes foreign and improper as I sip the burning oil and raise the flask in turn to the Pass. Certain traditions are meant to defy the place in which they're held; the act of drinking distillate that doesn't occur naturally thus becomes a validation of human life.

We sit on our packs and watch the sun move slowly, with nothing to challenge it, burning my face and searing the snow. I feel the radiation blasting down, almost visible. There's no sound but the maddening tinkle of invisible water under the snowpack. Nothing moves—wind, trees, animals, or clouds. Only the sun. And with only the sun's crossing to signify change, time seems to slow to the eternal memory of mountains.

▲ It is August 24, 1893, and Arthur Philemon Coleman turns his back to Mount Brown and the Punch Bowl. "How could Douglas be so wrong? The man could see, could he not? How could such a celebrated scientist make so monumental a blunder?"

"The failure was his, not yours," replies his brother.

Coleman mounts, practises turning his horse with his hands and not his legs.

"Such complete failure is rarely seen in my circles. Any effort, even a fraction of what we have offered, should provide some payoff. But to fail absolutely!"

Coleman leads the party down the trail, following home the trickle of doubt in his mind that he is at the correct pass. He descends from the high pass on his Map of Disappointment, on which there are several clouded peaks, rubbed raw from touching.

My thoughts distill down to breathing, then I rouse and shovel the snow into a tent site.

■ We decide to ascend Mount Brown while the weather is good, though it's already late afternoon. It doesn't look like a long climb, and not technical. The snow is soft, but our packs are light. We work our way through the trees and rock bands of the base.

"Do you think Collie was pissed when Outram scooped him on Columbia?" I ask.

"Of course. Collie found Columbia. Apparently, the natives didn't know of it. It was surrounded by glaciers, and they wouldn't set foot on ice. They thought it would absorb their hunting skill."

"Amazing how he never said as much. Too much the gentleman, I guess."

"Maybe not." The Lion shakes his head. "I mean, what could he say that would matter or wouldn't make him sound like a whiner? No one has dibs on a mountain. You can't reserve a first ascent. Telling a climber not to climb is like telling a kid not to try for the cookie jar. Especially a guy like Outram."

"He seems to have beaten Collie to everything."

"I love it. A man of science against a man of religion. Who

will win?" gloats the Lion, then shrugs. "Well, Outram beat everybody. That's why they call it a first ascent."

"It's just that I get the impression Outram was out to bag those peaks for all the wrong reasons. It's like he came for a vacation, did these climbs, and then he's done."

"That's one way of looking at it. Another is that you couldn't just buy those summits. There was hard work and incredible feats of endurance. Besides, Outram never left. He ended up staying here in Alberta. Collie went home to England. Outram was an inspiration, that's why they named a mountain after him."

"They named one after Collie as well."

"No. Collie named Mount Collie. Mount Outram is higher, closer to Columbia and beside Forbes."

"Wisdom and Peace, eh?" I taunt him.

The Lion kicks his up-hill ski around to start a switchback. It's becoming too steep to climb straight up. Our trail makes a scissoring path. We press on.

"I'm wondering what Collie and Outram would have said. Since they're not here, you get to be James Outram and answer for him. What were the two mountains that Outram strove for?"

"Well," the Lion says, "Outram was here in Canada recovering from the stress of overwork, which must be pretty hard as a reverend, and then he ends up overachieving on all these hard climbs. I'd say he was very driven and ambitious. So for his first peak I would say the Highest. He didn't seem to care much for the lesser peaks. As for his other, I will say Faith. I'm not sure why, just that as a reverend, and doing the climbs that he did, I think he would have to believe very deeply in something to do all that he did."

"And there is no mystery in Faith?"

"Perhaps. God moves in mysterious ways."

"So God is mystery, faith in Him is not."

"Nevertheless, at the end of the day, he went for the Highest."

The Lion steps aside; I lead. As I pass he punches me. "Ante up. What about Collie?"

Collie was a professor, a scientist. I'd read that he wanted to be remembered for two things: discovering neon and taking the first X-ray. He did not mention mountains at all, even though in Scotland and France and Canada he earned many first ascents. I had no doubt that he loved the game: the nature and the quest, whether it was a wild range on an unmapped continent or divining the microscopic structure of an element.

I say, "He liked exploring, liked finding the great challenges. He was driven by these searches. I'd guess his first peak would be Curiosity. Sometimes the mapmaking came before the opportunity of a first ascent, so for his second I'd have to say Order."

We stop above the trees. Before us curves a long flat ridge, dropping off precipitously to the right, or northern side, but sweeping over and into snowfields to the south. Already we can look down to the other side of the pass, to the steep descent that leads down toward the Columbia River and, eventually, through a thousand kilometres of mountain valleys, to the Pacific.

Below, the Ranger and Interpreter arrive at the Punch Bowl, following our tracks. The Interpreter skis out to the middle and starts to dance. Will she be able to see what it reflects?

Behind, above the black ridge that led to the pass, is the glacier-covered bulk of Hooker, the mountain we'd seen from the gravel flats, rising more impressively as it breaks free of the perspective of the valley. The reality that they're not seventeen thousand feet high is settling in. Their names don't seem to match them. The ridge is easy now. We ski side by side, slowly gaining altitude.

I'm impressed by David Douglas coming this far off the voyageurs' trail. Back then, there was no radio, no road, no contrails above. Even a twisted ankle would mean death. What had compelled him up here? The slope just didn't seem that special. Had he seen something else?

"I figure we need Hooker and Brown," I say. "So we create

the myth or, more importantly, perpetuate it. Men look up and dream because the mountains are there."

"Nice thought," agrees the Lion. "But try turning it on its head."

I try to judge his humour, but he's serious.

"The Greeks pondered the causes of things. If you had asked them, 'Why are there mountains?' they'd give you four causes. The Material cause is the ground has the potential to become a mountain. The Efficient cause is that mountains are just elevated earth standing up. The Formal cause is the earth raised them up. But the Final cause is where it gets interesting. They'd say the Final cause of mountains is they exist because men need to look up and dream."

"So, mountains exist for men to dream, instead of men dreaming because of mountains? That's opposite to the way we reason," I protest. "Who figured that? Plato?"

His voice is low. "No. His student. Aristotle."

"There seems to be two ways to see everything. Did you know your peaks right away?"

He shakes his head. We start the long ridge, climbing skins biting the wind-packed snow.

"I've always been fascinated by the why. You know, the oldest questions in the world. I could have said God and Truth, or Faith and Reason, or Synchronicity and Karma. Looking at why we are here right now, it occurs to me that I could have answered Cause and Effect, or Questions and Answers. Of those, Questions are by far the most important."

■ Nearing the top, we climb rapidly, staying back from the cornices that can break with a man's weight. It's a simple ski ascent, so the Lion looks forward more to the thrill of the descent than to ascending the peak itself. But I still hold out for the top, for a revelation. I slow as I approach, suspecting a false summit at the last curve, a higher bulge of snow and scattered rock. Then we're there, a rounded knob barely significant. Below, the tiny Punch Bowl, like a drop of shadow on the pressed spread of snow. The Ranger and Interpreter are setting up their tent. Hooker rises magnificent, the remains of its glaciers hanging amputated over the far side of the pass, its navy blue rock streaked with ice smears.

The weather has cleared, but it's bitter at the summit. To the west, in British Columbia, mountains fall away in a desolation of sharp snow peaks. To the northwest is the bulky fin of Mount Robson, but it seems slightly distorted, as if seen through water. Are the altitude and cold, thin air affecting me?

Why hadn't Douglas seen that? What could have been in the way?

I bundle up and sit, enjoying the end of the exertion and appreciating the brief time I'll have at the summit. The Lion digs in his pockets for food, squats on his skis, looks around.

"There's nothing," he says. "You can't see a single sign of civilization. We could be two hundred years ago. We could be Coleman."

"Coleman didn't see this."

"What inspired him, do you think?"

The two manifestations of his desire were made real before him in a way that many people never get. These peaks must have been so clear in his expectation. What gripped him when he sat in his classroom at the university looking at his maps? What made him spend many summers on difficult travels to find two lost giants, when all along that path lay pristine summits, a lot of which would have been a prize in themselves? Surely, finding and climbing the highest reported mountains in the Americas would solidify a climber's name in the annals. Perhaps Glory was one of his motivations? And yet I think Coleman sought them for the reason all mysteries are pursued: for the Truth, for the knowing.

I stand on the summit of Mount Brown, in the footsteps of Douglas, and cannot take in the view any more than I can remember individual waves in an ocean.

"You look like you did last spring, when the mountain you discovered turned out to be Assiniboine," says the Lion, sipping tea from his Thermos and watching the sky pale.

"The thrill is fading," I say. "If I want to uphold mystery, why do I follow it?"

"But mystery is all around us." He points south to a thin contrail like a golden thread parting the sky. "How do those things fly? It's incredible. If you never get used to a huge tube of metal flying people around the world in a few hours, then you will never be without the wonder of mystery. I bet Thompson would be amazed at how flimsy and warm our tent is."

"Sure. But eventually he would understand the tent, and the airplane, and the telephone, and gradually there would remain an appreciation but not necessarily a mystery."

"But mystery simply jumps to the next unknown. It's not about objects."

"Sure it is. If I don't know what's inside a box, then it has the property of mystery."

"To you, but not to me. I know what's inside the box. The mystery is from you, not the box."

"If there weren't maps in the first place, I wouldn't be here now."

"I always wondered why the great thinkers stayed around and taught normal Joes. Why make a map? But if the teaching is mysterious, like parables, and if they are the key to perpetuating mystery—and therefore motivation and meaning—it totally makes sense. Remember what you imagined Hooker and Brown and the Pass to be the very first time you heard of them, before you saw any photos or maps or read any accounts? Just that first flash of imagination, those first, childishly simple ideas of the mountains—perfect snowy pyramids, glistening with sunlight in rarefied air. That is the true form of these mountains: not their physical manifestation but their metaphysical truth."

We start down. The Lion makes a few sweeping turns, testing the snow. Down the ridge, two figures move up toward us.

We ski down in the fading day, the snow fast, the air frigid, my skin stretched by the cold.

The descent is on crusted névé; the skis speak strange vibrations as they prattle, sending shavings hissing down. To stray too far off our up-track would be to court the steep face and cornices or the open snow field and possible crevasses. Within a minute I'm leaning into a sliding stop, legs shaky after the first descent of the season.

The Lion, below, talks to the Ranger. The Interpreter smiles deep within her scarf. "Salut." I kiss her left cheek, then her right. Her skin is cool and smooth from exposure. Maybe Homer was right about the superlative beauty of Helen.

"I know you could not resist summiting," she says.

And then she's moving past, the Ranger stepping up. I wonder at their relationship. What I say is, "Little late to start?"

He nods. "There's a moon tonight." He has a heavy pack, looks prepared, professional.

Then they ski past, their climbing skins whispering. We watch them for a bit. I can still feel her cheeks, but the voices I hear are echoes from two hundred years before.

> He looks down and sees the others are far down the valley.
>
> David Douglas pulls his snowshoes up. He's speeded his descent through the heavy snow by sitting on them like a sled. There is pain in his knees and he'll lag behind, but behind his dread of being left behind is a quiet awareness of the sublime. This valley, full of new species, is just one in an endless sea of frozen waves. He has seen something that he believes no one else has and the knowledge calms him.
>
> He must be thousands of feet above the Pass. He feels wonder at crossing a pass in a wild land, forever and a day from where he started.

The Interpreter's presence lingers. The pass approaches rapidly. I think about her dream of nomads high in isolated valleys and tents.

On the last hundred metres I consider David Douglas—resourceful, brave, intelligent. A gardener. Born into a structured society rampant with the pollution and materials of the Industrial Revolution, the conviction of supply and demand, the dominance of the oceans. The unfortunate thing about the class system for those born to a low station is that when they reach for the stars, their other wrist is forever shackled to their caste. But Douglas was picked by a man of stature, with the influence to open privileged doors. What didn't Douglas owe his lord at Kew? What did his mentor ask in repayment? Or was Dr. Hooker a scientist who simply appreciated the value of quality instruments?

⌃ Surely a man's life is an uncharted destiny, Douglas thinks.

All his fortune, his travels, his fame for discovering and naming new species as he dared travel where the others of higher birth dared not, he owed to Sir William Hooker.

"I will name these mountains after my guides; after all, they have brought me here," he says aloud to the silence.

On May 2, 1827, he descends from what will prove to be the high mark in his Map of Notoriety, and from the summit of his career.

Douglas might have known that only fame could break the class chains. Only rare men can do that, and only through rare feats. That was his drive, his two peaks: Rare and Famous. Declare the heights, start a legend.

▪ The first stars appear. I'm not the only one to notice.

⌃ "Koo-koo-sint."

"Hmm?" Thompson turns. The Iroquois is looking at him.

"Stargazer. The men are afraid."

I drop a knee to begin my turn and start down the remaining slope. David Thompson hadn't skied. The man who mapped two million square kilometres of the northwest territory before there was a country, who travelled eighty thousand kilometres, did so on foot, snowshoe, horseback, and canoe in his pursuit to find the Great Western River. He travelled not for trade, or personal gain; he died penniless and forgotten. For what did he strive?

⛰ January 11, 1811. Thompson stands at the Pass and knows exactly where he is.

"They have no education," he says, turning back to his calculations, his face ruddy in the firelight. "Fear gathers on them like cloaks and they begin to believe all sorts of whispered things, despite any evidence in support and often plenty to the contrary."

Behind him the bearded face of a voyageur appears, staggering to his feet and pulling his buffalo robe tighter. It is 3 AM, time to start while the snow is hard. He realizes there are stars.

"Mon Dieu!" His face changes to childish wonder. "They are close enough to touch."

He sought the route through the mountains, the fabled Path to the West that narrated his dreams. This goal was the defining peak in his life. He is remembered for the diligence and excellence he brought to his work, his honesty and openness in his affairs with the natives, and the amazing accuracy of his map.

⛰ Thompson writes in his journal:

"Many reflections came on my mind; a new world was in a manner before me, and my object was to be at the Pacific Ocean before the month of August, how were we to find Provisions, and how many Men would remain with me, for they are dispirited, amidst various thoughts I fell asleep on my bed of Snow."

Thompson turns back to help clean the ice off the sled skids and check the equipment and dogs. He doesn't look at the gleaming glacier above him or the high corniced ridges sparking in the faint moon. His eyes are on the stars, his men, and the path. He leads them away, descending, another peak on his life's map. His own Map of Discovery is perfect.

Thompson succeeded because he searched not for the ideal, but for the real. Without maps, he had no expectation. His peaks: Path and Accuracy.

We drop through the rock bands pillowed with snow and start to track back to the Punch Bowl. We're almost there when there's a distant shout, cut off abruptly, and a crack loud enough to make me feel the world is splitting in two.

Up on Brown, near the top, a long section of compacted cornice begins a slow slump, small chunks underneath dropping like bombs. Then in a rush it falls, catching on the rock face and breaking apart in a cloud of pluming shards and glinting ice. It lands with a roar and a blast, sending spindrift blowing past.

I turn to face the sight to prevent myself from staggering in the wind. The Lion is ashen. "That was the Ranger," he says. I've no idea how he knows that. Did he see him fall? I prefer the Ranger to the Interpreter, so I don't ask.

The Lion pulls his hands off his ski poles and stands there. I want to race off but force myself to do the same. This is our training taking over. Stop. Breathe. Think. Don't waste time. Make a plan and then act. A person caught in an avalanche can survive, even though the force can snap trees. It depends on where they are, and the Ranger would have been on top of the mass. The face is at least a hundred metres vertical. Hard to believe anyone could survive, but there are stories to the contrary.

"Duvets. Slings. Headlamps. Probes. Shovels," the Lion recites. I already have all this.

"Hot water," I add.

"No time."

"Did you see where he fell?"

He nods, grim. We know the chances. The Ranger himself has spoken of avalanche recoveries where he found only pieces. But those were at the bottom of slopes. Up on the long ridge, a ragged section gapes in the arch. In the dusk, at the summit, I see a lone headlight, faint.

We ski quickly toward the debris. "Why was he so close to the edge? He knows better."

"Must've been distracted. C'mon. Focus."

We double-check our transceivers. The snow will settle fast, like concrete. Time matters. In the last light I follow the Lion at a distance as he angles up the broken pile toward the centre. He pauses and switches his transceiver to search. By default they're set to transmit. I hang back to keep my signal from interfering and in case another cornice breaks off and buries the Lion.

A thin cry emerges from the snow. I think of zinc bending, stressing the metal to the breaking point. The Lion waves within seconds, hurrying to a depression, and I arrive to see him pulling snow from around the Ranger, who sits, head up, shoulders clear.

I've been worried about how deep he might be, how long excavation might take. Now it doesn't seem so bad. The Lion is kneeling close, asking questions and feeling the Ranger's neck and head. I start to uncover the Ranger's chest, hoping his legs haven't been twisted. He's talking.

"Had to come to see it," he says.

"See what?" asks the Lion, calm, keeping the Ranger communicating. It's part of the training.

"Incredible. She said nothing of that."

"Where is she?"

"Not her."

"Can you move your toes? Do you remember what happened?"

"It's all right. I'm all right. I understand now."

His speech is slurred. His cheeks are frosty, mottled white.

The Lion looks at me from behind the Ranger and mimes a blow to his own head. The Ranger tries to excavate himself, like an exhausted swimmer treading water by force of habit.

"I don't want to move him," says the Lion.

"Get him out of the snow first."

"Can you bring the tents here?" the Lion asks.

I look at the mountain above. The sky is almost dark, the cornice an ominous white line, like a cresting wave, holding the light.

"We're still threatened. We gotta get out from under that." It's a bad location.

I hear a gasp, a hint of panic, like a spark spitting into the calm tinder of control. I wheel. Panic can turn the situation deadly. But the Ranger is still focused on pushing off the snow; it's not him. The Lion's face ripples, dissolves in the terror of responsibility. We are the unhurt, the survivors, we must take charge, we must get it right. It rattles me that he is losing his calm.

"Breathe," I say. The Lion clenches down, turns his face hard.

I grab his shoulder, bulky under the jacket. "Let's get him out. Fix his skis to a pack and make a sled. Get him to the tents, to the stove."

He nods. "But his back?"

The Ranger is still digging himself out, lolling his head.

"We've no choice." I worry about the Ranger's legs and back too. He's so vulnerable.

As we dig, the Lion checks the Ranger. I uncover his thighs and the Ranger starts to moan. I scoop deep to free his skis but can find only one. I pull it free. He grunts. We both stop to watch. The Ranger breathes. "My knee."

The Lion doesn't move. He's intense, determined to make right from last year's accident. His past seems right there with us.

"Medial fascia," the Ranger gasps.

"Delirious," I mouth to the Lion.

The Ranger shakes his head, cradled back on the snow. "No. Shock."

We need to move him, but I hesitate. The Ranger looks back at me suddenly, clear. In that flicker I realize I'm dependent on him as much as he is on me.

I crouch close to his face. "You're the most experienced here. Can you guide us?"

"Pull me," he says. "Up. From behind."

The Lion looks stricken. The Ranger will die if we don't; he could be paralyzed if we do.

"No choice," says the Ranger. "Do it."

I stumble around the blocks of debris to the Ranger's shoulders, catch him under the armpits, bending close. The Lion comes. We both pull. It's like ripping a tree stump's taproot from sucking mud. The Ranger groans, passes out. We dig snow away until he comes free.

The Lion looks sick.

We tie the single ski to his pack, work it under the Ranger, slide him down the debris pile in a slipping sprawl. At the bottom, on our track, the Lion ties the slings to his waist and starts to pull. It's slow, dragging through the snow, underneath the high arched brow of the cornice above. The Interpreter's headlight is so faint up there, like the first star of the evening. We can't yell to the Interpreter because the cornice may be too unstable—the sound could trigger more collapses. As we come around the ridge I can see the whole line of the ridge. Her light is not descending.

"I'll ski ahead and get the stove on," I say.

"No," gasps the Lion.

I'm afraid his panic will return.

"She's still up there. Maybe in shock. Definitely hypothermic," he says.

I picture her at the top, looking down at smooth snow that could break away suddenly, spilling down to death. I can't leave the Ranger, it'd be like DuNord casting aside his load.

"Give me the slings. I'll get him to the tent. You go find her," I say.

"No. You go. You're stronger," the Lion says. "Give me all the gear you have."

I need something to help her if she is hypothermic after her vigil, stumbling with cold on the descent. I can't let her get near that edge.

"I need everything," demands the Lion. "I'll pull him. I have to do this."

He's expressionless.

"You don't need anything. Just get her down," he says.

My hands don't accept the orders. They hold back the two slings I've been pulling with. When I force them, they move slowly. The Lion takes the slings. I let go, fingers still curled and stiff. I look up at the ridge, then start off, numb.

I follow our up-track easily through the rock bands and onto the ridge. I'm light and desperate, moving steadily, without pause, a growing need propelling me up from the valley, a reverse form of Gravity, a Love, a Strife. How long can she wait, motionless in the cold?

As I hit the open ridge, I can make out the headlight and dark shape of the Lion dragging the Ranger. The Lion has become Hercules, shouldering his burden to earn his freedom. It could be a load of furs. He could be DuNord, plowing his load through the unyielding snow. The Lion is past thought, mired in his own retribution.

I keep away from the edge lest I trigger another slide, and the Lion falls out of sight. I switch on my headlamp so he'll be able to see my progress from the tents, and so she can see me coming and hope. It does nothing for me, the beam lost in the emptiness of vast space.

I worry my feet forward, hissing the climbing skins like a hundred whispered admonishments. I imagine her sitting, paralyzed to move for fear that another spot will give way and disappear into the night with a blasting howl.

Before me a ghostly shadow appears, a marionette of my own making. I turn, feel the shift of my toque and jacket and the moisture that bleeds my heat, to see the tip of a crescent moon rising behind Hooker, thin and yellow and curved, like a reptile's eye lifting from a crusted shell.

It casts an uncertain light in a stark world, a mottled mosaic in blue. Before me the dim white slope. Beside me the utter blackness of the void. Inside, the pounding of a heart and the bellows of breath. Above, the needling stars, watching, not guiding.

There are no two peaks. Life is murkier than such clear distinctions. Rock needs air, air needs rock: mountains form the essence of clouds as clouds form the mystique of mountains. I shake it off, all the dreaming. This is a rescue now. I need to be nothing but practical.

Only the length of shadowed white beneath my feet feels real, narrowing as I gain height. As I climb, the stars gather around, even appear below me as my horizons fall away. I feel lost in them. Thompson left the Pass, descending, under the stars. Up here there's no reference, no base for them to wheel around. Instead the ridge sways within the stars' stationary domain.

I feel the dread of consequence as Thompson must have felt it. He is gone now, trailing the brigades out beyond memory, safe, leaving only his ancient story to help me.

> David Thompson rocks by the fire in his daughter's house after telling stories. He's almost blind. Memories come back with startling clarity, terns exploding from their nests in a flurry of wings, blurred white against the snow but for sharp black beaks and eyes.
>
> Bulrushes sway fat at the start of the Grand Portage, the thousand islands of the Lake of the Woods, the maple leaves along the St. Lawrence, the mists of Lake Ontario, the storms of Superior. Walking on the thin shale scattered below the peaks of the Rockies that tinkle and break like china. Faces come close, then fade, flowing, as the rivers pour. His cheek tickles; it is wet. He is surprised to find himself smiling.

I feel an emptiness in the air around me. With Thompson gone, the last of the stories that have wrapped around me is suddenly gone. What came before I heard them? What is my motivation without stories? The ridge narrows and each step becomes harder than the one before. The Lookout's Ideal: Truth—always harder the closer we get. I wonder if I can do this. The night is so dark.

Then, in that bleakest moment, everyone is with me: Thompson, leading, guiding. Douglas, snowshoeing, determined. Coleman and Outram and Collie, all clustering in the feeble light, urging me on. They are surrounded by voyageurs and outfitters. Thompson limps close: *Stay on the path, create the map*, he says. Douglas, smaller, with a flash of red hair: *There is a rare flower you must reach.* Coleman, under his battered felt hat, his white beard alight in the moon: *Keep trying, the map is in you.* Collie and Outram, together: *Do not lose the inspiration. You must see.* As I climb they come in close; the voyageurs are singing.

> *J'ai trouvé l'eau si belle*
> *Que je m'y suis baigné;*
> *Sous les feuilles d'un chêne*
> *Je me suis fait sécher*
> *Il y a longtemps que je t'aime*
> *Jamais je ne t'oublierai.*

Their chant is repetitive, endless, like my climb, like *a fleuve* that flows forever.

Up on the summit, I see the Interpreter huddled in that cold, small place, drawing me in. I aim for the tiny singularity of snow that's all that remains up in the stars. All these forces pull me. It's only the stories that I learned to tell the Interpreter that keep my focus: a mélange of trappers, mappers, and climbers walking after one another, blending toward a point. She's heaped like a solitary cairn marking the loss of her guide, sitting in her pit of snow.

"You never told me about this," she says softly.

She's slumped on her knees, as if on a vision quest. Head down, but eyes upward, transfixed on the stars. I imagine it's the trauma of seeing her guide disappear. My heart is breaking.

I bend to her face, needing a connection, needing her to come back and understand her situation. She sways away, refusing to break her view.

I move in front of her, my words invisible in the night, her breath a light mist, serene. The urgency builds, a wave surging. I need to get her down, to the safety of tents, of warmth. I try to pull her up from under her arms.

"Regarde la lune!" She points, like a child seeing a magical figure.

My heart drops; she's pointing the wrong way. The moon is rising to the southeast, behind Hooker, with the same murky effect as if shining through water. My eyes strain in the dark. She's further gone than I feared. Her life's slipping away as the hypothermia reaches into her core and distorts her reasoning and motor skills. Then she reaches and hits me hard. Her eyes are huge.

"Regarde."

She points.

I turn. Over my shoulder the stars quiver, subject to the lens of altitude. But it isn't the altitude. It's the moon. A smear of radiance, transmuted in the middle of the void, bent by a prism.

Mathematics collapse.

The moonlight burnishes the edge of . . . something. Some icy edge far above. It's not seen directly, more like translucent glass that is only known by the light it reflects. Below this, the faintest refraction shows me the inside of a cathedral, a mass rising beside us, the structure of a gemstone.

I stagger in recognition: on an up-thrust of the Earth's mantle is a bulge of basalt, and from that towers a spire of dolomite high into the stars, the sort of rock that forms steep cliffs and resists erosion, the kind that is sky blue, transparent when not subject to weathering, when protected from the elements. The kind of rock that could have gathered ice like rime. And wrapped around the dolomite column is a thick sheath of ice, perhaps gathered from the ice age, when all mountains were buried, and only the highest stood like trees, attracting the windblown hoar. The ice has been compressed over eons into flawless glass, binding the rock.

The stone inside the ice, as clear as air, is a soaring knife edge with an invisible blade, arching up like the crest of an angel's folded wing.

I can't see the base of the mountain, just the faint edge of crystal above, shifting the stars. I can only see where it stops by where the distortion ends.

This is the real Mount Brown. The highest.

■ It is the thing not seen, known only by its effects. Untraceable on maps but far more important, like clouds, like love, like gravity.

The moonlight is tenuous, a shimmer on a blade that flares and is lost as the metal turns.

It's my turn to be transfixed, twisted around at my knees, without even the presence to stand properly. A lower creature under a giant. I realize I'm on a mere buttress of the true mountain.

The Interpreter grabs my sleeve. How long have I been standing like this?

"Tell me the story," she asks. Her voice so quiet.

She must be hypothermic. A story, now? Here?

"Tell me the story," she says, louder.

I turn back and take a while to find the summit of Brown, wanting to trace it up, find a route, see the summit. It is faint as a comet trail. I can hardly believe it.

She pulls hard. "Tell me the story," she demands.

I turn back to face her. "What use is a story now? We're here. It's real."

She won't let me pull away to look up again.

"Because it's not a map," she insists. "Stories are about the future too, not just the past."

I barely process that. I just want to look.

"Tell *me* the story," she pleads. Her small face is insulated by softness, but her eyes are coals, fierce beneath her toque, brighter than the glint off Brown. Something there brings me back to the situation, how cold we are, how dangerous this is. I see her legs pulled under her and understand how scared she must be. I think of the Ranger asking me questions to help me out of my hypothermia after the bridge episode, how he said some people need stories. I think of all the stories that she's relied on for her reality.

"They don't exist," I hear myself speak. My voice is from the past, but I'm telling a story to get us both off the mountain now.

▲ Listen. A long time ago, a group came to these mountains, looking.

They all wanted something different, but when they got off the train they looked up and forgot what that was. All they could see was this ocean of stone.

Peaks: High. White. Distant.

Like hope. Like curiosity. Like fear.

They sent out their best explorer and he found the Pass.

Then a collector who named it.

Back in camp a patron publicized it.

They were like diamonds: compressed, structured, justified.

Like gymnastics. Like mathematics. Like philosophy.

They created a dream that wouldn't die because it was needed.

Years later the group heard the tales of something as grand as God.

Out went a seeker, with a full heart, who became disillusioned.

Then a scientist went forth who mapped it with a cold mind and determined his own reality.

Finally a pastor, who ignored it, and missed its truth.

They were like coal: combustible, practical, dependable.

Like body. Like mind. Like soul.

These are all facets of the same precious stone.

But none of them found what their imagination promised. So they reported that, marked it on maps. Made it physical. Climbable. Stabbed their fingers at it. Smudged it. Blurred it. Folded it. Tried to make it real even as they diminished it with writing. When they got to the top of their maps, they found what they sought wasn't there.

The mountains reveal that. Like the clouds the peaks make, they evaporate.

What you see isn't real, it isn't climbable.

You came for the pool. This is nothing but the reflection of the water.

Not a muddy mirror, but a clear vision.

I look at her, feeling the deep chill slip under my jacket, see the frost lining her scarf, and the night recedes out, expanding out into nothing.

"Look away," I whisper to her. "Now. Stand. Survive."

"Yes," she says sadly.

I help her up, get her skis turned around. I chance one look back, until she tugs.

"No, you know what is there. You are the story now."

The speed of the descent is frightening. It feels like the snow is giving away and we're falling. We rest halfway down. I feel drunk. My heart pounds warmth out my face to freeze against space. She kisses my cheek. Smooth as aluminum, warm as coal.

Back at the tent we're warm, but the chill has bitten once and won't be far away all night. The pale moon shows her tent, dark and frail. My own tent glows yellow. She is desperate to know about the Ranger, and the Lion waves over reassurance. I help her out of her skis and into the tent. She seems stable and takes time getting into her down bag. When I'm sure she's settled I hear a crunch of snow behind.

"Can you come?" the Lion asks quietly.

I walk on a trampled path to our tent. The Punch Bowl is barely the size of a hockey rink.

"How is she?" he asks, careworn. After I answer, he tells me the Ranger's been asking for me.

"Should we try to move him?" I ask the Lion.

"No. Both legs." He shakes his head. "I used his satellite phone and called the Service. They're sending a chopper at dawn. I won't leave him."

I poke through the double-walled flap. The Lion crouches, filling the door. Inside it's dank, smelling of soup, tea, and sweat. The Ranger has a sheen of fever. He's brushed his toque off. I put it back on, wondering why he looks strange, like a newborn, wet and vulnerable. Then I realize I've always seen him with a cap, a toque, a helmet. He looks younger. His cheeks are ruddy and seem to bleed meltwater. I'm exhausted, reeling, but I kneel beside him, hands on his shoulder.

"Tell him what you just told me," says the Lion to the Ranger.

"That crazy bat in her belfry," he mumbles.

I look back at the Lion. "Who?" I mouth. His eyes nod back to the Ranger.

"Weird old bird, sitting in her perch," the Ranger mutters.

It takes me a moment. "The Lookout?"

"She sees it all," he says. His voice is passionate but tired. The Lion withdraws, zips the flap.

"When did you go . . . "

"Vision and Respect," he says, silently laughing, as if humour is all reflective.

I wonder if he's delirious. "What did she tell you?"

"Those are my peaks, but no idea I'd see that."

I picture him there, up on the ridge, looking up and seeing the true peak of Brown far above. That would be such a shock to a practical mind that I can understand his straying to the edge.

"You're okay. We've got you," I say. My walls are down. I've let him lead me and he's let me carry him. "You're home, where you belong. You can rest now."

He smiles, focuses on me. His hands find mine and I'm impressed with his strength.

"Hey, Rumi. Hey, brother. She told me I'd find this. I didn't understand."

I wait. Is he drifting back to the vision of Brown?

"What did she say?" I ask.

He cocks his head over. He smells like the smoky ozone just before a big snowfall.

"'See yourself reflected in others and lose all fear. True leaders are in front, not ahead.' That vision . . . You guys have to transfer up here. People need to see this. We'll work the trails."

I grip his hand. He sinks back exhausted. I check his collar for damp, his pulse, his stomach inside the bag. He's warm, dry, sleeping. The gestures feel intimate. Whatever I had dreamt he was before today is now forgotten.

Outside the tent, I stand alone in the open night. I'm too tired to look up at Brown. I see movement in the Interpreter's tent and walk slowly over. My hands start to curl in the cold.

The Lion pulls open the door, draws it shut behind him. He looks up at the snow cap where we'd stood. He doesn't see the true peak. It's far too dangerous: a map of everything we desire is a not a map but reality. I realize how tired I am, how soaked.

He offers his hand. I unclench mine, pull off my glove, and shake his huge paw, so warm. The Lion hands me my gear. "Did you see why our Ranger fell? What distracted him?"

I'm lost for a moment. I think of small planes flying through these mountains and being found later as crumpled heaps at the base of big slopes. Maybe that's what happened to them. Images swirl like startled terns, until one settles. "The *Magnum Opus*," I say. "That which can turn other mountains into legends." I look back at the tent. "He'll be fine. He has a strong heart."

"The Philosopher's Stone," the Lion says, starting to smile. "You were right. The ideal is in the mountain. The *Magnum Opus* beats inside each of us. Go take care of her."

He has completed his penance, and redeemed himself from death. He's found equilibrium. I turn to the Interpreter's tent, dark beside the Punch Bowl. I stand at the highest point on my personal Map of Meaning. The Lion disappears into our tent, and in the flash of light from his headlamp are a hundred glistening peaks, one over each mountain in the valley. It isn't one ideal, or even two. It is thousands. The ghosts of the voyageurs and explorers and stories that have been just behind me vanish, as if joined to the ice peaks, as if lifted into the stars like the heroes of the Greek Parthenon, looking down benevolently.

"None but the brave deserve the fair," quotes James Outram.

She is already asleep when I enter. I check her temperature, pull the Ranger's big bag around me, sink into sleep.

In the middle of the night, I wake with a start. The Interpreter fumbles for a water bottle. I hand her mine, bury a headlamp inside a shirt to soften the glare.

She's revived, radiant in the glow, cheeks tanned dark, staring at the water in the clear bottle.

"She was right, you know. It is us who create the enchantment."

"Who?" I ask, even as I realize who she means.

"The Lookout," she says, turning the bottle in the light. "That beautiful seer in her tower of air."

"What did she tell you? To come here?"

"Not exactly. That was your doing, all your stories. But she was so sweet. She said, 'You are a creature of destiny, of the rivers, of water. You are the mother of oceans. Find your reflecting pond where you decide it should be, then create the enchantment.'"

"The reflecting pool."

"Yes." She looks into the circle of water through the mouth of her bottle. She turns so she looks through it at me. I smile.

"You see," she says. "I sit before the little pool, seeing my future, and I can decide to pour this little drop and be the mother of oceans. She asked me what two peaks I search for in life."

I laugh. The Lookout's stolen my best lines. "What did you tell her?"

"Knowledge and Destiny."

"You have the Destiny."

"But not the Knowledge. What happened to everyone? All the others that you told me about: Thompson, Douglas, Coleman? How did these mountains affect them?"

I stretch under the tent walls. The enclosure within the snow pit and the double-walled tent makes the world feel close. The wind is gone. The seashell echo fills my ears.

"Arthur Coleman left Athabasca Pass disgusted, but returned for Mount Robson, the highest yet.

"James Outram settled in Alberta, doing nothing historically significant after 1902.

"Norman Collie returned home and never visited the Rockies again.

"David Thompson died penniless. Today he's regarded as the greatest land geographer."

"You see," she says. "Maps are necessary, they are stories read differently. I am going back to school. For Knowledge." She seems settled. "What about you?"

I suddenly want to laugh. "It's the stories," I say. "It's the stories I've been following. I want to pass them along. I think I will work here. As an interpreter."

"Everyone came here for a different reason. I bet you did not think you would search for these mountains. Or what they would do to you. Tell me," she murmurs, unbraiding her hair. It falls over her face and shoulders in a cascade of dark curls and shadows. "What are your two peaks?"

ACKNOWLEDGMENTS

To my wife, Anne-Marie, for encouraging me to write seriously, and giving me the space to do so.

To James Cieslak and J.T. Gill for the experience on Trail Crew.

To Brad Wrobleski for teaching me alpinism.

To the readers of various drafts who gave feedback, especially Kevin Hakl, Pat Morrow, and Don Wynn.

To Brad Bellows for the travels and the encouragement.

To Ruth Linka of Brindle & Glass publishing, for taking a chance on new authors.

To Lynne Van Luven, who helped edit the publisher's drafts.

To the triumvirate of exceptional reviewers: Marcia Delves, Katie Ives, and Joe Kadi for keeping me sane and on track through many working drafts.

To Don Gorman, of Rocky Mountain Books, for encouraging my project without boundaries.

To those who gave me a place to write when I most needed uninterrupted solitude: chez Fafard, chez Dionne, and the three houses of chez Dianne.

To the Banff Writer's Studio – all of you for the great community, and especially to Michael Helm for his expert guidance. To Edna Alford and Greg Hollingshead for your belief in the transformation of the story. And to Linda, Leigh, and Saleema for your friendship and advice.

To Bob Sandford, for your friendship, guidance, and mentoring, without which this story would not have seen the light of day.

Jerry Auld's short stories have been published in the *Alpinist* and in the *Canadian Alpine Journal*. He is a graduate of the University of Calgary and an alumnus of the Banff Writing Studio, where he worked under the direction of Michael Helm and Paul Quarrington. At the 2005 Banff Mountain Film Festival, Jerry was the co-recipient of the 2005 People's Choice Award for the independent film *Sister Extreme*. Jerry's knowledge of the mountains comes from full-time work on the trail crew for Kananaskis Country in the Alberta Rockies, as well as at the Banff Centre, Parks Canada, and the Banff Lodging Company. He is currently a self-employed consultant in website development and programming. *Hooker & Brown* is his first novel.